REBA: MY STORY

Reba

MY STORY

Reba McEntire
with Tom Carter

BANTAM BOOKS
NEW YORK   TORONTO   LONDON   SYDNEY   AUCKLAND

REBA: MY STORY

A Bantam Book / May 1994

Unless otherwise credited, all the photographs in this book are
courtesy of the Reba Collection.
Grateful acknowledgment is made to *People* Weekly for permission to reprint
its cover. *People* Weekly is a registered trademark of Time Inc.,
used with permission.
Grateful acknowledgment is also made for permission to quote from ''If I
Had Only Known.'' Written by Jana Stanfield/Craig Morris. © 1992,
1991 Jana Stantunes (BMI)*/ Alabama Band Music (a division of
Wildcountry, Inc.) ASCAP
*Administered by Bug Music
All Rights Reserved/Used by Permission

Library of Congress Cataloging-in-Publication Data
McEntire, Reba.
Reba: my story/Reba McEntire, with Tom Carter.
p.   cm.
ISBN 0-553-09607-9
1. McEntire, Reba.   2. Country musicians—United States—Biography.
I. Carter, Tom, 1947–   .
ML420.M34125A3   1994
782.42'1642'092—dc20
[B]   94-1466
CIP
MN

Published simultaneously in the United States and Canada

PRINTED IN THE UNITED STATES OF AMERICA
BVG   0 9 8 7 6 5 4 3 2 1

I would like to dedicate this book to Shelby.
For every second I have watched, laughed, cried, and marveled at every little ''sing'' you do. You have given me the greatest five years of my life.

Hopefully, these words will keep you familiar with your family, past and present, and also give you an idea of what it is your Mama does and has been doing for the past thirty-nine years.

I can't imagine what the next few decades will be like, but I pray, that along with your Daddy, we'll see it together.

"It's not the critic who counts. . . . It's not the man who points out how the strong man stumbled. . . . Credit belongs to the man who really was in the arena, his face marred by dust, sweat and blood, who strives valiantly, who errs to come up short and short again, because there is no effort without error and shortcoming. It is the man who actually strives to do the deeds, who knows the great enthusiasm and great devotion, who spends himself on a worthy cause, who, at best, knows in the end the triumph of great achievement. And who, at worst, if he fails, at least fails while daring greatly, so that his place shall never be with those cold and cruel souls who know neither victory nor defeat."

—THEODORE ROOSEVELT

ACKNOWLEDGMENTS

IT SURE TOOK A LOT OF PEOPLE TO MAKE THIS BOOK HAPPEN, starting off with Mel Berger of the William Morris Agency talking to Narvel about me doing a book.

After Narvel talked me into it, we chose Bantam as our publisher. Then we selected Tom Carter, whom I have known since the early eighties, when he wrote for the *Tulsa World* in Tulsa, Oklahoma, to be the co-author. Tom did a great job interviewing people, gathering all the facts, listening to all the endless stories, and typing it all up, in addition to keeping up with my unpredictable schedule.

I would like to say thanks to my family for helping Tom. To Pake for the time he spent interviewing all the family and putting it down on tape for my Christmas present. To Ray Williams for all the great memories you shared with us. To Daddy for your inspiration and great stories of our past. To Alice and Susie, though I'm sorry I didn't always use your versions of the stories you told—I remembered them differently. It's funny how much of a brat you both thought I was. I don't remember it like that at all! And to Mama, thanks for not hanging up on me from all the endless phone calls I made, sometimes to ask the same question. (I forgot where I wrote it down the first time!)

Thank you all for helping me find the best pictures. I love each and every one of you.

Narvel, since we made it through this book writing, I'd say we can make it through just about anything. But as you know, there were times when I wanted to choke the liver out of you for talking me into it.

To my friends, relatives, associates, enemies, fans, business partners, and acquaintances who contributed to this project, you're in it whether you like it or not—but I hope you do!

Thank you, God, for letting me keep my sanity and my memory long enough to finish this book. As I read over it for the thousandth time, I'm pretty impressed by how much of a life you've let me lead. Thank you for my story, I'm glad it all started with you.

To you reading this book, I hope you are entertained and learn a little more about me and what I do and how I think. I hope you close the last page liking me a little more and not too disappointed in my shortcomings.

So here it is—my story. Please read on, and
Read My Mind!

Love,

Reba

PREFACE

I WAS ON OUR PLANE HEADED FOR OUR SHOW IN ATLANTIC CITY, NEW Jersey, when my husband and manager, Narvel Blackstock, showed me an issue of the supermarket tabloid *Star*. "Now, Reba, try not to get upset . . ." he told me, but I could see that he was pretty upset himself. Usually we laugh off such gossip-mill stories—as the show-business saying goes, "There's no such thing as bad publicity." But this time, the press had gone too far.

A photo of me from an awards show was plastered all over the *Star*'s front page, and over it was printed an enormous, shrill headline "Shocking charge by two ex-wives . . . REBA STOLE OUR HUSBANDS." Inside were unkind interviews with Lisa Gilbert, Narvel's first wife, who has long since remarried after her divorce from Narvel six years ago, and Sherrie, the former Mrs. Charlie Battles, who's been holding a grudge, apparently, even longer—for a full eighteen years, since 1975!

Why these women decided to speak out now was beyond me,

and what they were quoted as saying was a hurtful exaggeration of the truth. But the truth doesn't sell these newspapers, I guess; and when you're a public figure, everything you do is fair game for what I might call "reinterpretation," if I was trying to be polite.

That's one of the reasons that I'm writing this book—to set the record straight about my marriages and other matters that have been reported inaccurately by the press. But I have some other, more compelling personal reasons, too.

The first is that I'm lucky to have had a remarkable journey through life and to have met some wonderful people along the way—some of them in my own family! My Grandpap, John Wesley McEntire, and my Daddy, Clark McEntire, are famous for their rodeo triumphs. I was raised on a ranch, which my Mama and Daddy built from forty acres at the time I was born to some seventeen thousand today, with us kids working right alongside them tending the cattle just as cowboys had done for the last hundred years. It was a family operation all the way, of a kind that is vanishing from the American landscape as ranching becomes big business and as technology is radically changing the old-fashioned cowboy ways. Recently, a Brahma bull got loose and Daddy roped him—I've heard him brag that he's "lost a lot of ropin' poise, but I could still get 'er done"; though nowadays, usually, instead of a rope he uses a tranquilizer gun.

Such advances have done a lot to ease the harshness of the ranchers' life, and so by the time my son, Shelby, grows up, the old methods may be lost forever. Part of the reason I'm writing this book is that I want Shelby to understand what the traditional McEntire cowboy life was like.

My second reason is that I've had a marvelous time in the country music business and have been blessed with a thrilling degree of success. I'm proud of that since I've worked hard for it and I've had plenty of challenges to face, not the least of which was being a woman in a business that's still largely dominated by men. Women are usually the ones who buy the concert tickets, and women naturally want to see men—who can blame them? So it makes me especially happy that women can relate to my songs, and that they seem to view me as a friend. I'm also writing it to give credit where credit is due—to the people who have helped and inspired me. I could never have done it alone.

Thirdly, I've had to face a terrible tragedy, and I've found that many people want to know what it has taught me. Those questions haven't been easy to address, but in this book I'd like to try. Narvel says, correctly, that I was taught as a child how to pull on my inner resources in hard times and that I have never rebelled against that teaching. My personal faith in God has seen me through when nothing else could help, and my music has also been a constant source of consolation. I'm not going to try to tell anyone to do things my way. I'll simply share what has worked for me.

If there's anything I've learned it is that there's no greater source of happiness than my family. I continue to get so much from them, emotionally and spiritually. But I'd like to tell you about a few of their more distinctly material gifts, which I will always treasure.

My brother Pake, for Christmas 1992, gave me three hours of tape-recorded interviews with Ray Williams, my Daddy's first cousin, who knows all the McEntire history. Ray's stories are heartwarming and hilarious, and I'm so grateful to Pake for making the tape. Imagine if those stories had been lost to us! It's so valuable to have a record of who your ancestors were and of how they lived.

My sister Susie recently gave me my old Bible with the inscription I made when I was "saved" at age twelve. She also presented me with a pair of old basketball shoes I wore when I played high school basketball. I can't figure out how Susie got hold of those! But she's the thoughtful type who would, and now I have some precious mementos of my own personal history.

And back in 1979, when I was making my first tentative inroads into the music business, my sister Alice gave me—of all things—a toilet seat cover. On it were monogrammed the words "The Twinkle." She promised that if I ever made it big, she'd give me another one labeled "The Star." But she hasn't yet.

That's my reminder that I haven't yet reached the top, that there's still so much for me to strive for and to achieve. Alice's gift—or lack of one, I guess you could say—shows me that, at nearly forty, I have so much more to work for in life, so much more to look forward to.

I sure can't think of any better gift than that!

REBA: MY STORY

CHAPTER 1

L OVE IS A LIVING THING. ANYTHING LIVING MUST BE NUR-
tured. It takes time, effort, attention, and sometimes
work, but the return is way over tenfold. I'm very lucky
that Narvel and I work together and that we can take
Shelby with us when we want to. All the rest of my family is still
in southeastern Oklahoma. I talk to them or visit them as often as
I can.

My oldest sister, Alice Lynn Foran, is the county director of
the Atoka, Oklahoma, Department of Human Services. She's
married to Robert and has four great kids, Vince, Garett, Trevor,
and Haley, whom I love dearly. Alice is the rock, the one you can
call at three in the morning, and she'll always be ready to help in
any way. The next in line, my brother Pake and his wife, Katie,
run cattle on their ranch outside of Kiowa, Oklahoma. Pake's real
name is Del Stanley, but he got the nickname "Pecos Pete"
before he was born. Mama and Daddy would refer to the unborn
baby as Pecos Pete, and we've called him Pake for short ever

since. Besides ranching, Pake sells insurance and sings with his three daughters, Autumn, Calamity, and Chism, all over the country. My baby sister Martha Susan, who we call Susie, sings too and records on Integrity Music. She and her husband, Paul Lucksinger, have an evangelical ministry called Psalms Ministry, so on their tours, she sings and Paul shares his testimony, often with rodeo cowboys. Their three kids, E.P., Lucchese, and Samuel Clark, go with them a lot of the time.

My Mama, the former Jacqueline Smith, stays home most of the time now. A yearling hooked her "in the short ribs," Daddy says, about ten years ago. Actually, Mama said, her ribs have been broken twice by steers and once when she stepped out of the pickup onto a log that rolled out from under her. "It took me two months to get over that one, and after that, I just started staying home."

She talks to her children or grandchildren almost every day. Our love is nurtured.

❧

MY DADDY, CLARK VINCENT MCENTIRE, IS A FORMER THREE-TIME world-champion tie-down steer roper. He began roping when he was a small boy and entered his first amateur roping contest when he was twelve, in 1939. It happened almost by accident, when Eddie Curtis, Daddy's friend, asked him, "Are you going to rope?"

"Don't guess," Daddy said.

"You are now," Eddie said, after pitching down three dollars for an entry fee.

"I don't have a horse," Daddy said.

"You can ride mine," said Dick Truitt, a former World's-Champion steer roper and friend of the family.

Daddy wondered what in the world he would have done if he had caught the calf. They were great big calves (350 pounds).

Daddy turned professional when he won the Pendleton Round-Up All-Around Cowboy roping contest at seventeen, and by 1949 he was the fifth-highest-paid steer roper in the Rodeo Cowboy Association. That year he won $1,222. In 1957—the biggest year he ever had—he earned $5,184.

I once asked him if winning the championship was as good as getting there. He said, "No, the fun to me was seeing if I could beat 'em and win the money. After I won, it was like, 'So what?' "

I'm a lot like my Daddy.

⁂

THE MCENTIRE CLAN BUILT A LEGACY IN THE COMMERCIAL RODEO world, but that story came a generation after my eccentric great-grandfather, Clark Steven McEntire. He was born on a Mississippi riverboat on September 10, 1855. Everyone in my family simply called him Pap. His family lived in Cairo, the southernmost city in Illinois, because of its nearness to the nation's largest river. I'm told he didn't like to tell folks he was born in Illinois because they would think he was a Yankee. The Civil War had erupted when he was a boy.

If he had checked a map he would have noticed that Cairo is as far south as western Kentucky or eastern Missouri. But in his day, an Oklahoman who was suspected of having lived in or even near the North had the same kind of social standing Benedict Arnold had during the Revolutionary War.

Pap had broken his back while riding a bicycle and carried a tremendous hump between his shoulders. Pap was married twice, fathered twelve children, and had numerous girlfriends, or so Ray

Williams says. He's Daddy's cousin, who lived with Pap until he was ten.

Ray tells a story about Pap traveling with his first wife and their two boys when one of the boys became ill. He decided the youngster needed chicken soup for medicine just about the time the group passed a house with a flock of chickens. Pap jumped from his wagon and began to chase a chicken, whose squawking alerted its owner.

The owner ran outside and demanded to know what was going on.

"We've got a sick child," Pap replied. "Please help us catch one of our chickens that got loose."

The chicken's rightful owner chased it down and turned it over to Pap, not knowing he had surrendered part of his own flock. The child eventually died, as did his brother. Within a month after burying the two boys, Pap buried his wife, the boy's mother, then went on with his life.

But for all his resourcefulness, Pap remained impoverished. He tried his hand at chicken farming, but spring rains made the land too muddy for man or chicken to wade. Chicks were nonetheless hatched. When the rain ceased, the land dried and cracked and the chicks fell through the cracks, taking Pap's dreams of raising chickens along with them. Eventually, they say, his farm at Cairo, Oklahoma, east of Coalgate, was repossessed.

❧

THE MOST FAMOUS STORIES ABOUT PAP ARE SO EXTREME THAT YOU have to wonder if they're true. But I'll tell them to you anyway. As my Daddy admits, "There just ain't no telling what all that old man did."

At one point he moved out of the big house, away from his wife and children, into a shanty filled with dogs, rats, snakes, chickens, bugs, and more—he fed every stray animal that came around. He castrated the males and threatened to do the same to young boys who ventured near. He didn't have a lot of visitors.

Actually, his shanty was more like a rock pile in the yard with a protruding stovepipe. He called that dwelling his Dutch oven.

Who knows what kind of germs Pap caught from the stray animals he took into his Dutch oven? Ray said that he and Pap more than once caught the mange from stray dogs. To try to get rid of it, they coated their bodies in creosote dip, my Mama said.

The creosote was probably an improvement on Pap's usual condition. He never washed his clothes or himself, never took a bath in his entire life, or so Ray says. He'd boil coffee in a filthy bucket on top of a wood stove, let it cool below a boil, then drink it in gulps as if it were a soda pop. At night, he'd put his coat or vest on the back of a chair and a chicken or two would roost on it. The garment would be covered with droppings the next morning, but he never would wipe them off. He'd just put on his spotted wrap and let the droppings fall off throughout the day, in time to be replaced that night.

Pap also had to allow for chickens that slept on the headboard of his bed. When a chicken is asleep, you can pick it up, turn it around, and if you're careful, it won't wake up. Pap would turn around several roosting chickens each night before he lay down to keep them from leaving droppings on his head.

Though he dressed in near rags, Pap was never seen without a necktie. It was stiff from dirt and never formally tied. He just wrapped it around his neck a couple of times and made a make-shift knot. Even his hat, a derby, was rigid with filth. He wore only clothes that he picked up—literally. Some had been thrown away, but others were permanently "borrowed" by Pap when the owner wasn't looking.

Despite Pap's habit of "borrowing" everything from others, he accused people of stealing from him whenever some of his ragged clothes or useless junk was missing, and he fought for their recovery. One time Pap was sleeping on the ground and put his false teeth on a wagon-coupling pole. At sunrise, he couldn't find his teeth and accused another man of taking them.

"Why would I take your teeth? I got a perfect set of my own," the guy argued. Pap threatened to pull the man's natural teeth to be sure they weren't false.

He was one tough old bird. Daddy contends that Pap was a first cousin to the outlaw Cole Younger and that he knew the legendary Jesse James and his gang. And Ray tells the story of the time that Pap stepped on a blacksnake during the night and picked it up by its middle instead of its head or tail. Doubling back, the snake bit Pap squarely in the face.

"He flogged it again' and again' the ground," Ray said, until the snake was dead.

Then Pap crawled into his three-quarter-length bed, whose mattress was only a pile of rags. The dead snake lay on the floor for three days until its stench became unbearable and the swelling began to ease from Pap's face. He finally threw the decaying reptile outside to the dogs. He never went to a doctor.

He just went on with his life.

But Pap could be kindly, I'm happy to say. In his later years, he had a vehicle, a battered truck that he cranked by hand. Its top speed was maybe ten miles per hour. He drove it down dirt roads past people walking to town with buckets of cream for sale. He and his motorized contraption, which he and the neighbors named "Truckie," were a familiar sight. People would simply hop on the back of the moving vehicle, and by the time Pap reached town, as many as fifteen people would be hanging from the truck's bed and running boards. Pap spared them the long, dusty walk.

I'm told that people used to say it would kill a human being to live in that Dutch oven. I don't know if it killed Pap, but that's where he died, at the age of seventy-nine.

Nathan Rhyne, the ancestor of Clark Rhyne, my high school teacher, fashioned a pine box that was narrow at the head and feet. Ray said he tacked satin inside, but my Daddy says it was tar paper. A cemetery lot was bought for two dollars at Wardville, Oklahoma, and Pap's remains are there to this day.

⚜

IT'S EASY TO SEE WHY EACH OF PAP'S WIVES STRONGLY DISLIKED HIM. I don't think I could be married to a man that "colorful." Daddy said his grandma, Helen, used to get on her knees and pray that Pap wouldn't return each time he left.

It was Helen, Pap's second wife, who gave birth to John Wesley McEntire, my grandfather, who became our family's first rodeo star.

In 1930, John Wesley McEntire, who us kids called Grandpap, traveled from Cairo to Limestone Gap, Oklahoma, so he could put his cattle out on "open range." "The Depression hit and his cattle weren't worth anything," Daddy recalls. "He couldn't afford to renew his leases where he was staying south of Ada. So he moved his old cows down to Limestone Gap, because that was rangeland and he didn't have to pay a grass bill. He was just trying to exist, but in the spring the bank came and got his cows. So he just stayed."

His wife, Alice Kate Hayhurst McEntire, came to join him, bringing Daddy, and got a job teaching school at Limestone Gap. When she first arrived, Grandpap said, "There's no place for y'all to stay." Grandma said they'd live in the Cake House, which Grandpap had built to store the processed cottonseed cake feed for the cattle. So they did. Grandpap built another room and then a third so Grandma's Daddy could come live with them, though he didn't stay long. Daddy still remembers playing on the sacks of feed stacked up in one end of the house.

The Cake House today is only a leaning building with sheet-metal siding, a tin roof, and a floor that is one-half dirt and the other half concrete. You can slide your hand through the cracks in its seams, large enough to allow snow to blow through in the wintertime.

The house once had a wooden floor. At night, rats would crawl from beneath the floor and steal Grandpap's socks. One night a rat stole his false teeth and Grandpap tore the floor out to find them. The teeth were located and returned to their proper place. The floor never was.

My Daddy grew up in the Cake House, although his Daddy never owned the house or the land where it sat.

DADDY WEIGHED OVER TEN POUNDS AT BIRTH, AND MY GRANDMOTHER had a terrible time delivering him. Due to the primitive medical techniques of those days, she never fully recovered and suffered from female problems for the rest of her short life. There were no more children after that. Mama has told me many times about how Grandma Alice would be so sore that she was rolled back and forth in the sheets to turn her over.

In 1950, as soon as school was out, Grandma went to Poteau, Oklahoma, to have a hysterectomy. Nine days later, while she was in the hospital, Grandma suffered a stroke. Daddy and Mama were at a rodeo in Marietta, Oklahoma, at the time. They decided to stop by home after the rodeo. As they turned off the highway, they met Bess Martin, a neighbor and friend, and learned of Grandma's condition. They drove over to Poteau to be with her, but she never regained consciousness. She died on July 1, 1950, five years before I was born.

After her funeral, Mama and Daddy went to Grandpap's house. They found him throwing her personal things, including some beautiful quilts she'd made by hand, into the creek behind their house. Mama retrieved as much as she could. She even found Grandma's watch—she has it to this day—which had been scorched because Grandpap also tried to burn some of Grandma's things. Though Grandpap had been a difficult husband, I know he missed Grandma Alice an awful lot.

I sure wish I could have known her!

⚜

THE SUMMER GRANDMA DIED, GRANDPAP WAS FIFTY-THREE, AND HE still roped quite well. He won the Woodward, Oklahoma, steer roping and won a day money at Pendleton, Oregon. A day money is like a go-round. If ten cowboys are entered in a calf-roping competition, for example, the first go-round will be completed when all ten have had a chance to rope once. The one with the fastest time of the ten will be paid, and his earnings are called "day money." There are usually two or three go-rounds in each event in a rodeo competition, and the contestant who has the fastest average or the lowest average wins a greater sum, called the "average money."

But then, Grandpap had been infected with rodeo fever since an early age. By the time he was in his early twenties, he had made respectable money on a horse in a touring Wild West Show. By about 1923, Grandpap's rope had taken him from southeastern Oklahoma all the way to Madison Square Garden in New York City.

I've thought about that whenever I have played in New York City, and my sister Alice has never missed a chance to remind me that I'm not the first McEntire to perform there.

Today, rodeo cowboys travel in air-conditioned trucks with campers and motor homes, and many have corporate sponsors and backers who keep them on the road no matter if they win, lose, or draw. Former Rodeo Cowboys Association All-Around Cowboy Larry Mahan used to travel in a private jet. But

Grandpap went to most rodeos on horseback, and his income depended on his winnings. There were plenty of times when he was just starting out that he paid his entry fee but then missed his steer or saw another cowboy rope his steer faster. Then he made the long ride back home with a packhorse whose supply bags were as empty as Grandpap's pockets.

That was before the days of the RCA (Rodeo Cowboys Association) and the Professional Rodeo Cowboys Association, the sanctioning organizations for today's championship rodeos. Back then the only association was the Turtle Association, which Grandpap helped get started.

Even though both families were friends, my family has told me how Grandma Alice's folks thought Grandpap was irresponsible because he wouldn't work the fields and cared little about anything that didn't involve riding and roping. They themselves were practical and hardworking people who were used to making sacrifices. When Grandma's Daddy lost his slaves because President Lincoln had freed them after the Civil War, the family took their places in the fields, even though my great-grandfather didn't know how to farm himself and lost a leg when a sorghum masher fell on him and crushed it. So they didn't cotton to Grandpap's ways.

Actually, Grandpap made so little money during the early years of their marriage, they might have starved to death if Grandma Alice hadn't been a schoolteacher. And if Grandpap did win any money rodeoing, he was liable to let the neighbor kids play with it until they lost it, or he might just give it away.

But Grandma was conservative with her money and scrimped and saved so they got by. And in time, Grandpap became a rodeo hero. In 1934, he took first place in the steer roping at Cheyenne, Wyoming, the indisputable championship rodeo in the world. Anyone who won his event there simply became the world champion in that event. In his later years, Grandpap was a constant presence on our ranch, and us kids got very attached to him.

MY OTHER GRANDFATHER, GEORGE ELVIN SMITH, GREW UP AN ORPHAN and stayed with anyone who would take him in. Maybe that's why he was very sincere about taking care of his family. Even during the Depression, he made sure there was plenty of food on the table to eat and blankets on the bed. He loved his grandchildren, but he had little patience with them.

I was very close to his wife, my Mama's mother, Reba Estelle Brassfield (born in Smithville, Mississippi). I am her namesake, of course, and I truly adored her. She had Indian-like features, with thick, black hair that time would streak with gray. She braided her hair every night, and it was almost like a ceremony to a little girl. I can still see her with her long hair parted in the middle and woven into braids on each side.

I also remember how, in the evening, we'd sit on the front porch facing the west. Grandma would have her gallon jar filled with fresh milk heavy with cream, which she'd churn until it was butter. The lightning bugs would flash on and off as the light faded and the moon came up. The butter would taste great on our biscuits the next morning or in the following night's black-berry cobbler—the best I ever had. You can be sure she picked the berries herself!

Grandma seemed to understand children in the way that only grandmothers can. I remember that my sisters, brother, cousins, and I once held a summer version of an Easter egg hunt by hiding and seeking our beachcloppers (which some people call thongs). During the hunt, I spied a beachclopper on top of some old boards at the back of the house, and I climbed up to get it. Accidentally, I stepped on a long nail in one of the boards, which stuck deep into my foot right between my big and second toes.

My cousin Diannia was with me and hollered for Grandma, who pulled the nail out right then and there and carried me inside. I don't know how she doctored my wound. But I remember that she kept the other kids outside while she had my Aunt Georgia read the comic papers to me.

She knew how to make a little country girl feel so special that I forgot the pain.

Grandma was also the person who introduced me to Jesus Christ. Some of my fondest childhood memories have to do with Grandma telling me Bible stories when she and I fished from the pond dam. That's where I learned about Noah and the Ark, Jonah and the whale, Joseph and his coat of many colors, and other thrilling stories from the Old Testament. I accepted Jesus Christ as my personal savior when I was little bitty, sitting on a pond dam with Grandma.

Grandma practiced the "speaking in tongues," the descent of the Holy Spirit. "And they were all filled with the Holy Ghost, and began to speak with other tongues, as the Spirit gave them utterance," says Acts 2:4 in the King James Version.

One night during a service at her Baptist church, she started speaking in tongues. My Mama said she didn't think Grandma even knew where she was because she was so involved in the Spirit.

Such experiences are becoming increasingly commonplace in contemporary churches, even in the old-line denominations of the Protestant faiths. But when I was a girl, some folks in the more established denominations thought folks who spoke in tongues were religious fanatics. So Grandma was warned about her religious practices by an outraged member of the congregation. When she continued them, she was asked to leave the Baptist church she loved.

She then joined a nondenominational Holiness church, where folks recognized that the speaking in tongues was a gift. My Mama remembers services where Grandma would speak in unknown tongues, and someone in the congregation would give an interpretation, translating into English whatever it was that

Grandma had said. Interpretations are still common in Pentecostal and other Holiness churches.

Maybe that's why Grandma understood so well—and taught me—that connection to God is deeper than simple words. I used to watch her get on her knees in her nightgown by the bed. After her prayers I asked her what she was saying and she said she was talking to Jesus, so I'd ask her, "What are you saying?"

"I don't know," she'd say.

"If you don't know, how are you talking to Him?"

"That's the way my soul talks to Him. I'm talking to Him through the Holy Spirit."

❦

I STILL HAVE THE LITTLE BROWN HYMN BOOK I USED AS A CHILD. WE worshiped at the wood frame country church house at Chockie—a one-room structure with a front and back door. While the church had a piano, no one knew how to play it, though one of our parishioners, Miss Stella McGee, could sight-read music. She would read the sheet music, hum the pitch to the congregation, and then we would sing a cappella. Everyone would then join in. In warm weather, after church we'd all have dinner. The women would bring food and spread it out over picnic tables, while the men would bring benches out of the church for us to sit on. I loved those Sundays.

I was baptized by immersion at the Baptist church in Kiowa, Oklahoma, when I was twelve, just as John the Baptist baptized Jesus in the Jordan River. Some folks don't think baptism is necessary, but Jesus thought so, and so do I.

Still, I don't go to church all that much today. I like a preacher to get up and talk about the love of God and how good it makes you feel, not the Hell, fire, and brimstone. I do believe there are physical places called Heaven and Hell, and that they are as the Bible describes them. But I have no doubt that when I die,

I'm going to Heaven, to spend eternity with Grandma and other friends and loved ones who have gone before me in death.

When I do attend church, I like to go to the Pentecostal churches with my mother-in-law and father-in-law, Gloria and Narvel Blackstock. I know that having God's arms around you when you're speaking in the Spirit is a wonderful experience. I'm familiar with it, and so I'm comfortable with it. It's only if you don't know anything about a subject that it scares you. I love to see the joyful way that people worship the Lord in those churches. I love the music, too.

Though I don't go to church much, I pray every day. God is one hundred percent part of my life.

People can leave Jesus, but he'll never leave them. He has been with me all these years through trials and tribulations. I'm convinced He has looked after me physically. I went through some reckless days in college as many young people do, and I knew Grandma wasn't too pleased with me as she looked down from Heaven. There was a time or two when I might have been seriously injured or even killed had it not been for Him. And there have been times when I would have gone insane if I couldn't have turned to Him.

I rededicated my life to the Lord one year at the Copenhagen-Skoal roping in Fort Worth, Texas. I think it was in 1978. Willard Moody, a great friend and calf roper, and I were talking and I expressed to him some religious confusion in my life. There at the horse barns, we stepped into a stall for privacy and he said, "Reba, if you're confused, repeat after me." He said a small prayer that asked God to take control of my life. When I repeated the prayer, it felt like a ton of guilt, stress, and pain had been lifted off my shoulders. The Lord is still in control of my life. I'm proud of it. I wouldn't want it any other way.

CHAPTER 2

J ACK PALANCE WON AN OSCAR FOR HIS PERFORMANCE AS A HARD-
ened old trail guide in *City Slickers,* the popular 1991 movie
that also starred Billy Crystal. Crystal was one of three city
folks who hoped that by wearing diamonds and denim in the
country and chasing cattle for a week they'd find their "smiles,"
or their manhood.

I knew a lot of working cowboys when I was growing up, and
most of them, I think, would enjoy the undeniable humor of that
movie. But none of them, especially me, would think that working on a real cattle ranch gives you a lot to smile over.

One of the most frequent questions I was asked when my
career began to take hold was whether or not I was a real
cowgirl. Some folks thought that I learned to ride a horse in
college just to compete in rodeos. The fact is, I rode horses about
fifteen years before I ever went to college, and it wasn't for the
fun of competition. It was because my Daddy said, "Get on him,
get in the brush, and find some cattle."

There was a time when my Daddy, Clark McEntire, us kids, Grandpap, and a ranch hand took care of 3,000 head of cattle by ourselves from morning till night, then would come in and "doctor" 200 head. No, ranching is not an easy life—and while it's a little softer, a performer's life can be hard too. My friend Clark Rhyne, who was my history and art teacher at school, likes to say that my toughness was instilled in me by my Daddy and the life we all shared on the ranch.

⁎

THE BEST THING THAT EVER HAPPENED TO MY DADDY WAS MY MAMA! They had known each other since they were young. Daddy remembers the first time he saw Mama, because he associates her with a yearling her Daddy was hauling to Oklahoma City. "I thought she was a great big ole kid," he jokes, "four or five years older than me."

Mama, in fact, is older by only one year and twenty-four days.

Mama can't recall when she first saw Daddy. "He was just a little fat kid who was always around," she says. But she does remember one day in the ninth grade, when he came to school in khaki britches and a khaki shirt. Then, three weeks into the term, Daddy disappeared—he had quit school forever. I think he got intimidated by high school because he had been sick in first grade and missed learning how to read. But what he lacks in reading, he makes up for with a natural gift for figures, although Daddy would say he got his education in the roping pen.

Somehow, they got together, but they've forgotten their first date. "We didn't date much back then," Mama says. "There was a little country church about a mile and a half from my house. The girls walked and the boys mostly had horses. And the boys would ride up to the girls and get off their horses and walk beside them. If the girl didn't jerk away, well, that was a date."

Eventually they started going to church services or to picture shows together. Mama couldn't get enough of Clark Gable, Joan Fontaine, Barbara Stanwyck, and those other movie stars of the 1940s. "And I hated picture shows," Daddy says. "I had to sit through them just to see her."

To see Daddy, Mama had to ride her horse for one and a half miles to the state highway, where she would tie the horse to a tree and loosen the girth, then flag down the Greyhound bus to Atoka for the movie. When the show ended, she would retrace her tracks and retrieve her horse from the tree.

They sure must have liked each other.

Still, their courtship lasted five or six years, depending on which parent you ask. After a while, Mama was looking for a marriage proposal, but Daddy stayed silent on the subject. "It's hard to take on a wife when you didn't have anything but a lariat rope and a horse and gone off rodeoing all the time," Daddy explains.

Finally, Mama's determination beat out her patience and she took matters into her own hands: "I asked him," she says.

They married on March 17, 1950, when he was twenty-two and she was twenty-three. Daddy's brother-in-law had married four or five years before and had suggested they use the same preacher, saying, "He'll charge you, oh, two or three dollars to marry you," Daddy recalls. Well, Daddy brought a twenty-dollar bill, his entire net worth, and gave it to the preacher, expecting change. The minister merely said, "Thank you." Daddy never had much use for preachers after that.

Mama bought her own wedding ring for twenty-seven dollars after making a three-dollar down payment. Daddy put it on her finger, and for forty-four years, it has never been removed.

They made their home in what they called the "Til House," just down the road from Grandpap and Grandma Alice. It was a two-room shack with a wooden floor but no running water and no electricity. On the door frame, you could still see where the previous owners had allowed their hogs to go in and out, rubbing up against the frame.

"But Clark's mother, Alice, thought we could make it livable and real cute," recalls Mama, "so we got us some lye and made us some lye water and scrubbed the place down. Then we got some building paper and we papered down the walls and it looked pretty good. At least it was clean."

Mama kept on teaching school while Daddy pursued his rodeoing. She had been working since she was seventeen years old, teaching grades one through twelve in a one-room schoolhouse at Tipporary. In the summer she would ride the Greyhound bus down to Durant, about seventy miles, to take classes at Southeastern Oklahoma State University. That's one of the reasons why, years later, I chose that college.

Then Daddy won a car in a roping competition and he told Mama to ask her brother Dale if he'd be willing to swap the car for his eighty acres down on Boggy Creek. Dale said yes, and it was a done deal.

Mama stopped teaching after my oldest sister was born in 1951. She was named Alice after my Grandma Alice, who died in 1950. Mama also had to stop attending rodeos then with Daddy because he simply didn't want her along. Daddy preferred to go with other cowboys, usually his friend Hugh Posey, so they could split expenses. She was so mad about that, she once threw a hammer at Daddy. She missed, luckily.

One day when Daddy and Hugh were preparing to take off, Mama and Alice snuck into the camper in the bed of the pickup. When he discovered the two of them, Daddy refused to speak to Mama for the entire trip.

On one trip, Daddy suffered a terrible tragedy. Few things are more important to a rodeo cowboy than his trained horse, and Ole Joe was the best steer-roping horse Daddy ever had. His winning momentum was up on that horse, and he expected to ride him all the way to the world championship.

Daddy, Hugh Posey, and another friend, Max Kinyon, were going to a rodeo at Strong City, Kansas. Max wanted to ride Ole Joe, so he tied him to the back of their camper. Ole Joe was real bad about rearin' back and trying to break loose when you tried to saddle him. As he ran backwards, Ole Joe yanked out the piece of angle iron that he was tied up to. He ran into a fence and fell back on the angle iron, which stabbed him in the stomach.

Daddy took Ole Joe to Manhattan, Kansas, where veterinarians tried to put the animal's intestines back in place. Daddy was sitting on Ole Joe's head to hold him down while they anesthetized him. But the man who administered the anesthetic was a student and gave the horse too much. Daddy heard the vet say, "Go easy on that stuff. He's weak." After the shot, Daddy said, "Hell, fellers, he's already dead." Ole Joe died of a drug overdose.

That horse wouldn't have been for sale at any price, Daddy has always said. When he lost his Ole Joe, Daddy became a changed man. Mama says he seemed to withdraw and lost a lot of his spirit.

Two years later, when my brother was born, Daddy had to leave to go rodeoing. It was a hard time for Mama—a lot of folks say there isn't a time more sad for a woman than right after childbirth. Postnatal depression, doctors call it. But Daddy had to try to bring home the money that would sustain his family, so Mama had to be understanding.

Daddy left right after bringing Mama home from the hospital with my newborn brother Pake, taking the only automobile they had. Since she had no car and no telephone, Mama would tell our mailman, Bob Weaver, if she needed help, who then, when he delivered her mail, would inform Grandma Smith to come get them.

Daddy got back home a few months later, and just as soon as he got into the house, he wanted to know where Pake was.

"He's on the couch," Mama said. "You walked right past him."

"That's not Pake, that's Alice," Daddy said.

Pake had grown so much that Daddy hadn't recognized him. He had to check a birthmark on Pake's left knee to be sure. Clearly, Daddy had been away too long.

❧

I WAS BORN ON MARCH 28, 1955. MAMA HAD A ROUGHER TIME WITH ME than with any of the others, because I was a breech baby. As it happened, that was the only year my folks were without health insurance, and so, as Daddy likes to tell it, he had to sell some hogs to pay for me!

Not long after Mama and Daddy brought me home, Oklahoma City took their Boggy Creek property to be the floodplain for a new lake, later to be called Atoka Lake. So Daddy and Mama bought 100 acres on the east side of Highway 69, south of Limestone Gap, about two miles south of where Daddy had grown up and five from where Mama was raised. By the time they brought my sister Susie home from the hospital, Daddy had a three-bedroom house roughed in enough for us to live in.

Susie's birth meant that Mama now had four kids under the age of seven. But by then she was an expert at coping during Daddy's absences. One of the times when Daddy was gone, I can recall Mama down at the pond chopping ice so the cattle and horses could get something to drink. She fixed water pumps, stoves, rigs, and washed clothes outside on a wringer washing machine. Her abilities were a balance for Daddy's—he can do almost anything he makes his mind up to do, and do it right, except be a mechanic. "If it can't be fixed with baling wire, it can't be fixed," he always says. He once tore his shirt and tried to mend it by pouring maple syrup over the tear and putting an encyclopedia on top of it.

Baling wire would have worked better!

We had fun, Mama and us kids. She'd play with us and then tell us to go out and play, because she had work to do. But she played with us first. We sang at the supper table, told jokes, and swapped stories about things that happened during the day. We didn't do that when Daddy was home. It got on his nerves. The only time I knew Mama would rather be alone than with us kids was when she was reading a good book. The best thing to do then was to get a book and lie on the bed with her.

Mama stayed home till Alice was old enough to take care of us, then she went back to work, selling fish bait down at Atoka Lake. I remember how she went to and from work in an old pickup that had no brakes or starter. It was the best we could afford.

Mama would park the pickup on a hill at night and scotch it with a rock under a tire, then in the morning us kids would push it down the slope so she could pop the clutch and force-start the engine. She parked it on a hill at work as well and had to pop the clutch to drive home. Sometimes, she went in before day-light and came home after dark. That's when fishermen want bait.

She earned six dollars a day, and the priceless respect of children who never heard her complain.

I learned from Mama that a child wants and needs to know who the boss is and that the boss has to be consistent, loving but firm. That was Mama. If I can be half as good a Mama as my Mama, I'll be thrilled.

People ask me what I would change about my life. And I've thought about it and usually say "nothing." But I would change one thing: every time I ever made Mama cry. That breaks my heart, that I ever disappointed her enough to make her cry.

BETWEEN MAMA'S PAY AND DADDY'S RODEO EARNINGS, THEY BEGAN to build up a cattle herd. Daddy says that he raised our family by rodeoing, but as he—and we—got older, that part of his life slowed down. With us there helping him, he was able to concentrate on raising cattle and putting together our place near Limestone Gap.

I can't remember the first time I climbed on a horse, but I do remember that the first time I rode I had to be pushed up on the saddle, a fact that makes me smile today. I have quarter horses and thoroughbreds now, and riding is as natural to me as breathing. And, strangely, for all the ranching I did, I was never taught how to ride. Daddy just took us kids when we were little and threw us up on a horse. We stayed up. It was your basic survival technique.

Grandpap used to sit on his horse with one of his legs thrown over the saddle horn. He'd put the reins in his mouth and pinch off a plug of tobacco. Then he'd pull the reins out and put the tobacco in.

Us kids would imitate him and each throw one of our legs across the saddle horn. But if Daddy caught us, he'd grab us off the horse, kick our butt, and say, "Now get up there and ride that horse right."

He didn't go for any fooling around.

❦

BY THE TIME I WAS SIX I WAS GATHERING CATTLE, AND DOING IT FROM before daylight until after dark by the time I was seven. Some days we'd help Daddy gather the cattle to sell. Other times, we'd go to the "pole pens," or corrals, at the top of the mountain and gather them up for pregnancy tests, or to ear-tag them, or to worm or to brand them.

It would be 4 A.M. and still pitch-dark when Daddy would get us up for breakfast. Grandpap, Uncle Dale, Uncle Slim, our

friends from Clarksville, Texas, Jim Clark and Bob Christopher-
son, and usually some neighbors would join us. It's a wonder I
can remember so much about the food, since I was like the other
kids, usually half asleep when we ate. Daddy would fry bacon,
then fry eggs in the bacon grease. The eggs would literally float in
bacon fat. He never blotted the eggs, just put them on a platter.
They had so much grease on them they would slide right onto the
plate.

We'd use paper towels to absorb the grease, but not Daddy.
He'd eat the eggs, bacon grease and all. He made "cowboy
bread," which is a mixture of flour, water, and baking soda, and
sometimes he made milk gravy. Talk about cholesterol!

Then Daddy would say, "You kids go get the horses," and
we would go whistle them up close to the feed trough because we
didn't have a barn back then. Then we'd catch them while they
were eating. Alice, Pake, and I would saddle the horses, tie them
up, and then go tell Daddy we were ready.

The sun still wasn't up.

After Daddy gave us our instructions for the day, Grandpap
would have to "translate" for us. Daddy was under a lot of stress
when he worked the cattle, and that early in the morning,
tempers ran short. When Daddy was in a foul mood, he
would always interpret the mere asking of questions as back
talk, so we didn't dare ask him anything. If one of us did, he'd
tell us to pay attention, or holler, "Pull your head out of your
ass."

I don't know what we would have done without Grandpap,
who was sort of our rescuer. We'd chase cattle all day in brush so
thick you couldn't ride through it. A lot of times we'd get lost.
We'd give a holler that was an imitation of Grandpap's special
yell, and he would respond, and we'd go back and forth that way
until he found us.

Many times, I had to get off my horse and pull his legs out of
the briars. He'd take a step, get tangled again, and I'd pull him

out again. I'd get scratches right through my clothes. Some days I spent more time on the ground than on my horse.

Alice was a better hand at working cattle than any man Daddy ever hired, and I've heard him say so. I've seen her ride a horse into brush so thick that she couldn't see the steer she was chasing. She could only hear it bawling. But she'd lean over on the saddle with its horn poking her in the stomach and press in headfirst. She might come out a bloody mess, but she'd come out with a steer.

Our land was that rough until Daddy finally had it "chained." A chain big enough to anchor a battleship was strung between two bulldozers. The bulldozers were driven across the land, and the chain bent or uprooted everything. Then the bulldozers would push all the brush up in piles and later on Daddy would set it on fire.

❧

OUR LUNCH WOULD BE WHATEVER DADDY HAD IN THE TRUCK. IT WAS usually bologna on bread—no Miracle Whip or any other seasoning. We drank pond water from a glass jug. The water was as hot as the temperature inside the truck.

We'd choke down our food, because Daddy didn't like to waste time. Then it was right back after the cattle.

We'd ride as far as fifteen miles away from the house until darkness forced us to quit for the day. Daddy would send us on home while he got the corrals ready for the next morning. Except for the moonlight there wasn't any light for us to see our way home. I'd see sparks fly from the horseshoes hitting rocks as we headed for the house.

We'd be so tired, it was a good thing the horses knew the way back. Pake would run his horse way past the rest of us, get off his horse, and sleep on the ground until the sound of our horses' hooves hitting the ground would wake him up.

WHEN I WAS SIX AND SUSIE WAS FOUR, I REMEMBER HELPING DADDY castrate some young bulls. Daddy would buy one- and two-year-old cattle in Florida, Mississippi, or Texas and have them trucked to our place in Chockie, usually in January or February. Most of them would be bulls. Daddy thought that the cattle would grow faster, wouldn't have the "stag," thick-neck look, and wouldn't mess around as much if they were castrated as soon as they got to our place.

I would stand behind the bull and hold his tail while Daddy sliced the sack and cut the cord that let the testicles fall. Daddy would pass the testicles to me and I'd put them in a bucket. Next I'd hand Daddy the penicillin to inject the "bull turned steer" with, to prevent infections; when I got bigger I'd draw the medicine myself. Then I'd hand Daddy the knife so he could slit the steer's ears. This was called "ear marking." It was a way to identify the cattle as ours, like branding.

Many times when we were done, I helped carry that bucket of testicles to the house and Susie, Alice, and I would sit outside the back door and clean them. We called them mountain oysters. Then we'd take them in to Mama and she'd slice them thin, roll them in flour, and fry them in hot grease in a huge cast-iron skillet. I was literally raised on mountain oysters.

There wasn't any pampering in the pens. One time, Daddy and I were there, worming and branding, and it was getting close to 11 A.M., the heat of the day. There wasn't a breeze at all. I was standing real close to the fire that kept the branding irons hot.

Next thing I knew, my legs went out from under me and I was out. I guess I had heatstroke. When I came to, Daddy was taking a drink out of the water jug. He saw I was coming to and handed the jug to me, helped me to my feet, and we finished our job.

I'VE BEEN KICKED AND RUN OVER BY CATTLE, BUT I'VE KICKED THEM too. I got so mad one day when the cattle wouldn't go in the chute like I wanted them to that I rared back, cussing, and threw the Hot Shot, or cattle prod, at the wooden fence. It flew into ten pieces and came back and hit me in the forehead. Mama and Daddy didn't say a word. Getting my head cut open was punishment enough for cussing.

I'll never forget once dropping a big bottle of worm medicine at the cattle chute and breaking the glass. It cost thirty-six dollars, and I sure felt bad. Daddy didn't say a word that time either. I got another bottle out of the box and went on giving the cattle shots. I guess he thought at least I was trying.

But usually, Daddy didn't accept any excuses, no matter how politely they were given. He kept a buggy whip above the door frame and he'd get it down and snap it across one of us kids' behinds if he thought we needed it. He never warned us. He never even told us we were getting on his nerves. He just let us have it.

The idea of disobeying Daddy never crossed any of our minds. We did what we were told, when we were told.

There's only one time I remember going against him. We had a dog, Tag, who got into a dangerous habit of chasing deer instead of cattle. Most cattlemen will shoot such dogs on the spot because they'll turn other dogs on to it. Daddy was going to punish Tag and told me to hold him while he trained on him. I refused. Daddy hit me across the back with a coiled rope that was used to rope a steer. I took off running and fell. I hit my knee on a rock, and by the time I came back Daddy's temper had cooled.

Some of this may sound cruel, but the cowboy life is harsh. It's an ongoing struggle with nature—against the weather, predators, disease—with the constant threat of poverty if your cattle somehow don't make it to market in good shape. It's not a life for the sentimental or the weak.

The last time Daddy disciplined me was after I was married and had recorded one or two records. I had my own horse, Sonny, and Daddy mentioned that he needed some help the next day gathering cattle.

"I'll help you, Daddy," I said.

I loaded up Ole Sonny and drove over with Daddy to Ashland, at a place Daddy had leased. I was cinching up my horse when Daddy said, "Come on."

"I'll be there in just a minute."

I loped up beside Daddy and he said, "Don't talk back to me, young lady."

"Okay," I replied, and we loped around and found some of the cattle.

"You see them over there?" he said. "Go get them and bring them to the gate." Which I did.

By the time I rode back to where Daddy was, he and Pake were into a serious cussing match. I don't know what sparked it, but they were angry.

"You dough-bellied son of a bitch," Pake said. "You can't rope 'cause you're too fat."

"Why are you even trying to rope?" Daddy fired back. "You can't rope."

I rode up beside Jim Clark and said, "I got chewed out just for saying, 'I'll be there in just a minute.' " I rode back to the house with Jim and never went back to gather cattle with Daddy again.

The next time Daddy had to gather, he said, "Reba, you gonna go help?"

"You gonna holler at me?" I asked.

"Probably," he answered.

"Nope," I said.

꿀벌

I'VE BEEN ASKED IF I RESENTED THE WAY DADDY WHIPPED US KIDS. I don't. That's just the way he was.

What I did resent were the times I had to work cattle with the men, then go in about 11:30 A.M. to cook dinner, which is what we called the noon meal. We cooked it, the men ate it, we cleaned up the mess, then returned to work with the men. What's wrong with this picture?

Me having to cook stopped when I was eleven. It was noon one day, and Mama was at work. I don't remember where Alice was, but if she had been there, Daddy would have sent her. Instead, he told me, "Reba, you go on up to the house and fix dinner."

I looked in the cabinets and found a can of green beans. And lima beans. And pork 'n' beans.

I honestly didn't realize that everything I opened was a variety of beans.

"Reba, are you partial to beans?" Daddy asked when he and the rest of the family came inside. Pake, who still tells the story to tease me, says, "Can you imagine a damn cattle outfit with no meat?"

Daddy wanted some meat and potatoes, food that would "stick to his ribs." Instead, they all got a vegetarian meal years before that kind of eating became popular. I don't remember Daddy ever sending me to the house to cook again.

꿀벌

WHEN WE WERE GROWING UP I USED TO REGRET THAT DADDY NEVER told us that he loved us. It bothered me that he never gave us kids Christmas presents, except one year when he gave Pake a pocketknife. But Mama took care of that like I found out later a lot of mamas do. Daddy was just too busy.

After messing with yearlings from daylight until after dark, Daddy would just lie on the couch and then he'd go to bed, to the quiet. On the rare occasions when he was rested and he felt good, we'd pile on him on the couch and wrestle. Sometimes, he even took us swimming in the pond on the top of the mountain after we'd been working cattle all day. I remember there was a creek just right for swimming up past Grandpap's house almost to Uncle Keno's, Grandpap's brother. We'd take a watermelon and throw it in to get cold while we swam. Then we'd cut it open and eat it. It was a lot of fun. Lots of great memories.

I think my Daddy never learned how to show love like a lot of people because of his upbringing and him being an only child. Back in 1987, when he had triple-bypass surgery, I went to see him in intensive care. He had tubes sticking out from all over him and was still groggy from the heavy medication.

I just sat by his bedside, thinking back on those tough days on the ranch and understanding how rough it must be for Daddy to see those years of hard living catch up with him. Work was his whole life. "You can't mess around," he used to tell us. "If you're in business, you tend to business first." I realized then how much like him I am.

Squeezing his hand, I leaned over to him. I explained that I had to go meet the bus, that I had a show to do in Chattanooga, Tennessee, the following night.

In a faint voice he said, "Okay. I love you, honey."

That was the only time I ever heard him speak those words to me or to anyone else.

But he's come close. "I don't know," he said recently, "I've seen Reba on television now so many times. I'll say it still just makes me go to pumpin' inside."

CHAPTER 3

I NEVER KNEW HOW ABNORMALLY ROUGH MY CHILDHOOD WAS until I went home with other kids. Most of my friends had time on their hands, to play with toys and things. The only time we got out of work was when we went to school. When I came home, I took my school clothes off—hand-me-downs mostly from my cousins or sister; the only time I received new clothes was at Christmas—and put on my everyday clothes to get to work.

I had a white sweatshirt with the sleeves cut out that I wore for a long time. One day I'd wear it correctly. The next day, I'd turn it around, and the next day I'd turn it inside out. Then, the next day, I'd turn it around again. Since Mama had a day job and her hands were full when she got home, I thought I'd help out as much as possible. But I was never clothes conscious anyway, and to this day I prefer to wear jeans when I'm not onstage.

I don't mean to suggest that we were dirty. On school nights our evening routine included baths for all of us, but we only had one bathroom for six people. We bathed in a galvanized bathtub and whoever got there first had clean water, which was pulled by gravity through pipes from our pond. The cattle also drank out of that pond, so I never drank the water when I was at home unless it was fixed as iced tea. The water did go through a filtering process Daddy had bought, but iced tea is clear compared to the water that we had running into the house. Grandma Smith got their water from a well at their house, and I remember watching her strain it through a cotton dish towel to remove most of the foreign objects.

But my story is not another attempt by someone in show business to tell you how hard she had it as a little girl. My friend Burt Reynolds talks about how successful folks try to "outpoor" each other. They sit around telling stories, something like, "We were so poor when I was a kid that we didn't have running water."

"Oh yeah?" another argues. "We were so poor that the wolf brought his lunch when he came to our door."

I can add to that: "We were so poor when I was a kid, we didn't even have a remote control for the TV." That's what I'll tell my son, Shelby, someday.

We got a color television when I was twelve. I'll never forget how excited I was! We stopped at a Pizza Hut in Ada, Oklahoma, to celebrate the purchase. I had never been to one before.

When the waitress came, Mama said, "Hamburger, please," meaning hamburger pizza. I'd just been to the bathroom and didn't hear what was going on, didn't know there was more than one kind of pizza.

"Hamburger?" I shouted. "I thought we was gonna have pizza!"

Everybody laughed and never let me forget my stupid remark.

That TV became the nighttime entertainment center at our house—Pake could take an entire bath in the flash of a commercial. It also taught me my first lesson in democracy. We would vote at the start of the week on which shows we were going to watch on which nights. The majority ruled. We made a list, and posted it above the heating stove. Believe me, no child today has ever enjoyed a video game more than we enjoyed our nineteen-inch television that received only two channels.

❦

THE TV WAS OUR ONE BIG LUXURY. BUT KIDS WHO ARE BROUGHT UP with as few material things as we had usually become very inventive. One of the most fun and resourceful things us kids ever did together had to do with deer hunters. Our ranch had about as many deer as rattlesnakes, and both were equally visible.

During deer season in November, we'd go to Mama's office at school and use the copy machine to print permits to sell for a dollar apiece to the hunters who wanted to come on the McEntire land. This is how we got our Christmas money every year. We'd put a rope up on our side of the cattle guard—boards like a bridge over the creek that keep livestock from walking across the creek—and when we'd hear a pickup approaching, we'd hop right up with our permits.

Then the lies and excuses would begin.

"Oh, we hunted on here last year and Clark said we could hunt again," someone might say.

"You can, but it will cost you a dollar," one of us kids would reply.

"Don't you recognize me?" another might say. "I'm your kinfolk. I'm Uncle So-and-So."

"Nice to see you, Uncle So-and-So, have you got your dollar?" Despite our serious efforts, sometimes hunters would come onto our place with us not knowing. So at night, us four kids and Daddy would load up in his pickup to raid the deer camps. Daddy knew the land better than anybody, and I don't think we could have found our way around up there at night without him. Daddy always knew where the camps would be.

There we were, bouncing over the roughness that was our land, searching for the brightness of a campfire. When we spotted one, Daddy would stop, and us kids would pile out of the truck.

"How you fellers doing?" Daddy would say, leaving the collecting to us.

"Have you got your permit?" Pake would say. Once again, the excuses and lies.

Most of the responses were in fun, because everybody always paid. Some years, we'd do very well, clearing twenty to forty dollars a day. But Mama remembers that Pake got discouraged when we first started collecting. He thought the men were really trying to cheat him, and if he hadn't persisted, who knows if they would have paid? It was Pake's first lesson in grown-ups' dishonesty, as he had never previously known anything but the integrity of the McEntires and their friends, most of whom could use their word as their bond.

❦

DADDY ALWAYS SAID THAT, BEING AN ONLY CHILD, HE WANTED TO have enough kids to have his own baseball team. But after having four kids that made as much racket as we did—that was enough.

And being normal kids, we were full of mischief. Next to the barn, for instance, was a shed where Daddy kept his sick yearlings. We would tie a rope to the rafters on the barn and Alice and Pake would swing from the top of the shed over the haystack. At the height of their swing, they'd let go and fall into the mountain of loose hay.

I always wanted to try doing things like that, but never had the courage. When I was ten, I stood on top of the shed and braced myself for the swing. Alice and Pake had already gone into the house for dinner. I had assured them I was going to take the swing, but I was simply too scared. I climbed down the way I had come up, and never did take the plunge that was the McEntire version of bungee jumping twenty-five years ago. I wasn't ashamed of being chicken. I felt it was the smart thing to do— not to get hurt.

But Alice and Pake called me a sissy for days.

Pake, especially, used to pull these derring-do stunts all the time. I recall feeling my heart in my stomach watching him climb up and down a three-hundred-foot tower just to prove to us he could.

Sometimes we'd play in the hay barn, where Daddy had stacked the hay from the ground to the rafters. There was no way for the smallest breeze to penetrate the hay when it was that tightly packed. Us kids dug tunnels through that mountain of hay. We'd crawl on our hands and knees through the maze of passages, which may stand as the dumbest thing we ever did. If the hay had shifted one bit, we would have been trapped inside and smothered to death. Haystacks are also a hiding place for snakes and skunks that burrow inside. It's a thousand wonders we weren't crawling through a tunnel to come face-to-face with a rattler. There is no way we could have gotten out of there.

A lot of our mischief came out at the roping pen. Once Pake and Phillip Miller, Pake's buddy, dared Alice to ride one of our old steers, and a dare was all Alice needed. But the steer bucked and pinned her up against a split-rail fence, cutting her head open. Pake ran down to the creek, jerked his filthy T-shirt off, doused it in water, and ran back and crammed it on Alice's head to stop the bleeding. They wondered why she didn't bleed to death.

Then there was the time we could have lost Susie, a subject we talked about just this past Thanksgiving.

As we remembered it, Alice, Pake, and Susie had been down at the roping pen. Susie was riding behind Pake on Ole Brownie and Alice was on Pelican. When they got to the gate between the roping pens and the house, Pake stepped off his horse to open the gate and Alice rode on through. So did Susie on Brownie. Both my sisters headed toward the house, leaving Pake behind. Brownie, in a hurry to get to the barn, took off, and Susie, who was really small at the time, couldn't stop her horse. Brownie ran right by the house. I know because I had stayed at the house that day and ran out the front door when I heard her scream. Right behind our house was a long, two-line clothesline. Brownie went right under it and the lines caught Susie full in the face. One caught her in the mouth and one on the nose. Susie flipped about two times in the air before she hit the ground.

Alice, as the oldest, had been left in charge of us that day while Daddy took Mama to the dentist. She knew she'd get in trouble if Susie was seriously injured, so she tried to persuade her she wasn't hurt. So she rushed Susie into the house and put a mirror up to her.

"Now see," Alice said, "you aren't hurt a bit!"

Susie looked into the mirror and saw her face dripping with blood.

"Then you never heard such screaming," Pake said. "They liked to never got her quieted down after that. Susie thought she was killed."

Susie easily could have been killed through a game we used to play in the pickup. We would ride everywhere in the back of the truck, and were forever saying, "Last one out is a rotten egg." Susie, the baby of the family, didn't want to be outdone. She got a couple of concussions by jumping out of the vehicle before it came to a stop. It took her a couple of times to figure out she could wait.

THERE ARE MANY NATURAL PERILS TO GROWING UP IN THE RURAL Southwest—the ever-present wasps (I recall how Grandpap would apply tobacco juice to our wasp stings to take away the pain), the spring tornadoes that would send us running to the cellar Daddy had built for protection in the dead of night, and snakes, which were a constant fear. We looked out for snakes the way urban children look out for playground bullies.

I once started down the hall from the bedroom and saw a snake curled on the carpet. Mama said later it was just a mouse snake. I began to scream, but she was in no hurry to kill it, seeing that it was harmless. I continued to yell until she cut it into two pieces with scissors. Bloodstains remained on the carpet for weeks after that, and I pouted for days because she had been so casual about the snake.

Another time, I was sitting in Mama's bed Indian-style drawing on a chalkboard. A movement caught my attention out of the side of my eye. Then I saw a snake slithering around Mama's magazine on the floor.

Again I started screaming for Mama, who was outside. I threw the chalkboard at the snake and the board shattered to pieces. Luckily it was a nonpoisonous blacksnake. The only harm to its potential victim might be a fear-induced heart attack.

Rattlers, of course, were our biggest worry. In Oklahoma they grow to a frightening size. Okeene, Oklahoma, 168 miles from Chockie, hosts the world's largest rattler hunt every spring. An average of one thousand pounds of snakes are picked up off the ground in three days' time, some of them longer than seven feet. Our hired hand, Louie Sandman, once killed a rattlesnake that was six feet two inches long, holding a live rabbit in its mouth. Mama tells me that the largest rattlesnake ever seen around Chockie was killed by Grandpa's uncle, Belt Love, in the 1920s. That happened about a mile from where we lived. They laid the snake across the tracks, and he reached the full length from rail to rail.

A rattler's venom can sometimes cause instant death. We've even found cattle lying in the pasture that Daddy figured had died of snakebite. And rattlers can be hard to stop. Recently, Pake ran over a rattler as big as his arm with a four-wheel-drive vehicle. The snake slithered off. Daddy once hit a rattlesnake, which was coiled up, with a big rock. It bounced off like the snake was rubber. The snake slithered off under a rock, so Daddy left him alone.

AS WITH ALL KIDS, THERE WERE TIMES WHEN WE TURNED OUR MIS-chief on each other. Being the youngest two, Susie and I naturally tended to get picked on. Alice used to trick Susie and me into going out into the yard, then lock us out of the house. Susie and I eventually figured it all out and started unlocking our bedroom window screens and climbing back inside.

I have to confess that I sometimes started trouble myself. Once, with Pake's help, I convinced Susie she was adopted. I pointed out that, unlike the other three of us, who resemble Mama, she didn't have red hair or freckles, and that that must mean she wasn't a McEntire. She was so upset that she went to her doll for comfort. Her dolls were her life. She'd dress them up and talk to them. I think they were as real to her as her living, breathing brother and sisters.

When she picked up her doll and started to change its dress, she saw that Pake had painted its navel green. She began crying, hard. She packed her suitcase and she left home. She was seven. Susie got as far as the cattle guard and just stood there, bawling. She would have gone farther than that, but Mama had always told us that we could leave but if we ever went farther than the cattle guard we couldn't come back. Only later, when she was older, did it dawn on Susie that she might not look like Mama, but in looks and temperament she was just like our Daddy! And her baby pictures looked just like Grandma Alice's.

Unlike Susie, I was a tomboy and never had any interest in

dolls or in talking to anything that couldn't talk back. Maybe because our interests were different, or because we were so close in age and shared a room, she and I fought often as kids, arguing and pulling each other's hair. Come to think of it, though, Pake and I used to get into arguments a lot, too, usually while we were gathering cattle. He was bigger and no telling how many pounds heavier than me, but that didn't scare me one bit.

Our arguments often turned into fistfights. The horses would be going around and around as we'd try to hit each other and knock the other one off his or her horse. Our favorite game was Anything You Can Do I Can Do Better.

❧

MORE OFTEN THAN NOT, THOUGH, THERE WAS A LOT OF FUN AND laughing coming out of that little house in Chockie near Limestone Gap.

I recall how Mama had a pink record player, a Motorola, and a 45 of the Singing Nun singing "Dominique." Now, Susie and I couldn't understand a word of French, but my folks had this big dresser in their bedroom with a big old mirror. We'd stand in front of it and, using hairbrushes as "microphones," we'd lip-synch the song. And once a week, the four of us would come parading down the hall in our pajamas, dancing and singing to the music of "77 Sunset Strip," while it was coming on TV, all the time careful not to let our bare feet touch the hot floor where the furnace was. That was our idea back then of a "pregame show."

But I especially remember several New Year's Eves when friends and family came from miles around to dance in our brand-new living room, a large room built onto our house with money Mama and us kids had saved.

Putting the new living room on the back of the house would give us a lot more space. The old living room would become

Mama and Daddy's bedroom, so Pake could get their old one and Alice could get Pake's. Susie and I would still share one, but it was better for two than for three. So Mama put back money from work. Uncle Peck, Grandpap's brother, had given each of us kids a heifer calf when we were little, so when the calves grew up and had babies, we could sell them. We did, and it was our decision to put the money into the living room account.

On those New Year's Eves, someone would bring a guitar, another a fiddle, but everyone was required to bring either a "pie or a pint" (of whiskey). Nobody got out of line. There were kids everywhere. I watched those people play music, sing, and dance until daylight, and we sang along too. If someone got sleepy, he would pull up a piece of floor to sleep on. It was straight out of "The Waltons."

Special times like these make me realize that music has always been a huge part of my life.

SINCE MY DADDY WAS A RODEO CHAMPION, NATURALLY WE SPENT A lot of time attending them with him. Some of my fondest memories are of those trips my family made to rodeos. At night, Susie and I would sleep on each side of our green Ford's hump on the floor, while Pake slept on the shelf under the back window and Alice got the back seat. Going down the road in the dark, listening to the hum of the highway with our parents in the front, was a magical and safe feeling. Sleep and security came easily.

But often we'd get jolted out of that peaceful sleep. In those days there were no interstates, so we'd be traveling on two-lane highways that passed through small towns. When we'd come up on a red light, the heavy two-horse trailer we were pulling, which had no brakes, would be tough to stop fast. So Daddy would hit the brakes and Pake would fall off the shelf onto Alice and then both of them would wind up on the floor along with me and Susie. You can imagine the wrestling that went on after that.

Our daytime rides had their share of wrestling too. We were spirited children, and when boredom and restlessness set in, we could get bad about fighting, scuffling, and "Don't touch me" and "Pake did this" and "Mama, Pake did that." So when Daddy had had enough of it, which wouldn't take very long, he'd let his arm fall from across the back of the front seat and pinch whichever kid he made contact with first. So Mama would get us to singing to keep us occupied, teaching us three-part harmony and songs like "Please, Mr. Custer. I Don't Wanna Go" and "I'm So Lonesome Every Day."

I don't know how old I was when I went to my first rodeo. I have a picture of Pake and me in front of a rodeo arena when I was three. But I know I'd been going long before that. And I can date the start of my professional singing life to a rodeo trip we took to Cheyenne, Wyoming, when I was four or five. We were staying at the Edwards Hotel, and back in those days there were no TVs in the room. So everyone visited and hung out in the lobby. My memory of it is as plain as day: There was one television, lots of windows, and green leather couches with brass trim. Cowboys were everywhere.

One afternoon, while we were in the lobby, one of the cowboys asked Pake to sing him a song. Pake sang "You Ain't Nothin' but a Hound Dog" and got a quarter for it. Not wanting to be left out, I got Pake off to the side and asked him if he'd help me sing a song too. So then I got up and sang "Jesus Loves Me." Everett Shaw, our family friend and a former world-champion steer roper, paid me a nickel.

Back then was just like today. The girl singer does as much work as the guy but she gets less money for it. I've been fighting that all my life!

RODEOS WERE ALWAYS A MAJOR SOURCE OF FUN FOR US, BUT WE NOT only watched them, we learned all the skills. Long before the roping pen on the ranch became our playground, my siblings and I would rope our tricycles, while Mama pretended to be a rodeo announcer, or we'd go down to the cattle guard, sit on the willow bushes, and play like we were riding on a bronc. That old roping pen is gone now—the new Highway 69 runs right through it—but nothing can ever take away the good times we had there.

All the time I was growing up, Pake would be roping (either team roping, steer roping, or calf roping) and Alice would practice running barrels or poles. Barrel racing is where the horse runs as fast as he can and then virtually stops as fast as he can, turns a barrel and accelerates as fast as he can, then does it twice more. Fifteen hundred pounds of horseflesh sitting on four ankles not much larger than a man's tries to hurl itself and a rider around barrels three feet in diameter. I started running barrels when I was nine.

A lot of folks don't realize that a cowboy or cowgirl is only as good as his or her horse. In my case the horse probably knew more about running barrels than I did. The horse has to be trained, which I usually did myself—with help from Daddy, who had come up with a good method for training horses to run barrels.

"Now, Reba," he told me, "it looks to me like it would be a good idea to set barrels up out in the open—in the pasture—and just walk your horse around them for a few days. Get him real comfortable and agile with the barrels. Then begin to lope him around the barrels for a few days before you take him to the ropin' pen."

So I did what Daddy said, and it worked. I used his technique, but I did later on borrow some ideas from other barrel racers when I'd watch them train their horses. That was after I married, and my husband Charlie and I would stay at a rodeo for a day or two, so I'd see the girls put their horses through the barrel pattern. I especially liked the way the world-champion barrel racer for many years, Gail Petska, trained. She'd spin a horse around a barrel, putting its nose right on the barrel, then letting its butt just swing around.

Of course, there were some scary moments in the roping pen. When you rope a calf, your horse stops real fast and jerks the calf down. Then you get off your horse, and while the calf is down, you get hold of him, help him up, flank him, and put him down on his side so you can tie his legs together. One day Pake was on Ole Brownie roping calves. He got mad at Ole Brownie for not stopping properly and had jumped off to train on him, still dragging the calf tied at the end of the rope. I had enough of that and jumped on Ole Brownie and rode him up to give the calf slack around his neck so it wouldn't choke him. Pake dragged me off and hit me in the chest, fracturing my sternum. That's the closest I've ever come to having a broken bone.

Another time Pake and his friend Bill Hamilton were team roping and Bill was riding Blue. When Bill was getting ready to rope the horns, the girth broke and Bill fell off and the saddle slid under Blue's belly. I didn't think the horse would ever stop. He ran through the back fence before he finally came to a halt. Bill was okay and so was Blue, but both were a little rattled.

But these mishaps were just part of our training, part of the practice that earned us money at rodeos and points at the horse shows. Alice won lots of "All-Around" trophies at the Quarter Horse Shows. She had so many, she used them as doorstops. She even gave me one for Christmas one year, but replaced her award plaque with one that said "#1 Sister."

Rodeo is simply in the blood of our family. By the time I was eleven, I was already competing in rodeos. My first one was an International Rodeo Association (IRA) rodeo at Atoka, which I entered as a local contestant. It was no secret that I was nervous. Not only was I a beginner, but I also faced the pressure of being a

McEntire. Grandpap and Daddy made rodeo history, and Alice and Pake were good performers too. I had a lot to live up to.

I rode Ole Pelican, one of Daddy's roping horses—all I ever seemed to ride were Daddy's or Pake's rejects. Well, I thought I had ridden fast at home, but in the arena I thought I was flying. I probably weighed all of seventy-five or eighty pounds.

Then we got to the first barrel and Pelican stumbled and fell. I fell off into the dirt. I got up on my horse and finished my pattern, spurring as madly as someone competing in the National Finals Rodeo. It felt to me like my legs were flying out far enough to form a right angle with my body.

I didn't win, but I had managed to finish my first competitive barrel race. I was proud.

I don't remember what the announcer said, but Daddy told me at the end of my ride, "Reba, you need to kick your horse more."

"It felt like my legs were out this far, Daddy," I said, raising my arms. He just walked away.

⚜

I WOULD GO ON TO RUN BARRELS UNTIL I WAS TWENTY-ONE. I WAS competing usually in about fifty rodeos a year after I got out of high school, and very seldom I'll get to run barrels now at home. Looking back, though, I think I was an embarrassment to Daddy because I never did all that well on the rodeo circuit. I was better in the practice pen than I was in competition.

Rodeoing can be so very scary and dangerous. I've seen girls run their heads into fences. It's a wonder that I lasted as long as I did, that I never got hurt. I'd always get so nervous before a competition that I had to struggle to keep from throwing up.

I've never been that nervous about singing, even when I've sung for millions of people on prime-time, international television, such as on the Academy Awards. But I still get butterflies when I sing the National Anthem or sing at an awards show in front of my peers. And it used to get me when Mama, who is my biggest critic, was in the audience.

But now that I'm a mama myself I realize that she'll love me regardless of how I do. And I can see that, back then, Daddy did too.

CHAPTER 4

EVERYONE HAS SPECIAL MILESTONES IN HIS OR HER LIFE, SUCH as their wedding day or their high school commencement. One of mine was my first day of school.

On that big morning, my shoes, clothes, and the rest of my attire were placed neatly in a line on the back of the couch in the living room so that I could dress close to the old brown heating stove. I wanted to be warm while I slipped from my pajamas into my clothes. The warmth I felt was probably no more than sheer excitement.

We didn't have kindergarten in the Kiowa public school system, so my primary education began in the first grade in 1961. My teacher was Mrs. Eula Kelly, whom I had met when she taught Alice and Pake. I thought she was one of the nicest women in the world, so it thrilled me when, thirty years later, my collaborator on this book, Tom Carter, tracked her down and learned that she's a big fan of mine. She is about ninety now, and she smiled and laughed throughout Tom's visit until he asked her what she thinks when she sees me on television.

"I'm so proud," she said. Then she began to cry, bless her heart.

In a way, first grade was the real beginning of my performing career. It marked the first time I ever sang behind a microphone —during a Christmas program held in the high school gymnasium. I sang "Away in a Manger." I must not have done too badly, because in the second grade, I got an even more challenging assignment—I sang "He" at the high school commencement! That came about because Mama's friend, Donna Rue Wilson, who lived with us quite a bit during high school, graduated that year. She put in a word for me, and so there I was, seven years old, singing for eighteen- and nineteen-year-olds. For a little kid, it was pretty scary, but exciting to be the center of attention of so many teenagers that I looked up to.

The commencement address that year was given by our congressman, Carl Albert, who was also the speaker of the United States House of Representatives. Mama remembers that in his speech that night, Congressman Albert commented on Daddy's success as a roper. Then he predicted that if I kept on, I'd be more successful than my Daddy. So I guess I sang okay!

And I was keeping on. In the second grade, Mrs. Canton, our music teacher and my first piano teacher, put a program together and I sang "My Favorite Things," from *The Sound of Music,* though I didn't get to see the movie itself for a few years. Then, in the third grade, I sang "Red Wings" for my teacher Miss Cason's Thanksgiving program.

I liked singing a lot in those days, but everyone who knew me in school would have thought my favorite activity was lunch. We had the most wonderful cooks at Kiowa, Marie McClendon and Ruby Horn Maxwell. So I would always sit by the weak-stomached kids and would say something unappetizing like, "You wanna play Lookie?" They'd say, "What's that?" and I'd say,

...mily will always be a big part of my life. *Top left:* Here is my ...ama's immediate family, from left, her parents, George Elvin ...d Reba Estelle Brasfield Smith, Aunt Imogene Thompson, ...o we call Aunt Jeannie, Mama, Uncle Dale Smith, and Aunt ...orgia Lawrence. *Top right:* My Mama. She was at sixteen, ...d still is, a handsome woman. *Bottom right:* Mama and ...ddy in 1958. *Bottom left:* John Wesley and Alice Kate ...yhurst McEntire (*right*) are my father's parents.

FERRELL BU

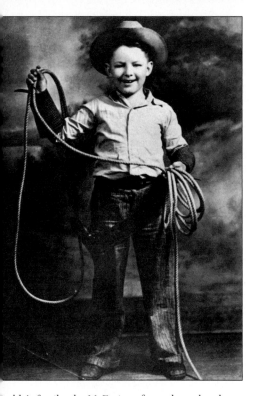

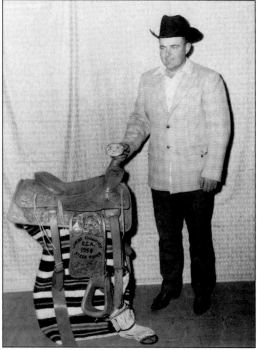

Daddy's family, the McEntires, formed a rodeo dynasty. *Facing page, top:* John Wesley "Grandpap" McEntire at the Cheyenne Frontier Days Rodeo in 1934. *Bottom:* Daddy tripping a steer at Pawhuska, Oklahoma, in 1963. *Above left:* Daddy in 1937—he began ropin' at an early age and even said he used to rope chickens! *Above right:* Daddy with his trophy saddle. He held the title of World Champion Steer Roper for the years of 1957, 1958, and 1961. We often went along to the rodeos. *Below:* This one was at Pendelton, Oregon, where Daddy won another saddle; from left are me, the Rodeo Queen, Mama, Daddy, and Pake.

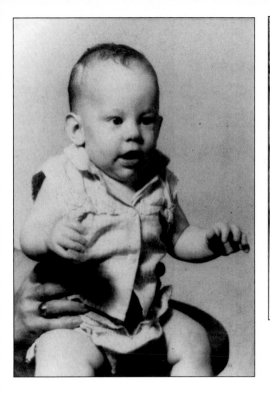

ing page, top left: I've never been camera shy, not even when I was a year old; that's Aunt Jeannie holding me. *right:* I'm celebrating my second birthday. *Bottom left:* My oldest sister Alice, right, and I are going straight the wrapping at my third Christmas. *Center right:* I always looked up to my cousin Gary Thompson. That's n holding me when I was a baby. It was a terrible shock losing him at such an early age. *Bottom right:* From *t,* Pake, Alice, and me in front of our black and white television set—look out Hollywood! *Above left:* Daddy, ma, Alice, me, and Pake pose in our kitchen soon after we moved to Chockie. *Above right:* One of my orite photos of us four kids—Pake, me, Alice, and Susie in 1958. *Below:* We were very close to our cousins, Thompsons. Here's the normal clan together: From left, Pake on the slide, Gary with the gun, Rickie hang-, Paula posing, Alice on her knees, and that's Aunt Georgia with me on the teeter-totter.

Ranching and rodeoing were as much a part of our childhood as school is for other children. *Above:* Pake started roping early but had to do it left-handed after breaking his right arm riding a calf that Doris Jean, our cousin, put him on. We all learned to ride a horse real quick. *Right:* Pake got to pose with Daddy on Ole Buddy at a steer roping in Laramie, Wyoming, in 1957. *Facing page:* I couldn't wait to go to school. *Top:* I proudly made my singing debut in the first grade, performing "Away in a Manger"; the girl wearing the bow in her hair at right is Brenda Lee, my buddy from fifth grade on and my first roommate in college. *Center:* My first grade class along with our teacher Miss Eula Kelly; I'm in the second row, third from left. The circles show the ten of us who graduated together from Kiowa High School twelve years later. *Bottom left and right:* My second and fifth grade school pictures plainly show that I had the freckles of a McEntire. Donna Rue gave me the initials, shown in the right-hand photo, for my birthday.

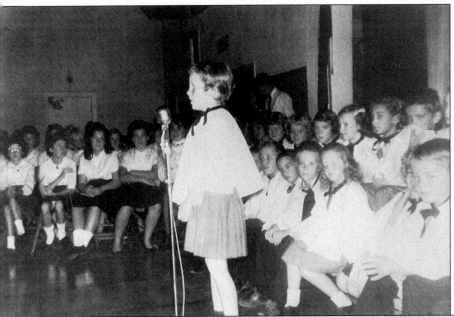

In the fifth grade, I started playing basketball and in junior high I went to basketball camp every summer. *Top:* Here I am at camp at the JFK college in Wahoo, Nebraska. I'd play ball and, after a crash course from Pake, entertain the other players on the guitar. *Center:* They picked me as a cheerleader mainly because I had a big mouth; I'm third from the left in the top row. *Below:* I played guard on the Kiowa Cowgirls basketball team coached by Bill Hensley. In this picture taken in my sophomore year of high school, I'm fourth from right.

"Lookie!" They'd look at me and I'd open my mouth. Of course, it would be full of food. Then I would ask them if they were going to eat their cake or beans or whatever we had that day. By the time I got through with them, I usually got their food.

It wasn't until the fifth grade that I truly got bitten by the show business bug. Mrs. Juanita Mackey was my teacher, and was also the 4-H Club director for grade school. In 4-H Club we did skits, practiced public speaking, showed calves and pigs, canned food, made aprons and pot holders—the works. Then, for the annual 4-H Share-the-Fun talent show, Mrs. Mackey let me borrow her daughter's prom dress and shoes, along with a rhinestone necklace and bracelet, to sing "My Sweet Little Alice Blue Gown." I felt like Cinderella. I won first in the Junior Individual Act division. It was my first trophy.

That victory made me like a hunting dog—I had tasted blood and now knew deep within my very soul that I was to be an entertainer.

Besides that, I recognized that singing was the best way to get any attention. I wasn't the oldest child in the family or the youngest, or even the only boy. I was the third child, so the only other way I could get noticed was to make trouble—but that was definitely not the kind of attention I was looking for.

❦

MY ENERGY AND AGGRESSION FOUND ANOTHER HEALTHY OUTLET IN fifth grade—athletics. I ran track that year and still hold the record for the seventy-five-yard dash in the Pittsburg County Conference, according to Paul Davis, my first coach.

I also started playing basketball, which indirectly helped to boost my musical skills. After hearing me sing, the coach of a summer basketball camp in Wahoo, Nebraska, invited me to come for three weeks. Mama only had to pay for the first week of my basketball training, and for the next two weeks I was to be a counselor and entertainer for the girls.

The catch was that I'd need to learn to play the guitar. Thanks to a crash course from Pake, by the time I got there I knew enough songs to get by, most of them from Dolly Parton's *Blue Ridge Mountain Boy* album. I must not have played too well—I still don't play the guitar much—but that summer, no one complained. The next few summers I went to Lindsay, Oklahoma, to Charles Heatly's Basketball Camp.

Back then we played half-court basketball—three on three— and I was a guard. I never had a lot of confidence in my ball playing, but apparently my coaches did. I was on the main team every year from then on, except when I was a sophomore in high school, and in my senior year, I even went on to the state finals.

Susie played basketball too, and her team made it to the district tournament. Pake recalled that the score was tied with only seconds left in the fourth quarter. Bill Hensley, the coach, called a time-out.

As the girls came in, Hensley struggled to be heard above the noise of the crowd, and it was hard to communicate with his exhausted players. He wanted the play to end with the passing of the ball to Susie.

She meant to ask him, "What do you want me to do, shoot?"

Instead, in her nervous excitement, she asked, "What do you want me to do, shit?"

Pake said the huddle fell out with laughter. He couldn't remember if Susie's team won or lost.

⚜

EXCEPT FOR ONE MONTH IN 1962 WHEN MY DADDY TOOK US ALL TO Okeechobee, Florida, where he bought cattle, my twelve years of education were spent at Kiowa. There were about thirty kids in the first grade, and ten of us graduated together eleven years later: Sherry Stiles, Melia Echelle, Joni Winslett, Roy Hatridge, Steve Phipps, Sue Fereday, Winford Hooe, Patty Ray, and Nathan Caldwell. My first cousin, Diannia Kay Smith, my uncle Dale's daughter, started with us in the first grade but was held back in the sixth.

Diannia, Melia, Sherry, and I were pretty inseparable in our early years. One time, Diannia and I hid in one of Daddy's trailers so she could spend the night with me. But when Uncle Dale and Aunt Virginia got halfway home, someone missed Diannia and they came back for her. We didn't get into too much trouble for that.

You could usually find the whole gang of us at Sherry's house on a Thursday night, when our favorite show, "Bewitched," came on. We did fun, silly things together, like read Ouija boards and have séances. Those scared us all to death. We'd get Patty King from across the street because she was the lightest of the group. We'd lay her on the floor, and with two fingers apiece under her, we'd try to raise her off the ground. One time, we did lift her off the floor. We were so frightened when that happened, we dropped her!

Melia, Sherry, and I still keep in contact yearly, one way or another. Old friends remind you of the past and all the fun and silly things you did. Sorta keeps you humble too.

I also spent a lot of time with our other cousins, the Thompsons. With the ten-year-or-so age gap between us, they were our baby-sitters as well as our kinfolk. There were four of them— Doris Jean, Gary, Paula, and Rickie—the children of Aunt Jeannie, Mama's sister, and her husband, Uncle Slim, whose real names were Imogene and Leslie Thompson. Doris was the oldest and the bossiest. She would put me behind the door whenever I'd get in trouble. Most of the time I'd fall asleep. She was also guilty of talking Alice into sticking her tongue to a frozen coffee can that was full of ice, and she was the one who put Pake on the calf that he fell off, breaking his right arm. I love Doris Jean with all my heart. She's a lot like Alice—I could call anytime I was in a tight spot and she'd be there to help.

Paula, also the second girl, was famous for her bedroom, where there were two twin beds. One she slept on, and the other stayed piled high with clothes, clean and dirty. We were a lot alike.

Rickie, the baby girl and a lot like Susie, used to keep big baskets of stuff in the top of her closet. Of course, I wanted to know what it was. I would shimmy up the sides of the closet, one foot on one side, one on the other, to find out—though finding out was never as much fun as getting there. I remember that, one time, Rickie was stuck taking care of me when she had a date with her boyfriend, Loyd. So we both got all dressed up—I was pretty excited, though not quite sure what a date was—but he never showed. Eventually they made up, and he is now her husband.

The only boy, Gary, was a very handsome young man and a good calf roper too. One night he and Alice were both up at the Bogata, Texas, rodeo, and I was honored that Gary asked me to hold his pocketknife, a cowboy's most valuable possession, while he roped. He won first place.

The U.S. involvement in the war in Vietnam was picking up, and we were all afraid Gary was going to have to go. Instead, on September 16, 1968, I got called to the office at school.

Gary had been in the roping pen behind his home in String-town, trying to put a tarp over some hay with his friend Greg Cochran (who later became one of my bus drivers). They were fastening down the hay with baling wire, and the wire accidentally connected with a high-voltage electric line. Thousands of volts shot through Gary as he caught the baling wire. Mercifully, he was dead before he hit the ground.

I remember the wreath of daisies, shaped like a horse, that stood beside the casket. I was only a sixth-grader, when, for the first time, my life was touched by the death of someone I loved. We had all worried that Gary would be sent to Vietnam, and then he was killed in his own backyard. I remember going to Aunt Jeannie and Uncle Slim's house and thinking how hard it was going to be for them to go through his things. It was a long time before I ever spoke about Gary around them. The death of a loved one is something you never forget. And Gary was my first.

❧

BY THE TIME I GOT TO JUNIOR HIGH SCHOOL, PAKE, SUSIE, AND I WERE singing more and more together around our house. Sometimes we were the entertainment when Mama and Daddy's friends came over to play dominoes. Alice didn't join us much back then; she was mostly concentrating on her barrel-racing. But she really has a beautiful voice. She sings with us if it's a family thing. She even sang at her oldest son's wedding last year.

Pake played acoustic rhythm guitar and sang melody. I sang the high harmony, and Susie sang the low. Some of our favorite songs were "Silver Wings," "Long Black Veil," "Stars in My Crown," and "Humble Shack." But Pake loved Merle Haggard, especially. He would watch and wait for Merle Haggard to come out with a new album and when he did, Pake would listen, write down every word and then learn almost every song. And we'd look at every little bit of it—album liner and everything—until we knew everything about it, every lyric, every song. I'd do the same with a Loretta Lynn and a Dolly Parton album. Those two ladies made you feel like they were your best friends. I loved their songs—and still do.

People used to ask Daddy where us kids got our talent. He'd say, "Oh, they got that from their Mama." That's so, but we got our lungs from Daddy, and we exercised them early and often during those years up in the hills gathering cattle and becoming lost, when that famous McEntire yell saved our hides more than once. On 8,000 acres, you didn't have a microphone with amplifiers. But it was Mama who taught us to sing harmony. I think that bloodline harmony is a special harmony—the McGuire Sisters have it, the Gatlin Brothers have it. It's the closest harmony in the world, I think.

MAMA BECAME VERY EXCITED ABOUT HOW WE'D TAKEN TO MUSIC, BUT she wished that we could get more formal musical training. At our school, there wasn't a marching band or even much of a music curriculum. Fortunately, that changed when Clark Rhyne came to Kiowa High School. He had been a McEntire family friend for years. He admired Daddy's and Grandpap's rodeo skills, and Clark's grandfather's sister was the former Alice Buie, one of Pap McEntire's wives. More importantly, Clark, in addition to being a teacher, is a professional musician, a fiddle and guitar player who played in honky-tonks around Oklahoma when I was a girl.

In fact, it was thanks to Clark Rhyne that I would make my first recording. It was of a song he wrote about Grandpap called ''The Ballad of John McEntire.'' The day after we heard it, Pake, Susie, and I went to Oklahoma City to record it. Clark had written it for experience and we recorded it for fun, but Clark did manage to sell a few around locally.

But that would come a couple of years later. Clark started teaching at Kiowa High School in 1969, when I was fourteen. At the time, Mama was working as the secretary to the superintendent of our school, the late Harold Toaz. So, with Clark's cooperation, she pitched her boss on the notion of setting up a school country-music band. ''She had a real knack of planting a seed of an idea in the old man,'' Clark Rhyne later recalled. ''And then he would think he thought of it. She planted a few seeds, and the old man called me in and asked me what I thought about it. I acted like it was the first I'd ever heard of it. And I said, 'Oh, that'd just be great, wouldn't that be great?' And he said, 'Well, we just might do it.' ''

Mr. Toaz's main concern was cost. There wasn't a lot of extra money in the Kiowa High School budget, and he didn't want to spend a fortune on instruments, microphones, and amplifiers. But Clark had an answer for that: He knew Smiley Weaver at Ada, who could get the band discounts on all the public address systems, and Bob Woods in Del City, who could give us great deals on instruments and amplifiers.

If it hadn't been for those guys, there wouldn't have been a Kiowa High School Cowboy Band, or maybe not even our family trio, the Singing McEntires. I'll even say there might not have been a solo career for Reba McEntire. Thanks so much, Smiley and Bob, for helping us out!

We were able to equip five musicians and three singers with three electric guitars, an electric bass, drums, three microphones, and four amplifiers for about five hundred dollars. And I'll never forget our speakers. Today I perform with about twenty speakers on each side of the stage. Each is about ten feet tall. The Kiowa High School Cowboy Band had two little bitty four-foot speakers, one on each side of the stage, for the entire band. The speakers were covered in electric blue padded patent leather with metallic flakes. We thought they were real cool!

Our early rehearsals were like music class, but held at the fairgrounds. Once our instruments and PA system came in, we moved over to the high school auditorium, which was also the cafeteria and which was where we'd have our concerts.

Our first order of business as a band was to decide who would play what. Kelly Rhyne could play drums, so he became our drummer, and David Jones was also a drummer. Pake knew how to play acoustic guitar, and Gary Raiburn became our electric guitar player. Carol Johnston, my cousin Diannia, and I all were there to sing, and my sister Susie would join us when she got to junior high school. Pake was the lead singer and also our band leader.

We didn't have a bass player, but Roger Wills wanted to try it. He already knew the frets of the guitar, so Clark Rhyne set out to teach him. Today, Roger is one of the top bass players in Nashville, thanks to that high school band. He was with me for five years and now plays and is the band leader for Alan Jackson.

Kelly Rhyne was not only our drummer, but most importantly he was my second serious boyfriend (my first was Doug Hull). Kelly and I wrote love notes back and forth to each other and he introduced me to Three Dog Night and Chicago—rock 'n' roll bands with great harmony. He was also a wonderful kisser! When he wasn't playing with us he was playing bigger jobs that paid him more. He was that good. When he was gone, Carol Johnston and I took turns playing drums and rhythm guitar. When she sang and played the guitar, I played the drums, and vice versa. But I could just barely keep the beat. I'd certainly never hire a drummer who played as badly as I did!

Our band's repertoire really had a range to it. Of the eight band members—Kelly, Roger, David, and Gary were into rock 'n' roll; Pake, Carol, Diannia, and I wanted to do country. So we compromised: "The song list ran all the way from Conway Twitty and Loretta Lynn to Merle Haggard, which is about as country as you can get, but probably about as deep as we got was 'Sitting on the Dock of the Bay,' " Clark remembers. "We were real strong on Glen Campbell—'Galveston,' 'By the Time I Get to Phoenix,' and 'Wichita Lineman.' I would go buy the songbook and the kids would learn the chords right off."

Once we got going, the band entertained during lunch breaks, until the noise got to Mr. Toaz and he put his foot down and made us stop, and at all the major high school functions. For example, the senior class would get us to put on a benefit to help them raise money for their year-end trip. We also played all of the school's home football games, performing before the kickoff and at halftime.

"And the band was so much better than the football team," Clark Rhyne said, "that at halftime if they didn't quit playing everybody would be down here watching the band and nobody was watching the football game. We'd just have to make them quit playing, because the crowd—there would be three hundred people gathered up around where the band was picking—the crowd would be requesting songs and saying, 'Well, don't quit yet.' And the football game was going on and we'd just have to pull the plug."

We had tremendous success for a group of high school kids. We won virtually every contest we entered, including both the county and district 4-H Club Share-the-Fun Contests. For one of these, we worked up a patriotic medley including "Okie from Muskogee" and wore red, white, and blue outfits. Where we came from, you couldn't get more patriotic than that. We were Okies too! We even wound up singing at the 4-H State Convention at Oklahoma State University in Stillwater.

⸎

THE KIOWA HIGH SCHOOL COWBOY BAND GREW SO POPULAR THAT IT landed some real, paying jobs in honky-tonks and dance halls. We couldn't have gotten away with that in Tulsa or Oklahoma City, because all of us were minors, too young to legally be inside those places, but in the small towns it was different. Mama and Carol Johnston's parents would take two carloads of teenage musicians over to the high school, where we would pick up the musical equipment. After the job, the equipment was returned to the school before our parents drove us to our various homes.

Usually, we were asleep by the time we got out of the parking lot of the club. We were a bunch of kids barely in puberty who didn't get to bed until almost daylight after some of our

shows. Once, we played a club in Ardmore, Oklahoma, from 9
P.M. until 1 A.M., passed the hat, then played two more sets from
1 A.M. until 3 A.M. We made thirteen dollars apiece.

The club audiences could be rough, but they gave us good
training in how to work a crowd. Some of those dances turned
into fistfights set to music. More often than not, it was so dark in
those clubs that we couldn't even see them fighting. We just
thought they were all dancing, and we'd play right through it.
When the truth was too obvious to ignore, Clark would tell us,
"If a fight breaks out to the left, you go to the right. Don't stand
there on the stage and watch it. Take everyone's attention to the
other direction."

And so we did.

Pake remembered a show where Mama told us on the way
home that she thought the crowd really enjoyed our music.

"Why?" he asked.

"Because I counted fourteen fights," she said.

We were playing in clubs at the time I was baptized at the
Kiowa Baptist church, and getting really serious about the right
and wrong things in life. I was twelve. One Saturday night when
we played the W-H Corral in Sulphur, I told Mama that when I
got onstage I planned to ask the audience if they were going to go
to church the next morning.

She just looked at me and smiled.

"Reba," she said, "what makes you think those people don't
go to church every Sunday?"

I was stunned. I had never thought of that.

"Do you think they do?" I asked.

"I don't know," she said, "but before I got up and started
preaching to them and telling them how bad they are, I'd sure
find out."

That was my first lesson about not judging people. How did I
know what they did when they left the honky-tonk? And anyway,
it wasn't any of my business.

❧

INDIRECTLY, THE KIOWA HIGH SCHOOL COWBOY BAND BROUGHT ME one of the first great highs of my career. The Harmon Jones Ford dealership in Atoka held a contest to choose "Miss Ford Country," hiring our band to play for entertainment during the day. And I won the contest!

My winning had less to do with my singing than with my writing, but that's not what the band thought. They said I won because I was a McEntire, accusing the judges of favoritism toward my family. I lived with that one for a long time.

The contest was actually an essay contest. Contestants were supposed to write why they thought they should win the use of a new Ford for six months. I wrote that because I was a singer and rodeo contestant, I'd drive the car all over the country. The car would carry the name of Harmon Jones Ford and be good advertising.

The judges were convinced, and at sixteen years old, there I was tooling around on my own, showing off my prize. I put 18,000 miles on that car in six months.

Mama, Daddy, Susie, my friend Kathy Mitchell, and I all piled in the car and took it to Cheyenne, Wyoming, for the annual Frontier Days Rodeo. As soon as we returned, I went with Debbie Boyd, Clark and Sue Rhyne, and their son, Jim Buie, who was two, to Colorado. I had a great time with that car.

❧

I MAY HAVE BEEN OLD ENOUGH TO HAVE A CAR OF MY OWN AND TO perform in nightclubs, but of course, I was still a kid. As serious as us McEntires were about our music, none of us lost our sense of mischief once we got to high school. Pake still likes to tell the story about how one of Alice's boyfriends, Jerry Wilson, talked me into trying chewing tobacco. I turned green and threw up, and Pake died laughing.

He also reminds me of the time he and I went to a calf roping and jackpot barrel race. In a jackpot barrel race, ten or so girls who want to run barrels put up money. The winner of the race gets most of the money, depending upon the split that was agreed on. I was always nervous while running barrels, and this time I got especially shaky when the announcer introduced me as Dorothy instead of Reba.

So what did Pake do? He leaned over the rail, and as I rounded the last barrel, he began hollering, ''Come on, Dorothy! Come on, Dorothy!''

A little thing like that can be real distracting.

I don't know why Pake does such things, and he can't understand why the women in the family get mad at him!

Of course, there were times I got back at Pake, but nearly always, Pake got the last laugh.

Once, Pake, Alice, and I went to a steer roping in Tucumcari, New Mexico, when Alice's boy, Vince, was only two. Pake was a grown man who was supposed to be in charge of the group. Well, that grown man took a piece of a radiator hose off the pickup's dash and put Vince's arm in all the way up to his armpit.

Then it wouldn't come off.

Vince was crying, Alice was cussing, and Pake, who was driving, wasn't paying the right amount of attention to the road. And if Vince wasn't upset enough, he became especially loud when his uncle Pake took out a pocketknife to cut the radiator hose off his arm. He probably thought Pake was going to amputate!

Once the radiator hose was removed and Vince's blood pressure was back down, we decided we should stop to eat. Afterward, Alice and Vince climbed into the camper, where she was going to try to get him to go to sleep. I had to go to the bathroom, so I was the last to come out of the café, and Alice had told Pake to be sure to wait for me.

But Pake pretended he thought I was in the camper with Alice and Vince. He knew exactly what he was doing as he began to drive away, leaving me standing in a deserted New Mexico truck stop parking lot.

I began to chase the pickup, yelling, "Pake, stop! Stop!"

The closer I got to the pickup, the more Pake gradually accelerated. I was running as fast as I could while he acted like he didn't notice me.

I couldn't tell he had me in the corner of his eye.

I finally got close enough to pound on the driver's window. Then Pake finally looked around.

"Oh, Reba!" Pake said, pretending to be surprised. "I thought you were in the back of the truck."

I won't tell you what I said to him.

❀

PAKE GRADUATED HIGH SCHOOL THREE YEARS AFTER THE BAND WAS formed, and shortly thereafter, the Kiowa High School Cowboy Band disbanded. It has never reassembled. Clark went on to become principal of Kiowa High School, and a few months before his retirement in 1993, he explained why he never put together another group.

"Our average class size runs twenty-five kids," he said. "So we're talking 150 kids in school. And how many times, in a school that small, do you find someone who becomes Alan Jackson's bass player? How many times do you find Pake, who had his own band and traveled and got songs in the Top Ten? His first song on RCA went to number five. And Reba's superstardom? Plus the Raiburn boy, who plays professionally around Dallas. My brother, Kelly, is playing part-time, and has traveled hitches with Reba on the road. Now how many times are you going to find that much talent in a school that small? It was a once-in-a-lifetime deal.''

I agree. I truly think the unlikely formation of a band that successful from a school district that small was an act of God. But, while I do have sentimental memories about the group, I can't really vouch for its musical greatness. Recently someone said to Pake, ''That band was popular, but was it any good?''

''We thought that Nashville was going to be coming into that cafeteria and signing us all any day,'' Pake said.

''Did you ever make a demo or anything?''

''No,'' Pake said, ''but we made a tape one time.''

''Have you listened to it since?''

''I listened to it about five or six years ago,'' Pake said. ''It sounded like a train wreck.''

CHAPTER 5

ALONG WITH SINGING, BASKETBALL, RODEOS, AND SCHOOL, I still helped out on the ranch, as we all did. My responsibilities continued even after I left for college. Not that I minded—as you know by now, it takes a lot of hands to run a ranch, and besides, I understood that a college tuition would put my folks under considerable economic strain. I did get some financial aid—fifty dollars a semester—but Daddy and Mama had to pay the rest. Although they would eventually reach a level of financial comfort as Daddy parlayed his rodeo earnings into new tracts of land and more cattle, it was a slow build and I wanted to do my share.

I went to college in Durant at Southeastern Oklahoma State University, where my major field of study was elementary education and my minor was music. I received my bachelor's degree, but never taught school as my Mama and Grandma had done before me, except for student teaching. Alice earned a degree in home economics and Susie in business. None of us ever worked a day in our fields of study.

Pake dropped out of college, but it was just as well. The only degree he could have earned would have been in partying.

⚜

DURANT IS ONLY ABOUT FIFTEEN MILES FROM CADDO, OKLAHOMA, where Daddy ran two or three hundred steers on some land he leased. "Reba," Daddy said, "it's more handy for you to drive fifteen miles every other day to feed those steers than it is for me to drive forty-five."

I said I would do it.

Daddy bought me a black Ford pickup when I graduated from high school. It had an orange and black interior and looked like a mobile pumpkin. It had a standard transmission, AM radio, but no air-conditioning. Every other day, I would load about thirty fifty-pound sacks of feed into that truck by myself and feed Daddy's steers.

I never lost one steer in the three and a half years it took me to earn my undergraduate degree.

The most fun I had while taking care of the cattle was when my roommates and buddies would go with me. One of my room-mates, Cindy Blackburn, was a beautiful girl who was always dressed to the max and was a member of one of the campus sororities.

One day, Brenda Lee, my first roommate in college and best friend since the fifth grade, Karen Watkins, my downstairs neigh-bor at college, Cindy, and I went to Caddo to feed the steers. We'd had a pretty good rain the day before.

The dirt in Caddo, Oklahoma, turns to black, gummy mud when it gets wet, and it's real easy to get stuck. I was driving and the girls were in the back of the truck when I hit a boggy spot. The tires started spinning and we began to slow down. I hollered

at the girls to jump out and push. Brenda and Karen had done
that before, so they knew better than to listen. They stayed in the
truck, but Cindy jumped out in her sorority sweatshirt and saddle
oxfords and began pushing with all her heart.

When we got out of the boggy spot, I looked back and Cindy
was standing there—feet apart, arms out, and covered in black
mud. From then on, she always rode in the front of the truck.

I kept a horse at college so I could keep him in shape for
weekend rodeos. I went to some college shows and PRCA rodeos. One of my sophomore-year roommates, Beth Crump, also
had a horse at college. We had a lot of fun with that.

⚜

OF COURSE, MY FAMILY WAS STILL AN IMPORTANT PART OF MY SOCIAL
life, college or no college. And I was dating a few guys—having
my first serious, grown-up romances.

I had always been very naive about guys. I usually didn't even
know if their advances were directed toward me. "Nobody ever
hits on me," I used to say to Alice. I don't know if I was proud
or curious about that.

Alice would try to remind me about a man or a place where
someone had made a pass. I never knew what she was talking
about. I rarely even remembered seeing the guy.

Still, I had a few boyfriends. I can recall vividly each of my
high school and college ones. In high school, there had been
Doug Hull, who was a good-looking rodeo bulldogger and very
good at sports. After ten months, I broke up with him for Kelly
Rhyne. Then Kelly broke up with me and I started dating Rick
Wilson, a guy from Hartshorne, Oklahoma, who took me to my
senior prom.

Rick and I met on a blind date. On our third date, he proposed to me. We dated off and on after I graduated from high
school and broke up during my freshman year of college.

After I had been in college for a couple of years, he called from New Jersey and said, "All right, I'm going to fly in and pick you up and we're going to get married in Dallas and go on a honeymoon in Hawaii."

His timing was bad, as I had been partying the night before. His call came about 7 A.M.

"Rick," I said, "I'm not going to get married. I'm having way too good a time in college. Don't call back."

And I hung up.

The telephone rang almost instantly.

"Don't you ever hang up on me again!" he shouted.

"Rick," I said, "I love you like a brother, but I don't want to get married. Good-bye."

Rick had been a jockey long before I met him. With Mama or with his parents, I had watched him ride at Ruidoso, New Mexico; Hot Springs, Arkansas; and Henryetta and Stroud, Oklahoma. Eventually he made it into the major leagues of horse racing. Funnily enough, in 1993, when Narvel and I were at the Aqueduct Racetrack in New York City, to watch one of our thoroughbred horses run, our agent Jimmy Gladwell said, "Now, Reba, your jockey today is a guy I think you know."

"What?" I said.

"All the other jockeys said you used to date this guy," Jimmy continued.

"What's his name?" I said.

"Rick Wilson."

I couldn't believe it. I saw him down at the paddock area before the race, and we gave each other a big hug. And wouldn't you just know it—he rode my horse to a first-place finish!

After Rick came Bobby Shillings, who I'd met at college. He was good-looking, but somewhat of a renegade—not quite what Daddy and Mama had in mind for me for matrimony.

One time Bobby and I were going to Mama and Daddy's house at Chockie but first stopped in Stringtown, where my sister

Alice was living. No one was home. I figured everyone was at Mama and Daddy's, so I decided to have a little fun. I called up there and Susie answered the telephone.

"Susie," I said, "tell Mama that me and Bobby are going to Shreveport, Louisiana, to get married. I'll see you later."

And I hung up.

Susie liked to have died. She started crying, and went to Mama and told her what I had said.

Mama was a little more calm. She called the Highway Patrol to have Bobby and me picked up. Bobby and I didn't know about all the commotion I'd started, and just calmly drove up to Mama's house.

"Here they come!" Susie yelled, and everybody met us at the door. Susie couldn't talk, she was crying so hard. Mama jerked the quirt off the wall. A quirt is a braided leather cord used by jockeys to whip horses. Daddy had gotten it in Mexico.

I was nineteen, and I really thought she was going to whip me with it.

"It was a joke! It was a joke!" I hollered.

"What do you mean scaring your little sister that way?" Mama said.

I felt terrible for Bobby. If he didn't know before that my family didn't want me to marry him, he definitely knew then.

And Susie wouldn't talk to me for a long time after that one.

⁂

WHILE I WAS IN COLLEGE, I CONTINUED TO SING. THIS WAS ALSO THE first time that I'd ever formally studied music. It was new, unfamiliar—and I learned plenty. In music theory class, for instance, we dissected symphonies. In chorus and choral group, we sang a lot of classical music—that was a lot of fun. I also became a member of the Chorvettes, a singing and dancing group that performed on campus and in neighboring towns. The group still exists, though its members change almost every year. Our leader was my voice teacher, Bob Pratt, whose techniques on breathing and posture have helped me throughout my career. After Bob Pratt died, Mary Ann Craige took over the Chorvettes.

❧

DURING MY SOPHOMORE YEAR AT SOSU, IN THE SUMMER OF 1974, I HAD been talking about going up to the National Finals Rodeo in Oklahoma City in December.

Daddy asked me, "Why don't you get a job up at the Finals? Do something more than just having a big time."

Now, I think Daddy knew I enjoyed "just going up and having a big time," but I was getting smart enough to know when he was making a point and that I should pay attention. "What do you think I should do?" I asked.

"Why don't you sing the National Anthem?" he said.

It seemed like a good idea to me. With "The Star-Spangled Banner," everyone stands up, stays quiet, and—the best part for any performer—there are 20,000 ears tuned on *you*. So I called Clem McSpadden, a rodeo announcer we'd known for years. He had served in the Oklahoma Senate for eighteen years and had narrowly lost the governorship. At the time he was running for a seat in the U.S. House of Representatives, and Pake, Susie, and I had helped him campaign by singing at fund-raisers. With Clem's help, I was hired.

The NFR is the World Series of rodeo, with the top fifteen money-winning cowboys in each event for that year competing for top prize money in Oklahoma City. It was exciting to be there, and while I didn't know it at the time, it was my first big break.

I'll never forget how nervous I felt driving up there with Daddy and Mama. What happened on the day we were supposed to rehearse didn't help my nerves either. I had gone around to the conductor, Al Good, and explained that I sang the National Anthem in the key of E. He insisted I sing it the way his orchestra played it, in A. From the look on his face I could tell we were gonna do it that night in A.

Well, the rehearsal started and it was time for me to begin. I strained to maintain an uncomfortably high falsetto as everyone kind of looked around like, "Is this what it's gonna be like for the next week?"

Stanley Draper from the Oklahoma City Chamber of Commerce heard me straining for the notes, and went to see Clem. Clem took up for me, telling Stanley that I'd get it and not to worry. The next night, the orchestra played the song in E.

A few years later, I began to sing the National Anthem from the arena floor, and sang it a cappella. I also sang it a cappella at the World Series in Kansas City. It's my favorite song.

⚜

During the middle of NFR week, I ran into Ken Lance, owner of the Ken Lance Sports Arena in Ada, Oklahoma. I had seen many country celebrities at Ken's place, including Loretta Lynn. Loretta heard us sing at the Ada Pow-Wow one year, and someone later asked her manager, David Skeptner, what he thought about me. His verdict: I shouldn't quit my day job. I've kidded him about that ever since.

I was hurrying off to get ready to sing the National Anthem when Ken stopped me. "Hey, Reba," he said, "I want you to meet a friend of mine."

There was Red Steagall—a big ole redheaded guy with a gentle look in his eyes. A longtime favorite on the rodeo circuit who did Western Swing in the tradition of Bob Wills, he had recorded several Top Ten songs and had written hits for other artists, including "Here We Go Again" for Ray Charles. I liked him immediately. I went on about my business, but I would see Red again later during Finals week.

Cowboys are both competitive and social. They'll try to beat each other in the arena, but they'll socialize and help each other when competition is finished. There are many stories about one cowboy lending another an entry fee, only for the borrower to beat the lender in competition. This happened as far back as Grandpap's day. And during the Finals, as a nightly event, cowboys go to clubs or dances, or they congregate in a hotel room to swap stories and songs.

During the 1974 Finals, the Justin Boot Company was sponsoring a suite and party at the Hilton Hotel where the rodeo contestants were staying. So one night after a performance, Mama, Daddy, Pake, and I went over to the Hilton. As we got out of the car, once again we ran into Ken Lance, who told us to come up to the Justin Boot Company suite.

Red was in the suite that night too, singing and playing his guitar and passing it around so some of the others in the room could sing. That's a tradition among country singers and is called a "guitar pull," as one singer will often "pull" the guitar from another to do a tune. Everett Shaw, world-champion steer roper, soon said, "Hey, Reba, do 'Joshua.'"

Red didn't know the chords for "Joshua" and I didn't play well enough to take the guitar, so I sang it a cappella. As Red put it later, "This little redheaded girl started singing, and it just blew me away."

Later that night, Mama got to talking with Bobby Steagall, Red's first wife, who asked Mama if I had any intention of getting serious about my singing. Mama said, "Oh yes, all the kids are very serious about their music." Later, Mama asked Red if he could help get a recording contract in Nashville for the Singing McEntires.

"At the time," Red said, "I just didn't think there was any

place for a trio in country music.'' But kindly, he kept me in mind.

❧

IN JANUARY 1975, WHEN THE OKLAHOMA GROUND WAS IN THE YEAR'S deepest freeze, warmth came to my world in the voice of Red Steagall. He called Mama and said, ''Well, Jackie, I've been thinking about it. I can't take all three. But I could take Reba. She's got something a little different.'' He was asking us now to come to Nashville to record a demonstration tape. Red Steagall was offering me a shot.

Almost anyone would jump at the chance Red offered me. I eventually did, but it took some prodding from Mama, because I was scared. I knew nothing about the music business or the people in it. I knew the voices of the recording stars on the radio, but nothing else about how the entertainment industry works. I didn't know the difference between an agent and an A & R man. I didn't even know what they were.

I was familiar, obviously, with my family and with rodeo. Those were the circles where I was comfortable. I had been very secure in my childhood and teenage world. As I got closer and closer to the big leagues of music, I knew that business wasn't going to be as protective and loving as my family had been.

So, when Mama and I set out for Nashville in March 1975, I kept coming up with reasons to stop the car all along the 700 miles. I suggested we stop to eat or to get ice cream. I wanted to pull over and see every tourist attraction. I came up with any excuse I could to delay my arrival.

''Now, Reba, let me tell you something,'' Mama finally said. ''If you don't want to go to Nashville, we don't have to do this. But I'm living all my dreams through you.''

That changed my attitude.

When she was a girl, my Mama was a wonderful singer whom Clark Rhyne has frequently compared to Patsy Cline. Her dream had been to go to California to try her luck, but no one was there to encourage or support her. Her folks said no; the war was on and she was needed at home. For Mama, responsibility had overridden opportunity—the opportunity I was taking lightly.

Four children and twenty-odd years later I wondered what, if any, regrets she held. And I realized a chance was being offered to me to do something bigger and maybe better with my life. When Mama told me that, it was just the kick I needed. I told Mama to drive on, and, except to get gasoline, I'm not sure we stopped again on that entire trip.

When we got to Nashville, Mama and I stayed at the Hall of Fame Motor Hotel on Division Street, just one block from 16th Avenue South, known as "Music Row." (The term Music Row today applies to about twelve square blocks encompassed by 15th, 16th, 17th, and 18th Avenues South.) I made my first demonstration recording in a tiny studio owned by Fred Carter, a Nashville studio guitarist who later played some road dates with Jerry Reed. For that session, Red had chosen "I'm Not Your Kind of Girl," written by Red and Glen Sutton, Lynn Anderson's ex-husband. The song was inspired by their ride on a Rock Island Line train from Amarillo to Memphis. Along with it, I cut three other tunes, including one that I'd written in college about one of the guys I had a crush on, called "Leave My Texas Boy Alone."

When we were done, Red said, "Go home and forget about it." In other words, don't call us, we'll call you. I returned to school and rodeoing, and waited.

"The first person I took the demo to was Jim Fogelsong, president of ABC Dot Records," Red remembers. The label's roster boasted Tommy Overstreet, Roy Clark, Freddy Fender, and others. "He put the tape on, but I don't think he ever listened to it. He said, 'Red, I don't need another girl singer.' That was our first rejection.''

Red also took my tape to Bob Montgomery, who had performed with Buddy Holly in high school and had written big hits such as Patsy Cline's ''Back in Baby's Arms'' and ''Misty Blue,'' the most performed song of 1967. By 1975, Montgomery was one of Nashville's leading independent record producers and owned a successful publishing company with Bobby Goldsboro.

Montgomery was polite but equally uninterested in the demo of yet another unknown girl country singer.

''I played it for a bunch of people,'' Red says, ''and everybody had the same remark.''

Finally, Joe Light, Red's music publishing partner, made a pitch to Glenn Keener, who was a producer at Phonogram-Mercury. ''We were pitching the song ['I'm Not Your Kind of Girl'], not the singer,'' Red recalls, '' 'cause Joe and I had the publishing on the song.''

''I really like this girl,'' Red quoted Glenn as saying.

Eventually, Keener took me, but never did take the song.

Keener was an associate producer under the legendary Jerry Kennedy, who in 1975 was producing Jerry Lee Lewis, Tom T. Hall, Johnny Rodriguez, the Statler Brothers, Faron Young, Roger Miller, Patti Page, Roy Drusky, Dave Dudley, and Jacky Ward. They were affiliated with Phonogram Records, now Polygram-Mercury.

As Glenn tells it, he ended up signing me almost by chance. He'd brought two tapes to the label's head in Chicago, who said he could sign one female singer. Glenn looked down at the tapes —one in one hand and one in the other. He can't remember who the other girl was. He handed them mine.

Jerry's recollection is different. He says that he recommended that Keener sign me after Jerry heard me sing ''The Star-Spangled Banner.'' Apparently, Jerry had gotten hold of a live recording made at that 1974 National Finals Rodeo.

Whatever the story is, thanks to Jerry and Glenn—and to Clem McSpadden, Ken Lance, and Red Steagall—I achieved every young singer's dream.

I signed a deal with Phonogram on November 11, 1975. My advances for each of my first four years with the label were $7,500, $10,000, $15,000, and $20,000, monies that were levied against future royalties. Only thing was, there wouldn't be any for a while—quite a while.

⚜

BUT WHAT ABOUT THE OTHER SINGING MCENTIRES? I'VE OFTEN BEEN asked the obvious and fair question: do Pake, Susie, and I have sibling rivalry? The answer is yes, but it hasn't spoiled our relationship. I love both of them with all of my heart. Both Pake and Susie sang harmony with me on my early records, and Pake was in two of my bands. Even after my first major record on a major label, "I Don't Want to Be a One Night Stand," came out in 1976, Pake and Susie continued to sing with me on occasion.

Then Pake came to think that we should split our earnings three ways, as we had when we were the Singing McEntires. But he and Susie weren't getting billing then—the bookings were in my name. I could see the arrangement wasn't going to work, and so our careers eventually went their separate ways.

In the middle 1980s, Pake got a deal of his own on RCA Records and toured for a while as my opening act—doing fifteen minutes solo, then falling in with the band to play behind me. He said recently that that was the best deal he ever had in the music business! But he also went on to say I always seemed to be mad at him in those days, which didn't bother him a whole lot, since I always got over it quickly.

I don't know what he was referring to—it might be I was angry at Pake because he quit the music business so quickly. He decided to stay at home with his wife, Katie, and their three kids, and I can sure understand that. But I wish there was a way he could have stuck with it. Call me prejudiced—but I think Pake outsings them all!

Susie is a talented gospel singer who has told me that she resents the fact that more people come to my concerts than hers, even though she sings for the Lord. I suspect that her turnouts have to do with the fact that secular music is more popular than Christian music. I'm not saying that's the way it should be. I'm just saying that's the way it is.

But richer or poorer, then or now, we have stayed a singing family. On September 18, 1986, Pake, Susie, and I did a special edition of "Nashville Now," devoted entirely to the McEntire family. It had been a long time since the three of us had sung together. Pake was on RCA at the time. Susie was singing only gospel music, so we harmonized on "Farther Along" and "Stars in My Crown," two of our favorite gospel songs. During the show, the producers got Mama on the phone from Oklahoma, so television viewers could hear her pride and excitement at seeing three of her four children performing together on one show. It was an evening that none of us will ever forget.

CHAPTER 6

DADDY DIDN'T WANT ANY OF US KIDS TO RODEO, YET three out of four of us did. He didn't want his kids to suffer the financial insecurity that rodeo cowboys had back then, when most of them couldn't get by on their own earnings. And only a few of those who could, saved or invested their money, like Daddy did, instead of wasting it on women and whiskey. Daddy didn't want us exposed to that rough behavior.

That's the dark side of rodeo life—but the brighter and better side is that you'll hardly ever see a kid in trouble with the law if he has a horse. That's been an old rodeo saying for years, and I believe it.

If a child has a horse, he has a buddy, a friend, and a companion. For years, I kept a horse in shape and rode for long hours. There were times when my horse and God were the only ones for me to talk to. I got very close to both.

Still, I can't think of anything associated with rodeo that isn't dangerous, including riding in the Grand Entry, which is the opening ceremony featuring a parade of every rider and horse. I've seen a horse break loose and run through the rest of the horses. Then maybe a rider is knocked off and somebody else's horse steps on him.

I'm sorry to say that, when I was young, I didn't always recognize those dangers. One time Brenda Lee Turney and I went to a rodeo at Stratford, Oklahoma. Brenda was not a very good rider, so I got her on one of my family's most gentle horses, then led her into a big bunch of people on horseback. Riders were milling in every direction, and I could see that Brenda was confused.

Then, being the mischievous young person I was, I told her, "Just keep on going, we'll get through here." So she went with the flow of riders and didn't know I had put her in the Grand Entry. She ran into the pivot horses and like to fell off her own horse because she was so mixed up and scared.

Luckily, she got through it okay, and we even laugh about it now. But at the time I was too immature to think about the fact that she could have been seriously hurt or killed. Rodeoing was so much my world that I couldn't imagine what it could be like for someone who hadn't been around it like I had.

⚜

IT WAS THROUGH RODEOING THAT I MET THE MAN WHO BECAME THE first great love of my life, Charlie Battles.

Although I didn't know Charlie personally, I knew about him long before we ever spoke. Charlie was a rodeo star, the world-champion steer wrestler in the International Rodeo Association in 1970, 1971, and 1972. He was ruggedly handsome, with a big build like Daddy's, while I was a wide-eyed barrel racer who was taken with the stature that Charlie held among the cowboys and cowgirls on the rodeo circuit. I never even considered that he could ever have a romantic interest in me.

I remember that our first encounter was something less than dramatic. I was at a rodeo with Alice, who was competing that night in the barrel racing. Everybody was out in the arena before the rodeo began, just walking around on their horses, warming them up. Charlie was riding his hazing horse and leading his bulldogging horse.

I walked down to the fence just to say, "Hi, Charlie."

He waved at me.

I thought he would be a great catch for Alice.

"Lord, Reba," she said. "He's married and has two kids."

I instantly forgot about matching him with Alice.

That was in 1971.

Then came that fateful National Finals Rodeo in December 1974, where I sang the National Anthem and met Red Steagall. After one performance, Mama and I went to Denny's in Oklahoma City. We were sitting at the counter as Charlie and his wife, Sherrie, walked by. They had just finished eating. We all began to talk, because Mama knew Sherrie from all of her rodeoing with Alice. Sherrie showed Mama pictures of Coty and Lance, Charlie's two boys, and Charlie and I struck up a conversation. I don't even remember what was said. I know Charlie didn't say a lot.

Three months later, I went with Pake to a rodeo in San Angelo, Texas. Charlie was there, but I barely spoke to him. In fact, I remember more about a stunt that Pake and I pulled than I do about being around Charlie.

It all started one afternoon during "slack." Slack is the time when the contestants who didn't get to compete during the scheduled event get to perform. Usually there are only ten contestants for a performance, and any extras perform during the slack.

I was dressed in jeans and was wearing a bandanna, with my

hair pulled back, very casual-looking. I was walking back from the pickup and camper where Pake and I were staying at the coliseum. We didn't have a motel room and took our showers there.

"Hey, Reba, did you get our hotel room?"

The voice belonged to Pax Irvine, a calf roper from Wyoming. He was teasing me in front of a bunch of cowboys, and I was embarrassed. I have never liked sexual joking, and I'm not real comfortable about flirting.

"No, Pax," I said, "I sure didn't get our room," and I kept walking.

"Now, honey," he kept on, "I told you when you got here first to get our hotel room."

All the cowboys could see my embarrassment, and they died laughing.

I told Pake about the remarks, and he got real mad.

I won that night's barrel race, and Pake and I went to the Blue Diamond Bar to celebrate. We had a few beers, and I guess the thought of what Pax had said to me was burning a hole in Pake's gut.

We got back to the rodeo grounds and we were walking to our camper when we passed Pax's trailer. There, standing quietly in the moonlight and tied securely, was Pax Irvine's horse.

Pake cut off his tail.

Now, a horse's tail has a hard core and hair grows out of the core. Pake cut the hair off up to the core—and horse hair is tough; it's used to make fiddle bows. So Pake, using only a pocketknife, had to saw and saw on the tail. Pax's horse became a bobbed-tail nag.

The next day, Pax was furious.

I've never told that story until now. But Pax, nineteen years ago, you embarrassed me in the light, and my brother barbered your horse in the dark. And anyway, I couldn't have talked Pake out of it if I had tried, but I confess I didn't try.

Above: From left, me, Pake, and Susie when we performed as the Singing McEntires; we were also part of the Kiowa Cowboy High School Band. Mama (*below right*) who worked in the school superintendent's office then, and Clark Rhyne (*below left*) our art and Oklahoma history teacher who was a well-known local musician, convinced Mr. Toaz, our superintendent, to establish the band.

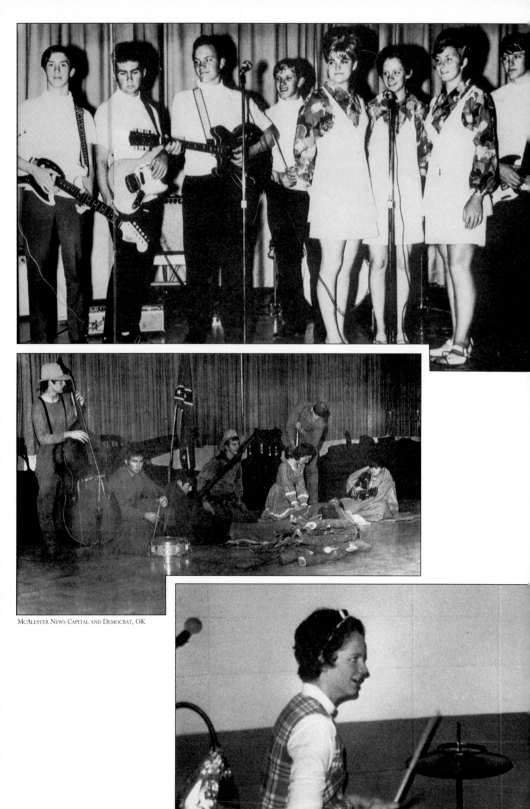

Facing page: Most of my time in high school was taken up by basketball, rodeos, my 4-H Club (*center*) shown here performing in a skit in the Share-the-Fun contest at Tahlequah, Oklahoma, and by the Kiowa High School Cowboy Band (*top*). The band's members were, from left, Gary Raiburn, Kelly Rhyne, Pake, David Jones, Carol Johnston, me, Diannia Kay Smith, and Roger Wills. I'm not sure if we looked like cowboys in those miniskirts. One of my jobs in the band was part-time drumming (*bottom*) though I had a hard time keeping the beat. *This page:* Then I started dating! Doug Hull (*above left*) from Stuart, Oklahoma, was my first go-out-on-a-date boyfriend, and my second was band member Kelly Rhyne (*above right*). *Center:* I proved better at writing than drumming. Thanks to one of my essays, I was crowned Miss Ford Country and won the use of a car for six months; the band was the entertainment for the day. *Below:* I also performed in the individual division for 4-H Share-the-Fun, but here, as the newspaper noted, I was "not myself" when I sang the Elvis hit "In the Ghetto."

NOT HERSELF is Reba McEntire as she sings in her individual 4-H club Share-The-Fun act, but the guise, plus some good singing, put her in district competition at Murray State college at Tishomingo Saturday. Dressed in old clothes with a wig, she sits on a garbage can as she presents "In The Ghetto" in front of props decorated like those in big cities. (Staff Phtoto by Hugh T. German)

Daddy didn't want his children to rodeo, but three out of four of us did. *Left:* I was thirteen when I ran barrels in Antlers, Oklahoma. *Below:* Pake roping calves in Burwell, Nebraska, on Old Bay, Daddy's steer-roping horse. Pake roped left-handed and Daddy roped right-handed—that horse was smart enough to know the difference! *Bottom left:* Here Alice is running barrels on Joe Dan at the Fort Worth Stock Show and Rodeo in 1971; she was runner-up for the World Championship in the International Rodeo Association. *Facing page, top:* In 1974, at the National Finals Rodeo in Oklahoma City, I sang the National Anthem. Red Steagall heard me and it kicked off my musical career. *Right:* I would return to sing the National Anthem for the next ten years, except for one year, until they moved the National Finals to Las Vegas, Nevada.

FORT WORTH STOCK SHOW AND RODEO

FERRELL BUTLER

1980
NFR
OKLAHOMA
CITY
©FAIN PHOTOGRAPHIC, LTD. (80) AX 7740

L. MAYOR

ing page, top: After hearing me sing at
National Finals Rodeo, Red Steagall
ped me make a demo tape and got me a
ord deal. *Bottom:* A few years later, I
formed with him at the
penhagen/Skoal Roping in Fort Worth,
as, where he jumped off his horse and
ted his zipper—Fruit of the Looms
ning through! *Above:* In 1977, I recorded
first album *Reba McEntire* for Polygram
ords. *Right:* In my early years at Fan
r, I had to wear a name tag so fans
uld know who I was.

Singing at the world famous Grand Ole Opry in 1984. I made my debut there on September 17, 1977, and I became a member in 1986.

The cowboys had laughed at me because Pax had suggested that he and I were shacking up. But they laughed harder when it was Pax's time to rope on his horse with a tail shorter than a cocker spaniel's.

❦

THE WEEKEND FOLLOWING SAN ANGELO I WENT WITH BETH CRUMP, my college rodeo-team buddy and roommate, to the PRCA rodeo in Lubbock, Texas. Charlie and Pake were there as well. They often rodeoed together, Pake roping calves and Charlie bulldogging. Silky, Pake's roping horse, wasn't doing so well, so Pake let me run barrels on him. I had a permit in the Girls Rodeo Association (GRA) and was traveling the circuit that March hoping to qualify for full membership. To do that you had to win $200 in accumulated prize money.

That night at the rodeo I finished with the evening's fastest time. And by the time the competition was over two nights later, I was in third place overall. I was so happy! With my third-place finish at San Angelo the weekend before, I had more than filled my permit. I was now a professional cowgirl.

That night, after we put the horses up, we wound up celebrating at the Cow Palace, a dance hall well known for country music and dancing. We were drinking lots of beer and having a real good time, when Pake pulled Beth into the men's room just to be funny. As things had played out, I'd been around Charlie all day.

The houselights came on, the signal for everybody to leave because the place was closing. As I walked by Charlie's table, he pulled me onto his lap.

We were all laughing, and I turned around and kissed him—full on the mouth. Mike Saltzman, a bulldogger from Eufaula, Oklahoma, was sitting at the table, and I'll never forget how his jaw dropped. I don't know why I did it—I was swept up by the excitement of the rodeo, and the music and the beer. It was impulsive, but kissing Charlie just seemed like the right thing to do at the time.

One of the next rodeos that I went to was at Fort Smith, Arkansas, and I once again went with Pake, who was once again around Charlie. I remember the rodeo because Pake did something there I'd never seen him do.

We had gone to a bar and were playing pool and eating beans, when Pake got to drinking beer—and he was scheduled to rope that night. He never drank before he roped.

"This will be good, to see what Pake does because he's relaxed," I thought to myself, as I climbed on the back of the chutes to watch Pake rope his calf. And Pake made one of the best runs I'd seen him make in a long time. Usually he got real tense.

A week later, I was back at Chockie practicing with Pake out at the roping pen.

"Reba," Pake said, "Charlie left his wife."

I was shocked. Flabbergasted. Astonished.

Eventually, I would decide that he had left his wife for me, but I honestly had no such thoughts at the time. I just hadn't been around Charlie enough even to think he'd be interested in me. I'd heard that he was unhappily married, but there had been no talk about him getting a divorce.

Sherrie, Charlie's wife, was a hardworking gal from a big family who was a good housewife. But I couldn't have lived with her myself. Sherrie and I were as different as night and day!

It was a while before Charlie and I really got together. In June, Patti Prather, a barrel racer and horse trainer from Texas whom I've known for years, and I took off on the rodeo trail, going up around Colorado, Wyoming, and Montana. I saw Charlie at almost every rodeo. We went to a dance together in Greeley, Colorado, where David Houston was performing. After we got home in July, I flew with Susie to meet Pake in Cheyenne to sing for the Christian Athletes Association and continued to see Charlie at the rodeos.

Then Charlie started coming down to Durant pretty often to visit me at college. I finally told him I didn't want to see him anymore. Charlie is a very persistent man and wanted to know why. I said, "Mark Thompkins," who I liked but hadn't really dated. That same night, we were all at a party together. Charlie confronted Mark about his intentions.

Mark told Charlie he was planning to marry soon—but the girl in question wasn't me. He had no claims on me whatsoever. I could have killed him: Mark was my out. If I'd had any backbone at all, my relationship with Charlie would have ended right then and there. But it didn't.

By the end of July, we were an item.

Despite the ten-year age difference between us, Charlie and I had a lot in common. Like Daddy, he rodeoed but also bought and handled cattle. Like me, he had a funny, lighthearted side but could also be serious. And I think another part of his appeal was that Charlie was so protective.

We were at a dance one night, for instance, after a performance at the National Finals Rodeo in Oklahoma City. Bobby Shillings, my old college boyfriend, was there with another girl.

We were all on the dance floor when Bobby and I happened to make eye contact. He shot me the "bird."

"Charlie, let's just leave," I said from out of nowhere. "Let's get out of here."

"What for?" Charlie said. "What's the matter? What's wrong?"

I wouldn't tell him, but Charlie was never one to let anything lie.

He kept pushing. "You'd better tell me. Something is upsetting you. I want to know what it is. Did Bobby Shillings do something to you?"

I said nothing until Charlie and I reached the pickup. Then I thought there would be no harm in telling Charlie there what had happened inside.

"Bobby flipped me off," I said.

That did it! He slammed the pickup door and stormed back into the dance. But the dance had ended and Bobby was gone.

A few minutes later, Charlie and I walked into the lobby of the Holiday Inn. There stood Bobby Shillings. Without a word, Charlie just went for Bobby like a little bulldog and threw him through a double plate-glass window. The glass shattered and then the lobby fell quiet.

I looked out the window, and Bobby stood up and quietly walked away. No security personnel or police came. No one said anything to Charlie, and he and I left the lobby.

I was a little shocked and embarrassed by Charlie's actions, but kind of impressed too. No one had ever fought for me before.

❦

BUT CHARLIE COULD BE MORE TENDERLY SUPPORTIVE, TOO, AND THAT was the side I was increasingly drawn to. During our courtship, I lost my Grandpap, and I was glad I had Charlie to help me through. Grandma Reba Smith had died when I was fifteen, and I was thirteen when my cousin Gary died. But I was older and more sensitive when Grandpap died. At that point, nothing had ever hurt me as much in my life as the death of the man who had been one of my major anchors.

I rode with Charlie in his pickup to the funeral. As I got out of the truck and started toward the church house, I somehow converged with Pake, Alice, and Susie. We just came together like magnets. We did it without thinking. It was like we were in a trance because we were grieving so hard over Grandpap's death.

All we could think of was our times with Grandpap: how he'd let us drive his old car he called his "hoopie" even though we were underage, how he'd put tobacco juice on our wasp stings, or give us a dime for a soda water, and of course how he'd rescue us when we were lost in the mountains while gathering cattle. But he sure could be aggravating too. He would do things to get attention, most of them directed at Mama, his daughter-in-law. Pake and my son, Shelby, are a lot like him. They love attention!

He spit tobacco juice in the water cooler fan one time, when it was running. He'd spit behind the heating stove and wink at us kids. When he ate at our house, he would intentionally sit two feet away from the table. His hands shook and he could not get the food from his plate to his mouth without it falling off his fork onto the floor. But you were wasting your breath to ask him to sit closer to the table. And he'd walk through our little house with footsteps as heavy as those of a three-hundred-pound person. His boots were two sizes too big, and he slammed them down with every step he took. The whole house shook. Us kids loved to imitate him.

But it was Mama, the target of most of Grandpap's antics, who stood by his deathbed and took care of him until the day he died. She even moved to Oklahoma City, approximately 140 miles away, and rented an apartment so she could watch over him in the hospital.

There is a special place in heaven for people as unselfish as Mama.

I'll never forget being in Grandpap's sickroom with Mama and Preacher Ward. Brother Ward stood over Grandpap, who was in a daze from sickness and strong medicine. His mind was wandering. Grandpap thought the preacher was Lowry, one of his old rodeo buddies from years ago.

"Lowry, is the girls here?" Grandpap asked the preacher.

"Yes, John," the preacher said. "Jackie and Reba are here."

Grandpap wasn't asking about Jackie and Reba. He was asking about the party girls that he and Lowry used to know.

Mama and I had to laugh.

Grandpap was buried next to Grandma Alice in the cemetery
in Coalgate, Oklahoma. Except for his last days in the hospital, he
lived and died within a few miles of his house. His tombstone was
engraved, as clear as day, with the words that describe him best:
"Lifetime Cowboy."

⚜

I WAS GROWING TO RELY ON CHARLIE VERY MUCH AND TO LOVE HIM.
He was becoming my whole world. So no one was really surprised when we announced our plans to marry. The date we
chose was June 21, 1976, the first day of summer.

We married at the Stringtown Baptist Church, in Stringtown,
Oklahoma. We had a tough time finding anyone to marry us,
since Charlie had been married before. It was a real short
ceremony, and I didn't even have a gown—I just wore a green
summer suit.

About all of my family attended—Mama, Daddy, Aunt Jeannie, my cousin Don Wayne Smith, my sister Susie and her boyfriend Kevin Bacon, Alice and her children Vince and Garett and
her second husband Brent, my cousins Patricia Ann and Rickie
Joy and Rickie's daughter Bridget and our friend Cody Miller.
But not Pake. He didn't think I should be marrying a man with
two kids, and time proved him right about that. I personally asked
him to come. He said no, and I said no more. I didn't beg, but I
was terribly hurt.

Looking back, I've decided there might have been more to it
than Pake's disapproval of Charlie's having kids. Pake and I had
been extremely close, traveling all over the country together
rodeoing and singing. At that time in my life he was my best
friend. Pake had also just lost Grandpap, and maybe he thought

he was losing me too. Maybe he resented Charlie coming into my life because he thought Charlie would come between us and Charlie would take priority. Charlie did.

Yet during the first week of our marriage, Charlie and I spent more time apart than together. After the "ceremony," we drove to Whitehouse, Texas—in separate vehicles. Charlie pulled the horse trailer and I drove another truck. I had a singing job that weekend, and he had rodeos to go to. We left the horses and trailer at Whitey Bob Walker's house and spent our wedding night in a Holiday Inn in Corsicana. It wasn't an especially romantic time, as we'd gotten in late. No roses, no champagne. I had to be up early the next day to promote my song "I Don't Want to Be a One Night Stand" during an interview on a Houston radio station.

By Thursday, Charlie was back rodeoing and I was traveling alone in my pickup, on the way to a show and dance at the Do-Drop-Inn in McAlester. I finished the show about 1 A.M. and was at home asleep by 2:30 A.M. I did the same thing Friday, and Charlie showed up from his rodeo by the end of my four-hour dance set on Saturday night. That was my honeymoon.

⚜

I WOULD COME TO MISS CHARLIE SO BADLY WHEN WE WERE APART. I would cry for two days before he left for a rodeo if I knew I wasn't going along. Once, early in our marriage, I went to Nashville to record "That Makes Two of Us," one of my duets with Jacky Ward. "I played this song and Reba just broke down and started crying," my producer Jerry Kennedy remembers. "The bottom line was that she got so melancholy about wanting to go home that she went home. We canceled the session and I took her to the airport."

I was insecure and just plain immature when I got married,

I'll tell you. I was scared of the dark at twenty-one years old, had been afraid of the dark all my life in fact, ever since Alice pushed me outside on the front porch, locked the door, and turned off the lights.

I'd sleep with my sheet pulled tight to my chin, and would never, ever, once I'd said my goodnights, put my hand outside the sheet. I was still gripped by a childhood memory of a movie I'd seen. In it, two sisters are sleeping in twin beds in the bedroom of a big house. Then one sister asks the other to turn her hand loose.

"I'm not touching you," says the other sister. It is a ghost that is clutching her hand.

So I would ask Charlie not to go to sleep until I did. And he wouldn't. I'd lie next to his big and breathing body, secure and safe by his side. I had never felt so safe.

THE FIRST "HOME" THAT CHARLIE AND I SHARED WAS A BEDROOM AT Mama and Daddy's house, where we stayed for a few months. Then we moved into the "Chockie Shack," which I could call a glorified dump except that there was nothing glorified about it. The ceiling literally fell in twice during the four years that Charlie and I lived there. I think the walls remained standing because the mice were holding hands. The rent was $10 a month.

We didn't even have running water. Charlie got our drinking water from the water plant in Atoka and brought it home in a big tank on a trailer. He put it into a cistern, and then it was pumped into the house. We used it for washing dishes, showering, and to fill the commode. To wash clothes, I had to go to Mama's or to the Laundromat in Atoka.

We had hand-me-down furniture and two hand-me-down

televisions. One had a picture, the other had audio, and they sat one on top of the other so we could see and hear. We thought we were pretty inventive with that one.

In those days we had nothing, but we wanted for little. For a long time, just having each other was enough.

CHAPTER 7

THE YEAR I WAS MARRIED, 1976, ALSO BROUGHT ME ANOTHER great joy: my first hit song.

On January 22, 1976, I did my first professional recording session with Glenn Keener at Woodland Sound Studios in Nashville. He assembled Nashville's finest recording session players of the day, including Pig Robbins, Pete Wade, Ray Edenton, Bob Moore, Buddy Harmon, Lloyd Green, Leon Rhodes, and Tommy Allsup.

We recorded the 1950s Roger Miller/Ray Price song "Invitation to the Blues," because that's a song that Pake, Susie, and I had done a lot before. And we recorded "I'm Not Your Kind of Girl," "I'll Give It to You," "A Boy Like You," and "I Don't Want to Be a One Night Stand," which became my first single.

Glenn and I had listened to a lot of songs before settling on these. I'd sing three or four songs, and I'd come out of the recording booth and we'd find some more songs and do another session. It wasn't at all like I do it today, where in five consecutive days I'll record ten songs.

Then it was back to Oklahoma. I didn't sit around on pins and needles waiting to become a star. I didn't even expect it. If it was going to happen, it was going to happen.

I'll never forget one afternoon in June of 1976, the same month I got married, when Mama, Susie, and I were sitting on the floor in the hall at Mama and Daddy's house. We had the old static-filled AM radio tuned to KVOO, the 50,000-watt powerhouse in Tulsa.

The disc jockey announced a new record by a new singer, and then I heard "I Don't Want to Be a One Night Stand" on the radio.

The three of us sat there and cried.

Pake, Susie, and I were still performing together, so we incorporated the song into our show. It rose to number eighty-eight on the *Billboard* country charts, then dropped off after five weeks.

RIGHT AFTER OUR FIRST SESSION, GLENN KEENER FELL VICTIM TO A personnel cutback at Mercury. I never worked with him again. I was inherited by Jerry Kennedy, one of Nashville's top producers, who was a great teacher for such a green talent as myself and later became a great friend. He included me as a part of the family at Mercury and at his home. He used to call me "R-Nell," short for Reba Nell.

Jerry is famous for taking his craft, but not himself, seriously. One time, when he was producing Jerry Lee Lewis, the studio security guard approached him and said, "Jerry, there's a carload of people outside who've driven here from Connecticut. They say they want to come inside to watch Jerry Lee record."

Most producers would have told the guard to send them

away, and at first Jerry did. But then he found out that, during a show in Connecticut, Lewis had invited everyone in the audience to come to his recording session in Nashville. Kennedy honored Jerry Lee's promise.

He also has a sense of humor. I remember us recording a song titled "I'm a W-O-M-A-N." The song contains a line that says, "It gives me the shivering fits." I got a little tongue-tied with that and sang, "It gives me the frivering shits." I jerked my head up to see if someone was gonna say "cut," "stop," or anything, but no one did and I finished the song.

When it was over, Jerry said, "That's a keeper." I thought my life was over. What would my Daddy say about me recording a song with that word in it? But then they all started laughing. I could take a joke pretty well. Jerry still has the tape.

One time, when I was recording "I'm Not That Lonely Yet," one of my early Mercury songs, I had brought my niece Garett, Alice's daughter, to Nashville. It was her seventh-birthday present.

"She was just a typical six- or seven-year-old," Kennedy recalls, "bouncing off the walls, you know, and having a big time. But Reba was not comfortable."

Jerry said that I told Garett that her behavior constantly reminded me to take my birth-control pills.

He got a big laugh out of that one.

⁂

MY NEXT MERCURY SINGLE, "NOTHIN' LIKE THE LOVE BETWEEN A Woman and a Man," came from a session I did with Jerry. It wasn't released until 1977 and was on the *Billboard* survey only four weeks, peaking at number eighty-six. My third single for Mercury was "Glad I Waited Just for You," which topped out at number eighty-eight on *Billboard*.

Hitting the *Billboard* charts sounds good, but in fact, I was a flop. Today, an artist can sell 500,000 records and not make it to number one. But in the middle 1970s, he or she could sell as few as 25,000 and have a number-one song. So, at the rate I was going, I wasn't making any money for Mercury.

I don't know why I wasn't dropped from the label. If that had happened, my career might have ended right there. Many labels are hesitant to sign an artist once he or she has been dropped by another one. But Mercury stood by me, and instead of letting me go, they put out an album. In August 1977, *Reba McEntire* was released. It produced not one significant hit.

When I finally got a Top Twenty song on Mercury, it was a duet with Jacky Ward called "Three Sheets in the Wind." Jacky was just like a big brother to me, and I loved to do shows with him. I always wished I could talk and tell jokes and funny stories to the audience like he did. When I'd try it, Mama would tell me, "Reba, don't talk, just sing!"

But that one Top Twenty song didn't make me a commercial success. In fact, I didn't earn a royalty check from Polygram-Mercury until 1988, thirteen years after I was signed to the label, and long after I had left.

People have asked me why I think my career took off so slowly when compared to today's singers. Nowadays, an artist will cut one record, have a hit, and be working for $10,000 a night within a year.

The answer is that the recording industry is totally different today. First, the coverage we get with videos is unbeatable. You'd have to perform in a lot of different cities in front of a lot of people to match the visibility you get from the life of one video. Secondly, TNN, The Nashville Television Network, didn't exist when I started back in 1976. It's another wonderful way to showcase new and established acts. I wish we'd had it back then.

Nowadays, country stations are often number one in their markets. That means more people are listening to country music than ever before. And they're also buying more country music.

Currently, the MCA country division, which I'm part of, is the largest branch of MCA Records, bigger than the pop and rock divisions. That means that country artists get a bigger proportion of the company's promotional and marketing dollars, so they get much better exposure than we did. Today the record labels will even give country artists financial help on their tours, to purchase buses and to pay their bands, and will even find them management.

It sure wasn't that way eighteen years ago.

When I was starting out, I had two strikes against me, one because I was female. With the exception of Loretta Lynn, Dolly Parton, Barbara Mandrell, and Tammy Wynette, there weren't many women who were headline acts in country music. Country concert promoters had to "package" several acts just to draw a crowd, and the package usually contained no more than one female act, if any. It's the general rule: Females don't sell like the males. I've worked a long time to change that theory.

Secondly, I wasn't famous. Nashville didn't have the surplus of songwriters in the seventies that it has today, and the good ones wouldn't pitch their best songs to an unknown. Why blow a possible hit on somebody not selling records when they could have a guaranteed moneymaking hit with a superstar? All the good songwriters were wanting to give their material to George Jones or Tammy Wynette, or Willie Nelson and Waylon Jennings, whose careers were a lot hotter than mine. But Jerry did his best to find great songs for me. He called me "The Queen of the Waltzes," because I recorded so many songs back then in waltz tempo. Recently he said that I could "get inside a song better than anyone I've ever met."

Fact is, Jerry never gave up on me; and I never gave up on myself. And that's a piece of hard-won wisdom I'd pass on to anyone wanting to chase a dream.

DURING THE YEARS AFTER I CUT MY FIRST RECORD, I HAD TO BUILD AN audience the best I could with scattered dates. Then Red got me a booking agent, his friend Ray Bingham, and in 1978 I found some guys from Coweta, Oklahoma, to back me when they could. When Ray couldn't book me—and there were times when he booked me without taking a commission just so that I would have a gig—he'd try to get enough work for the band so it could stay together. He put me in VFW halls, rodeos, and honky-tonks— anyplace he could get.

Our biggest-money job was at a fair in Missouri for a "show and dance." That's what they were called back then. We'd do three sets of songs from 9 P.M. until 1 A.M. On the first set, the people would stand near the stage to listen. The rest of the sets, they'd dance. We got paid $1,500 for the night. I was thrilled.

That's because many of our dates—and we didn't have but three or four a month—were at places I can best describe as holes-in-the-wall.

I can remember playing one club in the early 1980s where the cigarette smoke was so thick I couldn't see the crowd. The "dressing room" was a storeroom with big rolls of carpet on the floor. When we'd go from the stage to the bus and somebody walked on one, a bunch of stinging scorpions would run out.

That night, my bus driver drove me to a grocery store be- tween sets to buy some lemons. I was hoping the juice would cut through all the junk in my throat so it would be clear enough for me to sing. The lemons didn't help, but it didn't matter. The crowd was dancing more than listening anyway.

Bingham remembers that in one club where he put me there were almost always two or three fights, always among women.

"Beat all I ever saw," he says. "No matter how hard they fought, Reba just kept singing right on through it."

That stemmed from my training with the Kiowa High School Cowboy Band.

A PERFORMER ALWAYS HAS TO BE ABLE TO IMPROVISE——OR TO SEE THE humor in any given situation. This is something Red Steagall taught me about.

He and I were playing the "Copenhagen-Skoal Superstars Ropin' " in Fort Worth in 1977. Red rode into the arena on horseback wearing a denim suit with maroon velvet insets. "It's an old Southern gentlemen's outfit," he said.

He had told me earlier that he needed a safety pin because he was worried about his zipper busting open. When he jumped off his horse, sure enough, his zipper broke, but he didn't know it. As he stepped into the spotlight and broke into "Miles and Miles of Texas," the crowd could see his white drawers shining in the spotlight. And they began to laugh real hard.

"There's nothing funny about that song," Red recalls thinking to himself.

Danny Steagall, Red's brother, who was in the band, began to whisper-shout at me, and got me to yell, "Red, your fly is open," above the band's music. He finally heard me and realized for the first time what 7,700 people had been seeing all along.

All Red could do then was to remove that expensive, specially made suit coat, let me tie its arms around his back, and finish his part of the show dressed like that. He looked like he was wearing a maroon apron, and the crowd still seemed to find him funny no matter what he sang.

I WAS TO SOON HAVE A BAD EXPERIENCE OF MY OWN, AND LOOKING back on it, it's still hard to find the humor in it. It was 1978, and I was doing a show, again in Fort Worth, called the "Cowtown Pickin' Party." I was the opening act. Ray Wiley Hubbard's band was supposed to back me, but they didn't want to. They had never heard of me before.

"Is there a band here that can back me?" I asked.

"Yes," I was told, "there is a rock 'n' roll band."

"Where are they?"

I met with the players and told them the songs I did. The musicians were truly in agreement. None of them had ever heard any of my tunes.

"Okay," I said, "do you know 'Proud Mary'?"

"Yep," someone said, "we know that one."

"Okay, do you know 'San Antonio Rose'?" I asked.

"Never heard of it," one of them snapped.

"Do you know 'Jeremiah Was a Bullfrog'?" I asked, meaning "Joy to the World."

"Three Dog Night," one of them said. "We know that song."

"Great," I thought silently. "They know two songs."

So, to fill my time onstage, I told jokes. I'd had three single records out on a major record label, and the high point of my act was a joke about a duck.

"Get off the stage!" someone hollered. "Shut up! Take a hike!"

"Well," I thought to myself, "they paid me to do thirty minutes, and I'm going to stick to my thirty minutes."

So I stayed.

Meanwhile, the crowd began to yell for John Conlee, who had a big hit out called "Rose Colored Glasses." When he came out they burst into applause. I don't know if they were clapping because he got onstage or because I got off.

I went backstage, crushed. Luckily, Mama was with me. At least I had someone on my side. She was furious at the crowd.

I had not been attracting a great deal of press attention through my little records on Mercury. Lord knows, they tried. But the label's publicist couldn't get any publicity on me because there wasn't anything to talk about. But on that awful occasion, a reporter happened to show up from the *Fort Worth Star-Telegram*, one of the largest newspapers in Texas. The reporter had seen and heard the crowd's response to me.

"Well, are you going to quit the music business?" he wanted to know.

"Quit?" I fired back. "Absolutely not. I'm gonna get a band of my own and never have this problem again."

And I did.

The following weekend I played in south Texas at a cattle sale, and they had a band called Southern Comfort backing me. I really liked them, and they were interested in becoming my band. The next weekend, when we all played Ardmore, Oklahoma, a new drummer joined them. It was Preecher Williams, who would become my road manager and my mainstay for the next seven or eight years.

⚜

NOW AND THEN, I GOT RAYS OF ENCOURAGEMENT. RAY BINGHAM'S partner, whom he later married, the former Kathy Bee, became my buddy. She liked to ride horses, so we had a lot in common. She helped me fix my hair, and we had a lot of "girl talk."

One night she and I were in the back of my bus getting me ready for a show when someone knocked on my dressing room door. I was told that Norma Jean was on board and wanted to meet me.

Before Dolly Parton, Norma Jean was the "girl singer" in "The Porter Wagoner Show," once the highest-rated syndicated television program to come out of Nashville. Norma Jean had recorded twenty-five albums for RCA during the 1950s and 1960s. Dolly Parton has often described how, during her early days with Porter Wagoner, the crowd would call for Norma Jean, who had left the show forever. Dolly would go to the bus and cry.

Naturally, I was a little starstruck by Norma Jean. Kathy remembers that I raced out of my dressing room with my hair still in curlers to see her. And I was so flattered that she would actually come to my bus to meet me.

In those days, there wasn't exactly a line of people, in or out of show business, who were trying to get onto my bus.

DURING THIS TIME, I DID MANAGE TO ACHIEVE ONE OF MY GREATEST dreams. I got my first chance to sing on the Grand Ole Opry! I had just signed with a new booking agency, Lavendar-Blake, one of the many I worked with in my early career; and it was the first job they got me. My debut was on September 17, 1977.

Mama, Daddy, and Alice drove all the way from Oklahoma to Nashville to see me, a round-trip of about 1,400 miles. They drove it for a three-minute song.

When we pulled up to the Opry gate, the guard asked if he could help us.

"Yes, sir," Daddy said, "we got Reba McEntire here and she's gonna sing tonight on the Grand Ole Opry."

The guard checked his list.

"Her name's not on here," he said.

"What do you suggest we do?" Daddy asked.

"I suggest you turn around and go home," he said.

"We can't do that," Daddy said. "We drove here all the way from Oklahoma."

But the guard wouldn't give in.

Daddy turned around onto the service road behind the Grand Ole Opry House on Nashville's Opryland complex. On the other side of the interstate, we found a phone and I called Dick Blake, my booking agent, at home. Dick, a veteran agent, told us to go back to the guard shack, and by the time we arrived, the guard's attitude had totally changed.

"Right this way, Mr. McEntire," he said.

That was one of my first lessons in the power of influence.

The Grand Ole Opry is broken up into thirty-minute performance segments, each with a celebrity host. I was on a portion of
the show hosted by Charlie Walker, who sang "Please Don't
Squeeze My Charmin."

Imagine, I had never had a real hit record, I was living in a
broken-down old shack of a house, and here I was with Minnie
Pearl, Roy Acuff, Hank Snow, and other country music legends at
the world-famous Grand Ole Opry. We were four "proud-to-be-
there" Okies!

Backstage, Daddy told me that exactly thirty years before—
on September 17, 1947—he had placed in the calf- and steer-
roping categories at the Pendleton Roundup in Pendleton,
Oregon, and had been named the "All-Around Cowboy of the
Rodeo." What a lucky sign! Maybe I could make history too.

Then I heard about Dolly.

Dolly Parton, one of the biggest stars in the entire entertainment industry, decided to make a surprise appearance on the
Opry the night I made my premiere. Most every artist sang two
songs on the show, but since Dolly was coming, I was cut back to
one. Things could get worse—and they did. I didn't even get
to meet Dolly. I wish I had been told to come back another
night.

Dolly looked magnificent, as always. She wore a black pants
suit with chiffon, transparent, flowing arms. The outfit was
dotted with rhinestone butterflies, Dolly's trademark. I wore a
straight denim skirt with a matching shirt.

Dolly went on, beaming and smiling all over the room. I was
totally in awe, since I was still very shy about performing. But
having to follow Dolly Parton wouldn't have been easy even for a
veteran.

That's what I said: follow. I actually had to go on after her!

The Four Guys, a quartet that sings regularly on the Opry,

had to physically help me to the center of the stage when Charlie
Walker introduced me. I was that nervous.

I sang "Invitation to the Blues," which I'd sung on my first
LP. I can hardly remember getting through it, but that song was
certainly a milestone in my career.

⚜

LOOKING BACK, THE WAY I FELT THE FIRST TIME I SANG ON THE OPRY
sort of resembled the way I felt on my first visit there, when I
was seven. Mama, Daddy, Aunt Jeannie, Uncle Slim, Pake, Susie,
Alice, and I all made the trip from Chockie to Nashville, jammed
into Daddy's old GMC truck with a camper on the back. It was
in the heat of summer, and there was no air-conditioning in the
camper or cab.

On the way we camped out in a little park on the Oklahoma
side of Memphis, where it was hot and muggy and mosquitoes
were just eating everybody up. Susie and I, being the two youngest, got to stay in the camper. Everybody else slept out on top of
the picnic tables. Aunt Jeannie slept on one of the benches. Then
it began to rain and the adults huddled together under one of the
tables, using a tarp to create a tentlike cover. But somebody
moved and pulled the tarp off, and all the water that had collected on top poured right on Aunt Jeannie. She was drenched.

In Nashville, we stayed in the cheapest hotel we could find on
lower Broadway Avenue, close to the Ryman Auditorium, home
of the Opry until 1974. I took it upon myself to go exploring and
remember standing in front of a souvenir store owned by the late
Roy Acuff. Roy's dobro player and sidekick, Bashful Brother
Oswald, stood outside the store handing out free rulers. I
remember him handing me a ruler and hugging my neck. I was so
excited.

By the time that night's Opry performance began, Alice and
Aunt Jeannie were sick. Alice couldn't even go to the show.

There wasn't an ounce of ventilation in the hot old building, except for the mild stir of air from people waving fans donated by a funeral home. We were in the cheapest seats, under the balcony where people spilled soft drinks on those of us below. When a good seat down front became available, someone in my group would take it.

Mama was sitting down in front by the time I became sick too. It must have been something all of us ate. I went down the slanted aisle to tell her, and she told me to go find a bathroom. She never took her eyes off the stage.

I began to run, and then asked an usher where I could find a ladies' room. I didn't understand his directions, and I knew I was on the verge of being sick.

So I walked outside. On the front steps of the home of country music and the world's longest-running radio show, I threw up.

I should have been incredibly embarrassed, but I was too sick to realize it. And things got worse when a stranger walked by and handed me his handkerchief. In my childish innocence, after I wiped my mouth off I offered to give it back.

"No, honey," he said, "you keep it."

Those were my introductions to the world-famous Grand Ole Opry!

CHAPTER 8

FOR A LONG TIME, CHARLIE WAS FAIRLY INDIFFERENT TO MY career. He wouldn't go with me on many of my shows—his attitude was, you do your thing and I'll do mine. It was almost as though he felt that he was a world-champion steer wrestler, and what was I?

One time, especially, his attitude bothered me. I was supposed to sing at a private party in Fort Worth, Texas. The day came, and it was snowing hard. I called down to Texas to ask if the gig was still on. "Oh, yes," they told me, "the weather's fine down here. If you can make it, come on." I needed Charlie to drive me down to the show. I felt he was more experienced than I was. But he was tied up with something, so I had to drive through the ice storm myself.

Then a turning point came, when I started making money and Charlie slowed down on his rodeo career, when he began to get involved. In the beginning, I was glad to have his help. My bookings and recording dates were now beginning to escalate, getting to be more than I could comfortably juggle. And equally important to me, his involvement meant fewer separations. It seemed like an extension of the protectiveness that had first drawn me to him. It seemed that sharing something so basic to me—my music—could only bring us closer. And it did, for a while.

But that's not to say that there weren't some major chinks in our marriage. One predictable problem was his children. Anyone who has ever been a stepparent knows that it's not an easy role. Inevitably there are resentments on all four fronts—both parents', the stepparent's and the children's—and most of those resentments are at least partially valid.

So it wasn't always easy when Lance and Coty, Charlie's sons by his first marriage, came to visit us on school vacation, in the summers, and on some weekends. Charlie worked hard to get them as much as possible, though once Sherrie advised me to quit bothering them when I was finding out over the phone if we could see the boys. She said, "Go have kids of your own."

I especially remember one visit the boys made when Charlie and I were living in the Chockie Shack. Naturally, I wanted very much for them to like me as Charlie's wife and as their stepmother. I was nervous, though I looked forward to their visit, and had made special efforts to make our little house as neat and as homey as possible.

One morning, Lance, Coty, and Charlie got into the pickup to go feed cattle. When I heard the engine running, I came out of the house, heading to the truck intending to go along. Charlie and I had always fed cattle together, in any and all weather conditions. We were a ranching team, and that was something that was as much a part of our lives as rodeo and singing.

Until that day.

"Where're you going?" Charlie asked me.

His sons were looking at me from inside the pickup.

"I'm going to feed with you," I said, and my voice took an "of course" tone.

"There's not enough room," Charlie said. He closed the pickup's door, and he and his sons drove away. I'll never know why Charlie didn't say, "I think the boys and I need a little time together today." I could have accepted that. Or, better yet, "Climb in" or "Scoot over, boys! There's room for everybody." Instead, he just left me standing there watching while the taillights faded off into the distance.

That just broke my heart.

⚜

WE WERE STILL LIVING IN THE CHOCKIE SHACK WHEN I HAD MY FIRST Top Ten record. Here's how it happened: Earlier in the year, I had gone to an estate sale and wound up buying a deepfreeze that was full of blackberries. The lady selling it had gathered and frozen them that spring.

So one afternoon I was setting out to copy one of Grandma Smith's famous blackberry cobblers, when the phone rang.

It was Jerry Kennedy.

"Hey, Reba, what are you doing?" he said.

"Hey, Jerry," I said. "I'm cookin', what do you know?"

Long-distance telephone connections aren't the best in southeastern Oklahoma. Besides that, I was paying more attention to that cobbler and really wanted it to turn out right, so I was watching it carefully. Our oven's heat was uneven. The thermostat was out of whack, and I couldn't rely on the timer. I had to cook by sight the way some musicians play by ear.

Jerry told me he had a "monster song," music business slang for a giant hit record. Of course, I wanted the lowdown right away, but my cobbler was about to burn.

So I had to call him back. When I did, through the scratch of rural long distance, I first heard "You Lift Me Up to Heaven."

I highly respected Jerry's ear for a song. If he liked it, most usually I recorded it, and he rarely steered me wrong. This time was no exception. "You Lift Me Up to Heaven" was my career-making record. It went to number eight on the *Billboard* charts.

It looked like I was finally getting someplace.

◦✣◦

I THINK CHARLIE WOULD HAVE BEEN CONTENT TO LIVE IN THE Chockie Shack all his life. The rent was cheap, $10 a month, which was important because Charlie had come into our marriage $40,000 in debt.

It wasn't his fault—he had gone into a partnership to buy some cows with a relative who couldn't pay his part. To make things worse, the mama cows didn't perform as expected. I won't go into the efforts that a lending institution made to collect the money from Charlie, who would have paid if he'd had it. But he was flat broke. I'll just say Charlie's inability to pay back the $40,000 was putting him under big pressure.

So I went to Daddy on Charlie's behalf. Charlie didn't want to borrow money, and Daddy wasn't eager to loan it. Instead, we struck a deal: Daddy would pay the bank note and Charlie and I would pay him back largely by working for him on the ranch. One winter, Daddy and Mama went to Florida to buy cattle, and every week they would send a load back home, where we'd receive them, straighten them up, and put them out to pasture. It was so cold, Charlie and I would be almost frozen, trying to save the life of a yearling that had just been shipped hundreds of miles to Oklahoma from Florida. It sure was hard on them.

Charlie and I would give the cattle worm medicine and their shots for various diseases. We'd try to mainline a steer, but the needles would freeze up. We'd blow into the needles to try to clear them; if any spit got into the needle, it would freeze up by the time we got it into the vein. If the spit didn't freeze, then the medicine would. When we finally got the cattle straightened up, we'd brand and castrate them and watch them for a week to be sure they were okay. The sick ones would go in a separate pen. When all the cattle were healthy, they were put out into the main pasture.

It was hard work, but that was something I had done most of my life.

STILL, BY OUR FOURTH YEAR OF MARRIAGE, I HAD BEGUN TO DREAM that Charlie and I could have a house of our own, not that we were even thinking of looking for one. Up to this point, our household income was still coming from Charlie's rodeoing, my singing about three nights a month, and my checking records for an oil-lease company out of Oklahoma City at Coalgate. And, of course, we were still helping Daddy to repay our loan.

But then I heard that my cousin Rickie's place in Stringtown might be for sale. We were on our way home from a trip to Fan Fair in Nashville—my cousins Rickie Thompson and Paula Daniel, our friend Jan Lancaster, and I—in Jan's Cadillac, "Ole Fred," when Rickie casually mentioned it.

Rickie and her husband, Loyd, were living outside of Stringtown on 225 acres. It was a beautiful place, with pine trees and the Chickasaw Creek running through it. I'd always loved it. I thought of the place as Stringtown's answer to the Ponderosa Ranch, and I became very excited.

"Well, Rickie," I said, "what do you think you'd want for your place?"

Rickie said she'd talk to Loyd and told me to talk to Charlie.

Charlie was spreading gravel on the driveway at the house when I approached him.

"Charlie, turn off the tractor," I said anxiously.

He did.

"What is it?" he said.

"Let's go down and visit with Rickie and Loyd," I said.

"What for?" he asked.

"They're wanting to sell their place."

"We can't afford it," he said, and turned the tractor back on.

"Turn it off," I shouted above the engine. "Let's talk about this. I think we can get the money if we go down to the Federal Land Bank in Durant and use my contract with Mercury as collateral," I said. "That might pull some weight. Why don't we just go over and look at the place and go talk to the bank?"

Charlie wasn't into the idea at all at first. He was afraid to get any deeper into debt. But at least he agreed to explore getting a bank loan.

Borrowing money against a recording contract in Nashville is one thing, because bankers are familiar with the collateral. Trying to borrow money in Durant, Oklahoma, in the 1970s against a contract that said you were obliged to sing for an income was something else. I'm sure the banker had never seen a recording contract, much less loaned against one.

"It's against my better judgment," the banker said. "I'll never get my money back. But I'm going to give you this loan."

The bank got its money back to the penny. We had an installment loan, and I made it my priority over all our other monthly payments. I can't say for sure how much money we borrowed from the Federal Land Bank. My collaborator, Tom Carter, asked Charlie, at my request, to talk about the particulars of our finances for this book. It seemed only fair for him to be able to give his side of everything. But Charlie refused.

In late June 1980, we moved into that beautiful ranch house in Stringtown. We had three bedrooms, running water, no mice, and a ceiling that stayed in place.

I was determined to have a housewarming party on the Fourth of July. I hung curtains, pictures, put groceries into the refrigerator and plates and glasses in the kitchen cabinets, and did all the rest that goes with a move from one house to another. All my family came over, and we ate homemade ice cream and swam in our new pond. I can still remember feeling the muddy bottom between my toes and the rush of pride that you get when you really have a nice place of your own.

❧

BY 1980, I WAS TRYING TO DEVELOP SOMETHING OF AN "OR-ganization." Red Steagall was sort of my career manager, and Pake was my road manager, though he was getting tired of the job. Eventually, he decided to leave and asked Preecher Williams to replace him. But he wanted to be sure my affairs were lined up before he did.

At that point, we were putting together another band. It included Preecher on drums, my sister Susie doing harmony, and Charkie Christian on lead guitar. Pake played bass, and we felt that we needed a steel guitar player, so we called Red Steagall, who recommended Gary Carpenter.

Gary had another job and recommended someone none of us knew. His name was Narvel Blackstock.

At that point, Narvel was an insurance agent who played music on the side. He had been married at sixteen and had three beautiful children by the time he was twenty-one. And he loved music enough to drive from Burleson, Texas, to Chockie, Okla-homa—three and a half hours each way—then two hours each way to Nowata, Oklahoma, where I was scheduled to play a dance at a Veterans of Foreign Wars hall. Imagine traveling eleven hours, sight unseen, to try out a gig with a girl singer you'd barely heard of and who'd only recorded one song that you had never heard.

The job paid $150, with no per diem—that's an allowance of so much every day for living expenses. Narvel would be lucky to clear one hundred dollars for a job requiring about twenty hours, including travel, rehearsal, and performance time—which is one reason why band members for up-and-coming singers, then and now, come and go. Yet Narvel was all gung ho. He even quit his steady job before he joined me!

I've been thankful ever since that he did.

Even as a child, Narvel's desire was to become a professional musician. I think it's really fascinating that he began playing steel guitar when he was eight. The steel guitar, with its foot and knee pedals, is one of the most complicated of all the stringed instruments. Narvel began his career playing in Pentecostal churches, going on the road with a gospel quartet about the time he began to shave. He missed most Fridays and Mondays of his secondary education, traveling all day Friday to a Friday night concert or church service and all day Monday coming home from a Sunday night engagement.

At fourteen, when other boys his age were going to sleep in their rooms, Narvel was dozing in the back of a touring bus, listening to the roar of an old engine and the snoring of men twice his age. And that bus wasn't air-conditioned in a climate where the nighttime temperature was often in the middle nineties. The steel exterior of the bus only made it hotter inside.

The entire group regularly rented one hotel room, not always daily, for showers. They were modern gypsies in a caravan powered by diesel fuel.

For all of the above, Narvel was paid $25 a day, and was occasionally given trousers and a shirt. The price of the clothes was deducted from his salary.

Those early experiences would be great training for the life he would be facing in my band.

...net my first husband, Charlie Battles, while I was rodeoing in the early 1970s. *Above:* On our wedding day, ...ne 21, 1976, in Stringtown, Oklahoma. *Below:* We ran cattle at Pine Tree, a 14,000-acre place we leased east ... Stringtown.

When Charlie became more involved in my career, our home life and work life merged into one. *Above:* That's me washing dishes while listening to demo tapes at our home in Stringtown. *Below:* I also shared the ranching duties as usual. *Facing page, top left:* Then I'd hit the road to perform at shows such as Fan Fair 1983. *Right:* Narvel Blackstock started working for me in 1980, playing the steel guitar. *Below:* On my first big rodeo gig in Ardmore, Oklahoma, in 1978, Preecher Williams played with me for the first time. After I sang each night, I'd ride around the arena.

JOAN AND GORDY GOODWIN

traveled mostly in trucks, cars, and vans,
in 1981 I got my first bus and named
Old Mae. *Facing page, top:* This is how
looked after we repainted her. *Center:*
rvel walking me to the stage from my bus.
d a great feeling of love and acceptance
en I saw fans waiting for me. *Below:* By
v, I'd also begun to assemble somewhat of
"organization." From left: Narvel,
echer Williams, Duke Burr, me, Wormy
ler, my sister Susie, Wayne Lewis, and
ger Wills. We traveled all over the coun-
Right: Performing at the Big E Fair in
st Springfield, Massachusetts. *Below:* Red
I needed a professional manager, so I
d Don Williams (far right). Next to him
Charlie. Eventually, Don was succeeded
Bill Carter (left).

ERNIE CETTO

JOAN AND GORDY GOODWIN

organization kept growing. *Facing page,*
From left are road manager Preecher
liams, bus driver Larry Jones,
idman Russell Hulme, guitarist Leigh
nolds, drummer Matt Martin (with
ses), me, bass player Roger Wills, steel
ar player Narvel Blackstock, guitarist
id Anthony, and piano player Wayne
is. *Bottom:* By 1986 it had evolved to
ude (background, from left) tour
ager Narvel, pianist Donny Howard,
tric guitarist Bill Cooley, acoustic
arist Leigh Reynolds, hairstylist Sheri
Coy, drummer Steve Short, vocalist Suzy
kins, bass player Roger Wills, fiddler
y Soloman, lighting designer Sherry
nreich, and (foreground, from left)
er Dale Byrd, me, monitor engineer
my MeLear, soundman Ricky Moeller,
steel guitar player Donny LaValley.
t: In 1984, I accepted my first Country
ic Association Female Vocalist of the
award on behalf of my Mama for all
love and support throughout the years.
v: Mama and Daddy celebrated with
when I received my star in the walk of
e at the Country Music Hall of Fame.

Right: One of the greatest nights of my career was my debut at Carnegie Hall on October 28, 1987. This black suede dress was the first one ever made for me by Sandi Spika, who does all my costumes today. *Above:* I flew (from left) Daddy, Mama, Gail and Red Steagall up to see the show—first class all the way. I wouldn't have been singing at Carnegie Hall if it hadn't been for these four people. I love them dearly!

NARVEL'S INITIAL GIGS WITH ME SHOW A PRETTY CLEAR PICTURE OF MY performing life in those years. Even though I had a Top Ten hit, you might call my operation somewhat less than professional.

On his first day, he pulled up in an Oldsmobile 98 to meet us at the Chockie Shack. Charlie and I had just moved to Stringtown, so Preecher was living there and using the place as a sometime rehearsal hall for my band. Narvel must not have slammed the door when he entered. The ceiling didn't collapse.

Beer cans, ashtrays, and various other litter was scattered all over the place. A bullet hole punctured the sagging ceiling, from the time Preecher fired a gun into the air to get the guys in the band to quit arguing about who would sleep where inside the shack.

As an agent for Prudential, one of the world's largest insurance companies, Narvel had grown accustomed to offices with central heating and air-conditioning and fluorescent lights. In his office, the furniture was comfortable. At the Chockie Shack, it was collapsible.

"I was so shocked at the sight of the place," he recalls.

Narvel had also grown accustomed to structure and organization. But though he had arrived on time for his appointment with Pake, Pake was nowhere to be found. And he certainly didn't expect that Pake, the band leader for a recording artist on a major label, would show up in a pickup truck pulling a horse trailer.

Things got stranger, Narvel remembers. "We loaded our equipment in the back of the horse trailer. We arrived in Nowata at four in the afternoon, where we were going to set up the equipment and rehearse for a couple of hours. Here we are, supposed to play this show that night, and we had never played a note together. Reba had bought a new Peavey Sound System, but nobody in the band knew how to hook it up. They finally got the

PA system hooked up about the time the people starting coming into the hall. We still hadn't rehearsed, and I still hadn't seen Reba.''

Narvel would learn later that I hate to rehearse. I prefer for the band to get the song down pat, and then I come in to learn my part. My voice gets tired if I try to sing with each run-through, so I want to save it as much as possible for actual performing. I guess you could say I'm pretty lazy in that respect.

Finally, I arrived with Charlie and Susie right before the show, and Narvel swears that we all just walked into the hall and never spoke to him. I don't remember.

"It wasn't that they were being rude," Narvel explains. "It's just that they didn't realize what a big deal this was for me. I was making a lot more out of it than they were. It wasn't that big of a gig to them.''

Our guitar player that night was Charkie Christian, a guy I had grown up with, who was filling in until Kelly Rhyne began the next weekend. His parents and mine had rodeoed together when we were kids. Charkie had some peculiar rules: He was willing to play anything except fills, kickoffs, and turnarounds. That's like a baseball player saying he'll do anything except throw, catch, and hit.

Actually, Charkie did play the beginning and instrumental break on "Johnny B. Goode." That was his only solo of the night.

So Narvel, who had never rehearsed with the band and who barely knew any of my recorded material, had to lead the introduction, instrumental break, and ending to every song I sang that night. We did three sets spread over four hours. Narvel says it was five hours, but I think it just seemed that long to him. Fortunately, most of the songs I sang back then were covers, hit songs by other artists, so he was familiar with some of the tunes. Otherwise, he might not have been able to improvise so well.

When the show ended, Narvel recalls that Susie, Charlie, and I left without ever saying more to him than hello.

"By that time," he says, "I was really sucking wind. I sure wondered what kind of a deal I had got myself into. So we start back home and Pake says, 'Look, I know it was weird, but don't worry about a thing. I'm going to get everything under control. The next gig is about ten days away, and by that time there is going to be some new guys joining the band, and things are going to be a lot different. I'm going to get things under control.'

"The next thing I know, I got a call from Preecher saying Pake had quit."

Amazingly, Narvel came back. Our next job was at a rodeo outside of Houston. This was Roger Wills's (on bass, who is now with Alan Jackson) and Kelly Rhyne's (on guitar) first date with me since high school. The band, with Narvel on steel guitar, was supposed to set up and perform for about an hour before the rodeo. Unfortunately, during that hour a tractor was "discing" up the arena to prepare it for the rodeo, so they could hardly hear how they sounded.

Someone came up with the idea for me to enter the arena on horseback and then take the stage to do my show. So I rode in on a pickup horse, but that old horse nearly ran away with me before I got him settled down. Some grand entrance! Then, after the rodeo, we had to take our equipment down and set it all up again, facing the opposite direction, to play the four-hour-long dance.

At that point, Narvel hadn't even been told the worst—that we only had ten dates booked!

<hr>

SUSIE AND I TRAVELED FROM SHOW TO SHOW IN A LINCOLN CONTINEN-tal. The five guys in the band rode in our leaky van, which pulled the horse trailer that carried the instruments. The guys took turns driving through the night. When we arrived at our destination, we would get two hotel rooms, one for me and Susie and the other for the band, who would split the mattress into two double beds and put the fifth guy on a rollaway. Their room would often be so jammed with bedding that no floor space would show, and the guys would have to walk across the tops of the beds to get to the bathroom.

At any time, Narvel could have gone back to the economic security and suburban comfort of the insurance industry.

"I was getting a lot of pressure at home to quit because I wasn't making enough money," Narvel says. "But I really had no thought of going back. I had gotten to the point where I knew that music was where my heart and love was. And as bad as it was playing with Reba, it was the only avenue I had at that time beyond the local club band.

"The first year with Reba was very tough," Narvel remembers. "We may have played fifty dates that first year. We kept thinking with each album, 'This is going to be the album that pushes her over the top.' I think the next one was *Heart to Heart*. Then we did a little better, but nothing big was happening. It was a slow, slow build."

That's how Narvel came into a band he never left. In 1982, Narvel told Mama that he believed in me tremendously.

"I'll be around long after everybody else has quit," he said. And he is.

CHAPTER 9

I'D HATE TO TRY TO GUESS HOW MANY MILES I TRAVELED DURING the 1980s. So when I got my first bus in 1982, a twenty-year-old Silver Eagle, it was a really big event. I got it in May, so I called it my Mother's Day present. I already had a busload of kids!

We had been traveling since 1977 in trucks, vans with trailers, and cars, which didn't give us much of an air of seriousness. You pull backstage in a bus and the guard motions you to a parking spot. You pull up in a van and the guard asks you for identification. And you can park buses in commercial spots when you sometimes can't park a van at all.

I nearly lost a van in 1981 over a parking space.

I was at home in Stringtown cooking supper when my agent called me to say that Tammy Wynette was sick and had to cancel a show in Wisconsin. He wanted to know if I could fill in for her, and of course I said yes—her deposit was more than we'd make in two months. So I rushed around and rounded up my band,

and we drove down to Dallas/Fort Worth International Airport.

Six of us pulled up to the curbside check-in and I told Preecher, the tour manager, to go park the van and trailer.

I don't know if it was because we had a plane to catch and there was little time to look for the right parking place, but Preecher parked the van and trailer in a one-hour parking slot.

We were gonna be gone for three days.

We returned to the airport, and everyone in the group except me knew what Preecher had done.

"Okay, Preecher," I said, "go get the van."

He walked outside the terminal and came back in about a few seconds.

"It's not there," he said.

We were tired from performing and flying, and still had a three-hour drive back home ahead of us.

"What do you mean it isn't there?" I said.

"It's been towed off," he answered.

"How do you know?" I fired.

" 'Cause I left it right there," he said, pointing to a sign that said "One Hour Parking."

"You mean you parked on the other side of the street from that sign?" I said.

"No," he said as he cleared his throat. "I parked it on this side in *front* of that sign."

I told him to find out where the van was, and to go get it. It cost him $75 to get it out of lockup. I didn't speak to Preecher for a few days, and I never planned to pay him back. Years later, he told me that Charlie sneaked the money to him.

Having a bus meant that everyone could travel together to our shows. We would talk about the show, everyday life, politics, religion, and what we were doing on the way to the next job. We'd never had that luxury before.

❦

FOR A TOURING SINGER, FINDING A GOOD BUS DRIVER CAN BE AS important as finding good musicians. I'm a light sleeper, and since we traveled at all hours, I had to look hard to find someone who would drive smoothly enough to keep from waking me up. Then, too, especially in those early years, my drivers had to be good mechanics. My first driver, Wormy Miller, once had to get under a bus with a broom handle to try to force the transmission into reverse while my piano player, Wayne Lewis, struggled with the gears from the driver's seat.

After Wormy, we got a driver who the band nicknamed Sominex Rex, because he was so slow. I can't remember his real name. But I remember how he used to make U-turns in the middle of four-lane traffic. He scared all of us to death.

Greg Cochran from Atoka was our next driver. Greg had been with my cousin Gary Thompson when Gary was electrocuted in Stringtown while they were trying to put that tarp over the hay. Greg had been shocked and burned in the incident.

He was a great driver, but we think he had an esophageal reflux: he couldn't swallow his food. We'd pull into a truck stop, he'd order a giant plate of shrimp, and take two bites. He couldn't swallow the rest. Whoever sat by him often didn't order a meal, because he knew he'd get to finish Greg's. He was a funny guy who all of us liked, but unfortunately, Greg didn't last long on the road.

Then, in 1983, we hired a real doozie. He only lasted seventeen days. There was a problem with the bus, or a complete breakdown, each day he worked for me.

For example, we were in Davenport, Iowa, and after our show, he drove through a side-street underpass and almost got the bus stuck in the tunnel. I could hear the luggage rack, on top of the bus, being scraped off as he tried to force the bus through.

"Stop! Stop!" everyone on board started yelling.

I was in my stateroom, counting concession money with Preecher, when Wayne Lewis came running into the room. That bus was Wayne's pride and joy, and he always kept it washed and shining. He loved to baby it. He would have done nothing to harm it.

When he came into my room, he was carrying the bus's luggage rack and the antenna that had been torn from the top.

"This guy is killing me!" Wayne sarcastically said. "We're jammed in the tunnel."

The new driver made things worse by trying to claim the bus had cleared the same underpass on the way to the show. "Someone has laid asphalt on this road while we were at the concert," he said. "And now the road is higher. That's why the top of the bus is caught against the bottom of the underpass."

We got out of that scrape by letting the air out of the tires and backing out, before heading on to Nampa, Idaho.

"This is about all I can handle," I told the driver.

"Well, I'm quitting," he said.

"That's a smart idea," I said.

By the time we got to Omaha, the battery was dead—the driver had forgotten to put water in it—and we had to use the alternator. That burned up too. At that point the driver saved his own life by catching a plane home, while I flew to Nampa, Idaho, where I had a press conference. Narvel, Preecher, and Wayne took turns driving the bus the rest of the way to Nampa.

Charlie flew into Nampa, and the search was on for a new bus driver. Thanks to Russell Hulme, my soundman, we found Larry Jones. Larry had driven trucks for his dad's business in Duncan, Oklahoma, and had mentioned to Russell that he would like to be my bus driver if the job ever came open.

Larry and Charlie hit it off immediately, mainly because Larry offered to work free for thirty days if we would pay his expenses. He was just that eager. He was so eager, in fact, that he showed up a day early. Charlie didn't see how we could lose on a deal like that.

But when Wayne began to show Larry the ropes, he quickly learned that Larry had never driven a bus in his life. He didn't know how to start it or how to put it into reverse. He didn't even know where the ignition keys were supposed to go. He had just figured that a bus couldn't be too much different from a truck.

Nobody told me at the time, and I'm not sure they ever told Charlie.

The next night Larry drove us to the rodeo we were playing, and all eyes were on the new guy. Folks who travel for a living have a way of watching the one who drives them.

"It was dead silence," Larry remembers. "I was thinking, 'This must be my big test.' I got down to this one place and had to make a U-turn to get back into the rodeo grounds. I thought, 'God, this is it, I'm exposed.' "

Larry turned as far as he could, backed against traffic, and completed his turn. The turn probably took an entire minute. Still, nobody said anything as he struggled with the bus, looking into the mirrors to cover his sides.

He finished the turn, and the bus broke into applause.

I wanted to get to know Larry, so I sat in the jump seat the first time he drove us during daylight. We came up on a construction site.

"Man," Larry said, "I hope this ain't a roadblock. I don't have a driver's license."

Preecher asked Larry to see his license later that day. Larry had only been kidding.

⚜

THERE IS NO RHYME OR REASON FOR SOME OF THE THINGS THAT happen on the road. Sometimes, you have to think God is behind them. Sometimes, you know He is.

One time, Sheri McCoy, my hairdresser, and I flew from Detroit to Kansas City, Missouri, where Larry met us with the bus. When we reached our hotel, which happened to be one of a chain of hotels in that area, we discovered we had no reservations. That's when we learned that Kansas City, Kansas, and Kansas City, Missouri, have hotels with the same name.

We were in the wrong Kansas City.

I remember that the weather was extremely cold, icy and snowy. We drove around awhile trying to find our hotel, and finally I told Larry to stop and call for directions. He pushed the 0 button on the telephone. It froze inside and wouldn't come out. We stayed lost.

Larry ended up driving around Kansas City, Kansas, for four hours—longer than it had taken me to fly from Detroit. We were lost long enough for me to watch on the bus TV a videotaped movie, another one-hour program, and the ten-o'clock news. But surely it was God's plan for me to see that news broadcast, with a feature on all of the homeless people who were freezing out in the elements. It really tore me up. Here I was in a nice customized bus with a heater running full blast, and these people were searching for shelter to save their lives. In a way I felt guilty, but changed my mind and decided to do something about it instead.

So the next day, Charlie's niece Renee Nelson, Sheri, and I went to Wal-Mart after my rodeo show. We picked out socks and compact cases with toothpaste, shampoo, and other stuff that a travel bag would hold. I also got lots of pillows and blankets.

When the girls and I were taking that stuff through the checkout line, the cashier recognized me. He asked me why I was buying so much, and I told him about seeing the homeless on the news the evening before.

Wal-Mart is a family-oriented kind of place, so the cashier offered me a 10 percent discount on everything I bought. Of course, I didn't *ask* for a discount. But the next day a newspaper story claimed that I had bickered over the price with the people at Wal-Mart. I thought that was kind of tacky of the newspaper. I hope they were simply misinformed, and naturally, I was hurt that someone would tell such a lie.

But that hurt was overshadowed by my gratitude that God had let me be in a position to help. The Wal-Mart folks volunteered to send the items over to the people at the Rescue Mission for me, since I had another show that night and since we were in Renee's small Mustang car.

The next day, Larry came to me to apologize about getting lost.

"Never mind," I told him. "If you hadn't been lost, I wouldn't have heard about the people having such a rough time in the weather. We might have been frustrated about being lost, but it wasn't nearly as bad as being in the cold. At least we were in a warm bus."

❦

I'M STILL HAUNTED BY A TIME THAT I WISH I COULD HAVE HELPED— but could I have helped, if I had only known? On March 30, 1980, two days after my twenty-fifth birthday, I came in off a weekend tour to receive some terrible news.

I called Mama as I usually did after getting home and said, "What's been going on?"

Mama quietly told me, "Diannia Kay killed herself."

Diannia Kay, my cousin, had walked freely in and out of my home and life for as far back as I could remember. Miles separate families today, as they have separated me from my brother, sisters, and parents. But when I was growing up, most of my family lived within driving, or horse-riding, distance of each other. Cousins, aunts, and uncles were expected to unexpectedly drop by. And they did.

I was shocked at Mama's news and flooded with scores of memories of Diannia. There were more than just ties of blood between us. We were constantly together as childhood playmates at home, from the first grade up through the Kiowa High School Cowboy Band.

She had married Bill Lewis and they had a beautiful daughter, Virgeana Dale. Apparently, Diannia and Bill began having problems after a while. Diannia was crying a lot, very depressed, and in her own way, in the form of a letter, tried to let us know. But as everyone tries to tend to their own business, people around her just thought that, like any couple, she and Bill would work things out. Then, late one night after the house was quiet, Diannia took the rifle outside. She walked silently across the grass to a dry creek bed. She put the rifle barrel to her head, the butt on the ground, and reached down to pull the trigger.

She was found after a long search the next day.

In 1991, I recorded *For My Broken Heart,* my biggest-selling album at that time. The record contains a song, "If I Had Only Known," which I dedicated to the eight people we had lost in a 1991 plane crash. It also fits Diannia Kay's situation.

Suicide always leaves the loved ones left behind feeling helpless and guilty. I felt both.

Here I had been busy trying to build a career when Diannia had been busy trying to build peace of mind.

⚜

I HAD BEGUN TO REALIZE THAT IT WAS TIME TO GET SERIOUS ABOUT MY career. I could see that the kind of haphazard planning and general roughhousing of my early years on the road weren't going to help me advance as an artist. I needed to take more control of my performing life, and I started by getting more choosy about the places where I sang.

A touring entertainer never knows what a place is like if he's never played it before. I learned that as far back as the Singing McEntires. Some places have swanky names. You drive all day and night to get there, then find out they're not so swanky. That was especially true in my early days when I was playing the honky-tonks.

It is not that I have anything against honky-tonks. It's good for performers to stay close to the grass roots, to see how the people respond, the songs that get them dancing, and—hard to take, but important to know—what bores them enough so they talk through it. But I always had a terrible time singing through all the cigarette smoke, which I had grown allergic to. For five years, with my burning throat and running eyes I'd felt like I'd been singing in rooms full of ammonia.

I remember the inside of the last honky-tonk I ever played. It was in 1982. Susie, the band, and I worked a club in Texas, and after the show my sinuses were inflamed and infected. They were killing me. I went to the motel and called Charlie that night.

"I'm not playing another club," I said. "Don't book me into another nightclub."

"You've just ruined your career," Charlie said.

"I don't care," I said. "If I continue to sing in that smoke, I won't have a career because I won't have a voice!"

Charlie insisted several more times that my career was over, because nightclubs were the places where I had played most. But I had made my decision, and I stood by it.

Much later on, I told this story to my movie stand-in on *The Gambler*. She had been saying that she would much rather learn the ropes of the film business by being a stand-in than by taking what she knew were bad acting jobs. Well, hindsight is always 20/20. I played all the bad clubs, and if I'd gone in and tried to find a job as a backup singer for a first-class act, I might have learned the ropes better and sooner. I might have been more experienced by the time I hit. But looking back, I wouldn't trade in one bit of it. The time it took let me meet lots of great people, and learning the hard way never lets you forget.

And I honestly think my low tolerance of smoke was God's

way of telling me to get out of the nightclubs and onto the concert stages, that I wasn't getting anywhere there. Then, on December 10, 1982, the Statler Brothers asked me to tour with them as their opening act. I know in my heart I wouldn't have become a part of their tour if I hadn't put my foot down about not singing in clubs.

At that time, the Statlers had enjoyed a remarkable recording career, and had been named "Vocal Group of the Year" more often by the Country Music Association than any other group. They still hold that record.

The brothers had always liked having a girl singer as their opening act. In the late 1970s, they'd used Barbara Mandrell. In 1982, they paid me $3,500 a night and they showed me the courtesy and professionalism that they're famous for.

I even got to do a television special with the Statler Brothers. The setting was a fictional place called McEntire Town, in which the Statlers were the bad guys and Mel Tillis was the sheriff. Everyone knows that Mel used to stutter badly, but in 1976, when he was named "Entertainer of the Year," he credited Minnie Pearl with giving him the confidence to act. He said that Minnie told him the secret of comedy was not to rush your lines, but to stand there and wait for the crowd to respond. He must have learned that lesson well, because he's one of the most entertaining and funny people I've ever known—on and off the stage. I've learned a lot from observing him.

Another great thing about Mel is that he doesn't put on airs —he's pretty much the same offstage as he is on. I once did a show with him in Rhinelander, Wisconsin, along with Janie Fricke. Even as recently as the early 1980s, that was something you hardly saw—two girl singers on a country-music package show.

Mel came by my bus to visit with a chaw of tobacco in his mouth. Lana Sheffield was my traveling companion, helping out with my bookkeeping, mail, and errands at the time.

Well, Lana took a paper towel and lined the bottom of a Styrofoam cup, then handed it to Mel. Mel was very impressed that Lana had known what to do. Here he was, a headliner and a big star, and yet he appreciated someone's knowing the old, country ways. Lana told him everyone knew how to do that in southeastern Oklahoma.

⚜

I FELT SO LUCKY, AS A GREENHORN IN THE COUNTRY MUSIC BUSINESS, to be hanging around the Statler Brothers and Mel Tillis. They sure were a lot of fun.

After I left the Statler Brothers, I opened for Conway Twitty, Ronnie Milsap, and then Mickey Gilley. All of them were great to work with, but the food provided at mealtime by each headline act was as different as their music.

The Statlers didn't provide food for their opening acts. We never knew from night to night if we were even going to get something to drink.

Milsap provided a deli tray and a loaf of bread. Susie and I would take the bread out of the wrapper, make sandwiches for us and the band, then put the sandwiches back in the bread wrapper and carry it with us to eat after the show. That would be our supper.

Conway provided a full meal, and Gilley gave us T-bone steak, soup, salad, and other vegetables, along with dessert. The meal was set out each day between sound check and show time. And by show time, not a bite was left!

⚜

I ALSO STARTED PAYING MORE ATTENTION TO HOW I SOUNDED, thanks to a lesson from Tom T. Hall.

Many folks think he was the best country songwriter of the

1960s and 1970s. It would be easier to list singers who didn't hit with his material than it would be to list all of those who did.

I was his opening act on one show where the sound system was terrible. There was distortion and feedback, and I couldn't understand a word I was singing.

I went over to Tom's bus after my set. His bus had air-conditioning, and mine did too, but it wasn't working very good that year. He did his show, and we wound up visiting again on his bus when he came offstage.

"Were the monitors bad when you were up there?" he asked.

"Oh Lord, yes," I said.

"Why didn't you say something?" he said.

"Well, Tom," I said, "I'm just the opening act. I'm just proud to be here."

"Well," he said, "you still should have said something."

When Tom did his set, he stopped his show and made sure they fixed the sound system before he continued.

"I'll tell you what," I said, "that's something I've been really looking forward to."

"What?" he said.

"When I get rich and famous," I said, "all I'm gonna do is bitch and sing."

Tom fell off the couch laughing.

❧

NEXT I TOOK A CLOSE LOOK AT THE WAY THE BAND BEHAVED ITSELF. When you're on the road, the people you take with you represent you. For example, if one of my band members gets falling-down drunk in a hotel after our show, and the public sees that, they won't say so-and-so was drunk. Instead, they'll say something like, "Reba McEntire's such-and-such player was in here, and he sure got drunk.'' They'll tell everything he did, and they'll attach my name each time they tell it.

So I realized that it's important that the people who travel with you represent you in a respectable way, both on- and off-stage.

In the early 1980s, the guys in my band used to ''party hearty.'' My motel room was often close to theirs. I'd have to tell them that if they couldn't be quiet when they came in, to go to the bus and sleep there instead of waking me up. It worked for a while.

Then there was the night, when we'd just finished a show with Johnny Duncan up north, that Preecher had to come to me. ''We've got a problem,'' said Preecher. ''Narvel left to go to a party, and we can't get into the van.''

The van was my group's only vehicle.

My band and I caught a ride with Johnny to the hotel, and Narvel showed up a few hours later.

''I've got the van keys,'' he confessed.

In the middle of the night, Preecher had to find someone to unlock the gate behind the auditorium we had played in so we could get our van.

Narvel was beat from the late hour, but I made him get up early the next morning to drive his annoyed boss to the airport. He didn't feel like hearing a rules lecture from me shortly after daylight, and I knew he felt bad enough and embarrassed enough about the whole situation. So I let the band handle it. They teased him for a long time after that one.

⚜

OF COURSE, NOT EVERY EMBARRASSING INCIDENT IS PREVENTABLE, AND some that happened to us are pretty funny. There was the time we did some shows in Quincy, California, followed by a show in Columbus, Ohio, for our first appearance ever at the Ohio State

Fair. Due to the distance involved, the band and I flew to another show we had scheduled somewhere in between, while Preecher and the others drove the bus to Ohio, stopping along the way at Nevada's Mustang Ranch, one of the nation's most famous spots for female/male "hospitality."

Preecher claims that he had gone to sleep, only awakening the next morning when he noticed the bus was not in motion. He says he looked out the bus window, saw where he was, and went back to sleep. That's what he says.

"Reba McEntire" was printed on the front of my bus. Someone later said that some of the Mustang girls stood under the sign to be photographed while wearing little more than a smile. Isn't that great publicity? For all I know, the photographs are hanging in the lobby of the Mustang Ranch.

One mishap for which Preecher was totally blameless took place in Texas. The band and I played Billy Bob's in Fort Worth and had stopped afterward at a truck stop near Arlington. The bus was being filled with diesel fuel as most of us ate. Preecher, who had a touch of the stomach flu, stayed in the men's room a little longer than the rest. He told Wayne Lewis that he'd be right out, but Wayne forgot.

We drove off without Preecher. We noticed his absence about the time we reached Pecos, 450 miles away, when we checked his bunk to find it empty. We hadn't heard Preecher yelling and screaming as the bus left him in a cloud of smoke. Since he was then the road manager, he had my travel itinerary and knew that we would be spending the night in El Paso. So he hitched a ride with a truck driver, and almost beat us there.

On another Preecher excursion when I wasn't along, he and Larry stopped at a truck stop, where Larry drained oil from the engine onto the driveway. That isn't allowed.

As Preecher later reported it, a trucker who had recently washed his rig drove through the oil and it splashed onto his rims.

He bounded out of his rig and told Larry he was going to "whip his ass."

Preecher said that Larry told the trucker "Nighty-night," and knocked him out.

Someone called the sheriff. Perhaps the lawman was a Reba McEntire fan, because when he saw the bus and realized who owned it, he took the truck driver to jail. Larry and Preecher kept this incident a secret until years after Preecher left my organization!

Larry and Preecher did seem to get into more than their share of scrapes. There was a time in Shreveport when I was ready to fire them both. I had ridden in a car from the hotel, with a friend of mine, Lisa Cacioppo, to the racetrack where we were to perform on a stage in front of a grandstand. The bus was running in front of me. I saw it stop suddenly.

I didn't know that Larry was staring at a puddle of water, wondering if it was shallow enough for him to drive through. But rather than get off the bus to check, I learned later, Larry turned to Preecher, the road manager.

"What should I do?" Larry asked.

"Go for it!" Preecher shouted. "Kick it in the ass."

Water sprayed higher than the bus as Larry slammed the accelerator to the floor and plowed headlong into a curb under the water. The right wheel was fine, but the left fender was dented and almost caved in.

I pulled around to the front of the bus when it stopped and got out of my car. Larry was still in the driver's seat, too high up to see what had happened. He was just casually looking around. "What the hell is wrong with her this time?" Larry says he was thinking.

I was astounded—and steaming. It was raining, but the falling water did little to cool my temper. I stomped on board.

First, I suggested that we all get together and wreck the entire bus. Larry had no idea why I was so mad.

"Why did you do that?" I asked him.

"Do what?" he said.

"Why did you drive through that water and wreck the bus?" I shouted.

He walked outside and stared dumbly at the damaged wheel. He couldn't believe his eyes.

By the time he got back on board, I had gone to the stateroom. Soon, there was a weak knock.

Larry was like a kid caught with his hand in the cookie jar. He kept apologizing all over himself, saying that Preecher had said it was okay to drive through the water.

I was still furious.

"Go get Preecher," I said in a low tone.

Preecher had some excuse about not knowing how deep the water was, and that, to me, was all the more reason he should not have told Larry to drive through it.

Eventually, everyone settled down. Although the incident happened on a Sunday afternoon, welders were brought in to pull the frame off the left front wheel and fix the fender. Larry confessed years later that not only the wheel but also the front end of the bus on the driver's side was damaged. But somehow the welders repaired the bus enough to make it drivable. And the miles and music resumed.

It was a long time before we were able to laugh about that one.

BUT IN A WAY, I COULD UNDERSTAND LARRY AND PREECHER'S CARE-lessness. Life on the road is so tiring that it is hard to keep your wits about you. It can also be real boring, and sometimes musicians stir things up just to pass the time. Myself included.

One night I worked a show with Steve Wariner at the Bo Jangles Club in Amarillo, Texas. It was Preecher's birthday, so we'd done a little celebrating that night. We were leaving the club for the hotel, and while the guys were inside getting their gear, I sat in the bus listening to the CB radio. When I heard the overcolorful language of the truckers, I decided to get on the air.

I pretended to be a nun and scolded them harshly for their talk. I had many of them apologizing for their awful language. Well, I had to laugh. It was so funny to hear those tough, burly guys say they knew better than to talk that way.

Another time when we were on the road, Charlie and I were staying at a four-star hotel in Los Angeles, down off Sunset. One morning we decided to take a swim in the rooftop pool. I was on a health kick and suggested we take the stairs.

We walked up several stories in our swimming suits, bathrobes, and house slippers. No one else could see us. Charlie was griping about the long haul when we finally reached the top floor.

He reached for the door to the pool. It was locked.

"No entrance to the pool from this area," a sign said.

He was grumbling as we started back down the stairs to the lower floor. That door also was locked. We found that to be the case with every floor until we reached the bottom. That door led out into the street, so we had to go around the hotel and walk into the lobby of the new Bel Age Inn in our swimming suits and bathrobes. The concierge pulled her glasses down and looked at us.

I was dying laughing. Charlie was just dying.

"Fine mess you got us into this time," he said.

⚜

BESIDES LITERALLY AND FIGURATIVELY CLEANING UP OUR ACT, THERE were other important measures I had to take to really get a grip on my career. Red Steagall, who had been overseeing my career, convinced me that the time had come to bring in a professional.

He was good enough to introduce me first to Gary Hart and then to his own manager, Don Williams.

Then, shortly after joining my show, Narvel approached Charlie and said he thought the band needed a leader.

"Well, if you think we need one and you want to be one, then you're it," Charlie told Narvel.

Later, Preecher, our road manager, got sick and wanted to go home. He said he didn't want to come back, because he had had his fill of road life.

Narvel knocked on our hotel room door one day while we were playing in Las Vegas.

"What's up?" I said.

"I guess Charlie told you that I now want to be tour manager," Narvel said.

"No," I said, "this is the first I've heard of it."

But Narvel and Charlie had discussed it earlier, and Narvel got the job.

By then Charlie and I knew Narvel very well and trusted him immensely. Even the story of his marriage was evidence of his integrity. When Narvel was fourteen years old, he dated a girl named Lisa Ritter off and on up until the time he got his driver's license, at sixteen; then he started dating other girls. But one night she and Narvel went to a Merle Haggard concert. A few weeks after the concert, Lisa called to tell him that she was pregnant.

So, with the persuasion of his mother, Narvel chose to quit music, school, and his apprenticeship at a print shop and marry her. Narvel's dad and Lisa's mom were not for the wedding. Gloria, Narvel's mom, knew that marriage was the right thing to do.

Despite all the strikes against him, Narvel was determined to prove himself. To support his wife and child, he took the best job he could find, selling Kirby vacuum cleaners door to door.

One day he stopped at the home of a man who was impressed by Narvel's selling techniques.

"Man," he said, "you're good. You ought to think about selling insurance."

That's how Narvel became one of the top salesmen at Prudential Insurance.

To other players, working for me was a job. For Narvel, it seemed to be a career. He was always coming up with ideas to improve the show or our travel conditions. That drive and enthusiasm are what made Narvel the best partner I ever had.

❦

MY FINAL STEP TOWARD PROFESSIONALISM WAS GETTING MYSELF AN agent, but I almost lost my chance, through no fault of my own. In March 1981, I was scheduled to do a show at the Mabee Center at Oral Roberts University in Tulsa, Oklahoma. The William Morris Agency folks were coming out to see me perform. A lot of artists feel that William Morris has more prestige than any other talent or literary agency, and after only five years in the business, I was nervous about performing for their representatives. Two had flown in all the way from New York City to watch me.

On that all-important show I appeared with Red Steagall, Darrell McCall, a local band, and George Jones. The show was sponsored by a radio station that gave away free tickets. The 17,000-seat hall was filled to overflowing.

George Jones has made no secret of the thirty-year battle he had with alcohol. Recently, he released a videotaped autobiography called "The Same Old Me," which mentioned a period of hospitalization shortly after that Mabee Center show. In it he said that his IQ was down to 74 because of the booze, and he talked at length about all the personal appearances he missed over the years because he was too drunk to go onstage.

He got the nickname of "No Show Jones" for all of those missed dates. After he became sober, he wrote a song called "No Show Jones," which he uses now to open his stage shows. Then he tells the crowd that he's going to quit singing that song because he's been sober for so long. That always makes for a lot of applause.

Tom Carter, who was reviewing the show that night for the *Tulsa World,* said that for the Mabee Center show, George rode all the way from Nashville to Tulsa for a matinee, and he arrived sober.

Then he started to drink.

George's road manager went to Kathy Bee, who had booked the entertainment, and told her she had better put Jones onstage while he was still in good shape. He was belting down drinks pretty fast.

"I can't," Kathy said. "Reba has got folks here from William Morris waiting to watch her, and Jones is supposed to be the headliner. He's supposed to close the show. He's the star."

Jones suddenly announced he wouldn't go on at all if Kathy didn't find him a girlfriend. Kathy became furious and told him she was running a concert, not an escort service.

Meanwhile, George kept drinking, and saying he would go onstage only if he could go right then, and only if he had a girlfriend first. And the girl, he demanded, had to be short.

Kathy is a wise ole gal who had been around drinking men before.

"Okay," she finally told George, "we'll compromise. You go onstage now and do your show. And when you come off, I'll have you a girlfriend here."

So George went out, did his forty-five minutes, and walked offstage directly to a bottle and to Kathy.

"Where is my girl?" Jones demanded.

"George," Kathy said, "that girl was a no-show."

He became angry and left. By then, the lineup was hopelessly out of order, and a local band closed the show starring George Jones.

But the next day, the *Tulsa World* published Tom's review that said, in part, ''Reba McEntire is destined to become country music's next female superstar. She has the vocal prowess of Patsy Cline, the natural charm of Loretta Lynn. The comparative new-comer eased through her repertoire with all the control of a diamond cutter on deadline.''

Now you see why I chose Tom Carter as my co-writer.

Not long after, I was signed by William Morris, and after some time away from the agency, I'm back with them today for all my movie and literary contacts.

And I'm happy and proud to say that with the help of his wife, Nancy, George won his battle with the bottle. They are a wonderful, happy, beautiful couple today. I love them both very much!

CHAPTER 10

IN 1983, THE BAND AND I WERE SITTING IN A GARAGE IN DE SOTO, Texas—and not by choice. The lug nuts on the front left tire of "Ole Mae," my bus, had loosened so much that we were afraid to go any further without having it checked. That bus looked good, but it had more style than substance. We were no strangers to breakdowns.

While the mechanic wrestled with the tire, I called my manager, Don Williams, just to see if anything was happening.

"Well," he said. "As a matter of fact, there is something going on. Your song just went number one."

I couldn't believe it! There, in that greasy garage, I began to bawl. I called Charlie. "Yeah," he said, "Don's already called me." I called Mama, and we laughed and cried. It had finally happened—the one thing Mama and I had waited a lifetime for.

My first number-one song was "Can't Even Get the Blues," and I had stumbled on it almost through pure luck. One day, I was in Jerry Kennedy's office listening to songs for my next album project. I loved to visit Jerry, because he told me war stories about veterans in the music business. His recollections were always hilarious.

"Let me play you a song I've got for Jacky Ward," Jerry said.

By that time, Jerry and I had largely fallen into a pattern of recording waltzes at medium tempo. Two of our biggest Mercury hits were waltzes, "I'm Not That Lonely Yet" and "There Ain't No Future in This." But the song Jerry played me was completely different, an up-tempo sassy tune I loved from the first time I heard it. It had a story line people could relate to, about a woman whose man has left her—again—and it doesn't bother her anymore. It was a strong-woman song.

"Why wouldn't you pitch me a song like that?" I asked. "Why wouldn't you think I could record it?"

"Well," he said, "could you?"

"In a heartbeat," I said.

So we recorded the song, and it almost didn't make the album. They chose it as the last single released off the album, but it hit. This business is a huge gamble. No one ever knows which song is gonna be "the one"!

The song belonged to Loretta Lynn's publishing company, and when it went number one, she sent me a beautiful silk-flower arrangement that I cherish to this day. Later, she sent me a beautiful diamond necklace, which was stolen from my suitcase a few years later along with some other pieces of jewelry I was very fond of. I had forgotten to take the bag out of the trunk of a rented car I'd just returned to the airport lot. By the time I realized what I'd done, the jewelry was gone.

I hated to lose that necklace, because it came from Loretta. I'm very proud to say that I'm one of her friends, and she certainly is one of mine. She's a sweet, fun person to be around, and quite a character!

◦◦◦

IN THE WAKE OF THAT NUMBER-ONE SONG, DON WILLIAMS, MY MAN-
ager, got me an invitation to "The Tonight Show," which was a
very big breakthrough for a country singer. In the days before
Country Music Television and The Nashville Network, country
entertainers rarely appeared on national TV. The reason was
probably the fact that country music wasn't nearly as popular as it
is today. But country music was very well represented on weekly
TV shows, such as "The Wilburn Brothers Show," "Ernest
Tubb's TV Show," "Glenn Campbell Hour," "Johnny Cash,"
"Hee Haw," "Pop Goes the Country," "Nashville on the
Road," and I was fortunate enough to have performed on some
of them.

In 1981, I'd gotten to be a part of a wonderful television
special, Johnny Cash and "The Ladies of Country Music"—
twenty of us—with Johnny being the only man. I was so honored
to be chosen, because I was really just starting out then; I hadn't
even done my first major tour. Johnny did a very generous thing
for that show—he furnished gowns for all the ladies and at the
end of the taping gave them the gowns to keep. Mine was a
beautiful aqua, slim-styled evening gown with spaghetti
straps.

Not many television hosts would have even thought to make
such a kind and sensitive gesture, and I, for one, was very grateful. It's that kind of openheartedness, along with his great music,
that has made Johnny Cash a legend. He has never lost sight of his
roots.

Then, two years later, came my chance to meet the other
Johnny, Johnny Carson, the late-night king himself and host of
the granddaddy of all the network television shows. On that first,
1983, "Tonight Show" date, for good luck—and because I
couldn't afford anything else—I wore that same dress that Johnny
Cash had given me for his TV special. Naturally, I was a bundle of

nerves, but when I met Carson backstage before the show, he was very nice and gracious.

I was to sing two songs, with Narvel playing the steel guitar with the Tonight Show Orchestra and Susie singing harmony from inside a sound-control booth. Neither of the songs was my number-one record "Can't Even Get the Blues." Instead, the producers asked me to sing "You Lift Me Up to Heaven," my first Top Ten record, and "Only You," the old Platters song I'd done a remake of.

I wouldn't get the real guest treatment—the chance to be called to the interview couch—until my third appearance. That time Johnny questioned me about my background in rodeo, and I explained that I had been a barrel racer. He seemed fascinated by the way I said "barrel" and kept asking me to repeat it, impersonating me and making fun of how I said "barrel."

Well, Johnny's from Nebraska, and that's about as rural as Oklahoma. I guess he lost his Nebraskan accent a long time ago. But, in hindsight, I can see that Johnny meant no harm—he was just trying to break the ice.

❧

I WOULD GO ON TO HAVE ONLY ONE MORE NUMBER-ONE SONG WITH Mercury—"You're the First Time I've Thought About Leaving" —among the seventy songs I recorded there. Not bad, but not exactly a terrific track record, either. I just didn't feel that Mercury was pushing my songs hard enough, and they in turn had to be unhappy with my sales. I was grateful that Mercury had stuck with me and had supported me for the eight years I was with them, but I felt it was time to move on. The taste of a number-one record was something I wanted to taste again.

So I called a meeting of me, Jerry Kennedy, Don Williams, and Don's lawyer, Bill Carter, to see what could be done. After a lengthy discussion, I asked that Mercury release me from my contract so I could get a fresh start somewhere else. Of course, I was scared to take such a strong stand and to leave my safe and familiar "home" of eight years for the unknown territory of a new record label. And I knew I would miss Jerry Kennedy, who after seven albums had become as much my friend as my producer. Later, though, Jerry said that he didn't blame me for leaving.

Looking back, I can see that the best things that ever happened in my life happened when I went with my gut feelings. I can sometimes "feel" what is right for me better than others can rationalize it. If I go by my heart or my gut, I usually don't go wrong—and this time was no exception.

Don Williams started pulling in offers from other labels, with the help of Bill Carter. "I remember vividly that we had a contract from CBS on the desk," Carter says. "And the negotiation was right up to being . . . well, had ended, and [we were] ready to sign."

But then Carter got a call from Irving Azoff, the ex-manager of the 1970s rock stars the Eagles and the new head of MCA. "I'm on my way to London," Carter recalls Azoff saying. "Don't sign that contract! You just take the deal that you've got from CBS, add a comfortable figure to it, and then telegraph me in London with your terms."

"And the next morning," Carter says, "about 5:30 A.M., the phone rang. It was Zack Horowitz, head of business affairs for MCA. He said, 'I'm sending you a confirmation that you've got a contract.' Actually, I nearly flipped. I had no idea that they might accept!"

This power struggle, going on without my knowing it, was for a singer who was leaving a record company that had never made a profit off her work. But Carter says that Azoff didn't care. He simply believed in my voice and even reached his decision without ever seeing me perform. I certainly had to respect the man's nerve.

And I also had to respect Carter's handling of the situation. During the time I had been looking for a new record label, I had also begun to think that I needed a new manager. Don had helped me a lot, but his offices were in Los Angeles, so Charlie and I rarely saw him. Since we lived in Stringtown, Oklahoma, there was no one "minding the store" in Nashville, where my professional life was based. Having been Don's lawyer, Carter knew how my business worked, and so it was natural for him to step in.

As my new manager, Carter had to field a call from Jim Fogelsong, the head of MCA's Nashville division, the day after I got my contract confirmation. Fogelsong had rejected me back in the days when Red Steagall was shopping my first demo tape around, and now his boss Irving Azoff had adopted me. All he could say to Carter was "I understand we have signed Reba McEntire."

But Fogelsong, for whatever reason, went along with it. It was under his direction that I cut my first album for MCA, *Just a Little Love,* in 1984. My producer was the creative and fun-loving Noro Wilson. Noro even came out on the road with me to observe my show and get a feel for my music. I loved working with him, but we never really got the chance to find my "direction" in music. The MCA officials didn't like the album, and I was told to find another producer.

I think if Noro and I had gotten another chance, we could have come up with something better—something more country. But the decision wasn't mine.

After Noro came Harold Shedd, the red-hot producer for Alabama. In those days, the early 1980s, everybody in country music was trying to record "crossover" songs—ones that would also attract the pop-music audience. So I thought to myself: "Do the opposite." Besides, country was the music that I loved and wanted to record.

When Harold wanted to put an orchestra on my new album, I put my foot down. "If everybody else is going to do this contemporary, crossover stuff, let me do something different," I told him.

The value of being different had been planted in my mind years earlier, when I was playing a wedding reception in Pampa, Texas. I met another girl singer there whose style of dressing was different from everyone else's there. Once we got to talking, I came out and asked her why she dressed the way she did.

"This is my theory," she said. "If everybody is dressing formal, wear jeans. If everybody is wearing jeans, dress formal. Be different. They'll notice you."

It was a good lesson. That girl's words, running through my mind, gave me confidence as I described my new vision for my music to Harold.

"I want to record my kind of country," I insisted.

My kind of country is the clear, pure, old-fashioned kind, emotional and gutsy and also sentimental. The songs tell about real human problems—love and the pain of heartbreak and loss—in a way that shows you that the singer is no stranger to pain, and is tough enough to suffer and survive.

One person I had to convince was Jimmy Bowen, the record industry legend who had just succeeded Jim Fogelsong as president of MCA's Nashville division. I'd heard that Bowen didn't like me; when he took over MCA, he had told Bill Carter, "I'm thinking of dropping the redhead." Today, he recalls, "Something bothered me about her voice." Those early tapes lacked the "little jazz licks" that he likes to hear in my singing. "That was back in the days when she went into the vocal booth, got to do the song, and left," Bowen says. "She wasn't in the overdub, she didn't go to the mix, she wasn't involved in the process at all."

Bowen would change all that.

When I met with Bowen about my problem with Harold Shedd, I knew I had to get him on my side. I gave him the tape I'd made of the kinds of songs I wanted to record—songs like Merle Haggard's "Mama Tried," Ray Price's "City Lights,"

Dolly Parton's "Jolene," and Loretta Lynn's "If You're Not Gone Too Long"—and he listened to it.

Then he said, "Well, we'll have to find you a new producer."

"No, sir," I shot back. "I want you to produce me."

"W-h-o-o-a!" he said. "I'll have to think about that."

"I don't want anybody else producing me but you," I said. "You're the main man, you can make it happen."

He told me no—that I was the one who had to make it happen.

"I can get great musicians for you," Bowen remembers saying, "I know how—I know who should work with each other. I can make you sound great. But if you don't know what a woman should say to cause another woman to get up from her house and drive clear across town to sort through the KISS posters just to find your record, then you're not going to make it. We do a half-assed job of helping men do that [select their songs], and we have no prayer of helping a woman do that. You've got to be able to do it."

That's what I wanted to hear—I love a challenge! So I told him, "Sure, I can do that. How do I do it?" He put me with Don Lanier, his artist and repertoire chief, who is nicknamed "Dirt," and we started to visit the publishing companies—lots of them—to listen, really listen to find the songs that would complete my mission. It was a process that Bowen started with me and then initiated with every other artist on the label.

We call those product meetings today. Now either I go over to the publishing company or the music publishers come to play their songs for me at the offices of my firm, Starstruck Entertainment. We have five or six appointments a day over a two- or three-day period, sometimes more if we need them and haven't found the right songs. When I hear a song I like, I put it on "hold" until I've gone through all the material, and then cut back my choices to thirty songs or under.

But for that second MCA album, I really had to search, with the help of Dirt. I didn't find really country songs, because the writers were trying for more contemporary-sounding music. So I had to go back a few years in the catalogs of the publishing companies and find songs written five to twenty years ago, to get the country music that I wanted.

Bill Carter had suggested that I approach the highly respected Harlan Howard, whom the Nashville media calls "Mr. Songwriter." In the 1950s, Harlan got inspired to write by copying down lyrics from Ernest Tubb songs as they were sung on the Grand Ole Opry. Whenever he missed a line, he made up a replacement. Eventually, he made up all of the lines himself.

I was in grade school when he wrote the classics "Heartaches by the Number" and "Pick Me Up on Your Way Down," as well as one of the most haunting country songs of all time, "I Fall to Pieces," for Patsy Cline. It would take too much space to list all of his hits, but he is just as productive today as he was when he moved to Nashville thirty-three years ago. He had a hit in 1993 with Pam Tillis.

In 1983, I felt like I was in the presence of royalty when I settled into a big, wing-backed chair at Harlan's house.

Charlie and I sat there quietly as Harlan loaded his tape machine. I listened carefully as he played me a batch of tunes, and I was a little disappointed. They weren't what I expected of Harlan Howard.

Harlan was just sitting there grinning at me, and after several passes on his songs, I said, "Have you got anything else?" And he said, "Yes." Then he played "Somebody Should Leave," a song Harlan had co-written with Chick Raines. I started tearing up, with chills all over me. I said, "Harlan, can I have that song?" He smiled real big and said, "Do you like it?" I said, "I love it."

He said, "Yep."

I know now that Harlan was testing me. If I had liked all

those other songs, he would never have played me "Somebody Should Leave." When I passed on all those others, he knew I knew a special song when I heard it.

Ultimately, Bowen didn't agree to produce me, but compromised by mixing (electronically arranging) the album, which we decided to call *My Kind of Country*. It was produced by Harold Shedd. Harold found one of the songs for that album, "How Blue," a song I almost didn't do! When Harold played it for me I thought it sounded like a man's song. Very wisely, Harold suggested we quit for the day. He knew I was really tired! When he played it again for me the following morning, I said, "Oh, Harold, I'm sorry. That's a great song!"

"Somebody Should Leave" and "How Blue" both became number-one hits. "Somebody Should Leave" taught me that Jimmy Bowen's words were true: "You've got to find your own songs, because nobody but you knows what you want to sing."

Up until then, I was more or less just a singer, leaving a lot of the creative decisions to the "professionals"—my managers, my producers, the label heads. I was really totally ignorant about the business. Then I came to realize that the difference between being a singer and being an artist could rest on something as simple— though hard to achieve—as my belief in myself.

But that took years of great education from my producers, manager, and record label heads. I think they taught me well. I owe a lot to Glenn Keener, Jerry Kennedy, Noro Wilson, Harold Shedd, and to Jimmy Bowen!

Thanks to Bowen, I even got some control in the studio. During the session work, it was up to me to communicate with the pickers—to let them know what I wanted in a song—while he stayed in the control room. He told the players that if they had a question, they were to ask me, not him. The album applied the newest electronic recording techniques to traditional country arrangements, and I sat right behind Bowen when he mixed the cuts, taking notes on just how much of each voice and instrument would be heard. That part was a little boring, but it helped me understand what really gives a record its sound.

Bowen gave me a very great gift—the right to control my own music—and a great deal of wise advice. He was a very patient teacher—or maybe I should say "preacher." Bowen has a well-earned reputation for talking a lot. He'd get you in his office, and you might not get the chance to say ten words. He'd start telling you his philosophies and his ideas about what works and what doesn't in music, and why. As a joke, I started numbering his speeches. That Speech #37 was a good one!

❦

MY KIND OF COUNTRY HELPED KICK OFF WHAT THE NATIONAL MAGA-zines called "the New Traditionalist movement," a revolution in country music that they credited to Randy Travis, Ricky Skaggs, me, and George Strait.

Randy had hit with "1983" and "On the Other Hand." The first two lines of the second song were no more than Randy's voice and a rhythm guitar. The simple arrangement was a far cry from the lush violins that Nashville had been using on records throughout the late 1970s and early 1980s. Ricky was named "Entertainer of the Year," the highest honor in country music, for reviving old mountain and bluegrass tunes. George, with his beautiful voice, revived Western Swing. His ballads and dance music brought "Texas music" back to the forefront.

Of course, none of us set out to spawn an entire musical movement. We never had that in mind. We had just been looking to record good, solid country music, the kind we had grown up with, the kind that ran steadily in our veins. Our kind of music also seemed to be the special kind that touched people's hearts.

❦

THANKS TO *MY KIND OF COUNTRY*, I WAS STARTING TO CHANGE MY billing status. When I signed on with MCA in 1984, I had played a date with Conway Twitty in Grand Falls, Wisconsin. I was paid $5,000—the most money I had ever made for a show at the time. I had been releasing records for eight years, had traveled more than a million miles back and forth across the nation, and that was my biggest draw. Some folks think $5,000 is a lot of money for approximately an hour's worth of singing, but consider that I had to pay five band members and a bus driver. I had to rent motel rooms. I had to buy the diesel fuel to get to the show. I had to give my booking agent and my manager 10 percent each off the top for booking the show. Of course, I had to pay taxes on what was left, and I was making payments on the bus. So those dollars didn't go far.

Conway Twitty, of course, was a major star, one who could pull in a large audience, and by opening for him I performed for about five thousand people a night. But at some point, I hoped to become a headline act myself, and Bill Carter thought that *My Kind of Country* made 1984 the right time. Charlie, on the other hand, thought I should work my way up, appearing as an opening act for a while longer, *with* a guaranteed fee. But I went with Carter's advice. It was a huge gamble—for my first headline show, I attracted only eight hundred people and everybody lost money, especially me—and eventually, that gamble paid off. We had some mighty lean times until then, though!

Still, I don't care how successful you are as a recording artist, it's important to keep bringing your music directly to the people. I've always believed that the heart of entertainment is performance, not just producing a studio version of your work. And one of the most important lessons I've learned is that you're never as good as you could be. There's always room for improvement. I've never stopped trying to improve my act—whether it would be my hair and costumes or sets or how my shows are staged.

Early on, for instance, I was very insecure. I would try to find nice clothes, but for a long time I couldn't afford them. I'd put everything I had into looking nice, but I just didn't know how. And when I'd go out to sing, I didn't know how to talk to audiences.

But from the start I wanted desperately to mature as an artist and performer, and, fortunately, I've had people around me who could help. They have been so instrumental in getting me where I am today.

Most important, I made it a point to be receptive to any advice that would help the show to grow or to improve my sessions in the studio. I might choose to do something one way— a music fragment, a piece of stagecraft—or maybe not at all. But I always listened very, very closely to what people had to say. Not that I did all they told me. I'd listen and take what I liked—and I still do.

❧

I STARTED USING CHOREOGRAPHY IN MY SHOW AT A TIME WHEN, except for Barbara Mandrell and the Mandrell Sisters, the idea was still foreign to country music. I met my first choreographer, Andre Tyier, through my then-manager Don Williams. Narvel and Preecher were with me when I walked into Andre's office in Studio City, California. After watching me sing, the first question he asked was "Why aren't you looking at me?"

" 'Cause you make me nervous," I said.

My stage presence still left a lot to be desired.

"Well," Tyier said, "don't you look at the audience when you sing?"

"No," I admitted.

"You should look at the audience," he told me. "Then take your eyes from person to person, and go down the rows like a typewriter. Then go up with your eyes to the next row and look them in the eye! That's the way to really reach an audience."

Those suggestions are obvious to me now, but at the time I said, "Good Lord, that's awfully personal."

"Well, where do you look?" he asked.

"At the Exit signs," I said.

One of the reasons I looked at the Exit signs was to keep from choking up during my delivery of songs like "Somebody Should Leave." Even now, I find it difficult to get through certain songs, like "The Greatest Man I Never Knew" and "For My Broken Heart," without choking up.

But I followed Andre's suggestions to the tee, and I know it's made a huge difference in performing.

I also began experimenting with stage lighting. By the time I signed with MCA, Narvel, then our road manager, had gotten the fever to make our show more theatrical. We tried out one of his ideas at a theater we played in Ann Arbor, Michigan. Narvel's plan was to turn off all the stage lights after our last song. Everyone would leave the stage in total darkness. Then we'd turn up the "moody-blue" lights and I'd come back on to sing my encore song, the Patsy Cline classic "Sweet Dreams."

The first night we tried it we didn't even have a stage curtain. Darkness was our only cover. I could barely see the Exit signs.

I started to shuffle offstage in the darkness, and I remembered something was to my right. I thought it was a microphone stand. I put my hands out to find it, but my feet shuffled right under a monitor speaker. I fell right over the top of it.

I hit my stomach and my shins, ripped my new satin pants, and then crawled over the monitor. The microphone was still hot, and it made a loud thud when it hit the floor. I said a little dirty word, but hopefully nobody heard it. My new pants were so tight that I couldn't get up, so I had to shuffle off the stage on my hands and feet.

Tom Bresh, who had opened the show for me, was sitting on a stool at stage right. I literally went hand-over-hand up his stool to stand up. He didn't even try to help me. He just looked down at me with his arms crossed and said, "Good show, Reba."

Somehow I managed to gracefully hobble out to do "Sweet Dreams," and later the band and I laughed for hours about our first try at a "big production" number.

Some of our later, more ambitious attempts had equally funny results. For one show in Lubbock, Texas, we planned to make onstage "fog," using a dry-ice machine. The barrel used for the machine we bought was broken, and so the guys in the band fixed it in my bus barn in Stringtown the night we left for a Lubbock show. To make sure it didn't leak anymore, they filled the fifty-gallon barrel with water from Charlie's diesel-fuel can. That made Charlie furious! You don't put water in a diesel can.

Charlie started grumbling about the time—it was raining, and we were running late for our show. So, without doing a run-through with the machine, we packed up and headed for Lubbock.

At the show, Larry Jones was going to run the dry-ice machine from inside a little bitty room just offstage. He was supposed to place dry ice into a basket, then drop the basket into hot water to make the fog. The fog would leak out of hoses that ran from the machine all over the stage, making the entire floor "foggy." Thus, a fog machine!

It didn't work that way.

Dry ice, which is actually solidified carbon dioxide, is hot and must be handled with gloves. But Larry didn't wear any, and when he picked up the ice, it burned his hands. So he quickly dumped the dry ice directly into the water, missing the basket. He also forgot to close the lid, which would have forced the fog to travel through the hoses.

In the small room, Larry was covered with "smoke." And very soon, the fog started billowing out of the room onto the stage. We could see Larry and his predicament and got so tickled that we couldn't finish the song. The audience had to be told what had happened. They didn't catch our humor! So much for dramatic special effects!

Just last year I had another funny mishap. I had only seconds to make a costume change, onstage in the dark behind a screen. What the audience didn't know is that in the rush of getting me ready, Sandi handed me the wrong black suede boot. So I ended up with the left boot on my right foot and vice versa. I realized this too late to switch them before the lights came on, and I had to do my next two numbers with my boots on the wrong feet. I won't tell you what I thought about doing to Sandi when I got my hands on her throat. But she didn't realize I couldn't see. Since her eyes were adjusted to the dark, she thought I knew which boot was which.

⁂

OF COURSE, PLENTY OF THINGS THAT HAPPEN ON THE ROAD ARE impossible to laugh off. One of the first things you learn about playing for pay is that not everybody pays. Such veteran entertainers as George Jones and the late Conway Twitty used to tell all kinds of horror stories about driving all night to play a show for a promoter who couldn't pay them. Then they'd have to pay their bands out of their own pockets. In my time, professional promoters have made life easier, but there were a few times early in my career when people just didn't want to pay.

It would fall to Narvel, as tour manager, to try to collect. One time, a promoter vanished after our show, so Narvel found a cop and went to the promoter's house—something he says he'll never do again. Lord knows, the officer and Narvel might have been shot going up to a man's house so late at night! But the promoter never came to his door, and since we had to leave town to go to another show, I don't think we ever got paid.

Another time, in 1984, we were more successful. We were playing a dinner theater in Minnesota for a second time, and since we'd gotten paid on the first trip, we trusted the owner. We took his personal check instead of a cashier's check for our show. The personal check bounced.

Every time we called him about it, he gave us the runaround, claiming that he'd sent us a replacement check. It never arrived. You know, the old "the check's in the mail" story!

I considered taking legal action against the man, but Carter, my career manager, and Charlie said to forget it. They thought it would be a waste of time. So when we returned to the state to play a different venue, Narvel, my driver Larry Jones, Pake, who was opening the show for me, and I went out to the dinner theater.

A security guard carrying a walkie-talkie stopped us, and when Narvel insisted on talking to the owner, the guard said he'd radio him to come down to meet us in the lobby. We knew that the owner would try to slip out the back door if the guard did that, so we followed the guard to the owner's office. It felt like a sting on "60 Minutes." Even as we approached, we could see the owner turning off his office lights. When Narvel opened the door, we saw him and his wife in the dark, gathering up their personal things while getting ready to leave.

"What brings you back here?" he said to us. He was obviously embarrassed.

"We're here to collect the money you owe us," Narvel said. He was the spokesperson for the group. My presence was enough —I didn't have to talk.

"Really?"

He told us that he had meant to pay us but had spent my

money remodeling his dinner theater and would pay us when he got ahead. We told him we didn't care to become his partners in the club business.

The man promised that he would pay up that night after his evening show, so Narvel and Larry were waiting at the theater when it ended. And they got our money—$5,000—in cash, much of it in one- and five-dollar bills. Sometimes in show business, it pays to persevere!

Larry thought I was pretty tough for going along on the collection mission. Well, that sure surprised me, because Larry is a pretty tough ole boy himself. He had been a bouncer in a bar before he became my driver, and once he actually got into a kickboxing fight over my honor. A man said a sexually lewd thing about me and Larry knocked him out—or so he thought. The guy, who knew karate, surprised Larry by leaping off the floor and kicking the side of Larry's face, taking off a good deal of his facial skin in the process.

All the way from Stringtown to Nashville, Larry drove with the injured side of his face held so I couldn't see it. It wasn't until the next morning at breakfast that I found out what happened. It looked like poor Larry had a giant rug burn. Yet he had been tough enough not to say a word about it to me for seven hundred miles.

Now, that's tough!

On the way back from our collection episode in Minnesota, we plotted to play a joke on Charlie, who didn't believe we'd ever succeed in getting that money. Somebody had given me a pair of cheap earrings, so we decided we'd tell Charlie the earrings were my past-due payment.

"Hey," Narvel told Charlie, "the guy didn't have the money, but he gave us his wife's earrings. They're worth $5,000, and I saw him take them off her ears myself."

Charlie studied the earrings, but he wasn't satisfied that they could possibly be worth $5,000. Finally, we had to tell him that we were kidding, that we had gotten the cash.

He was not amused.

❦

CHARLIE WASN'T ALL THAT AMUSING HIMSELF IN THOSE DAYS. I SOME-times thought that he felt demeaned by my becoming more successful, getting lots of attention, and making more money than he did.

So I let him take charge of things, but he didn't always make the right decisions. As Narvel recalls, "Things could have been so much easier, but Charlie didn't want anything to be easy." For example, Charlie would insist that everyone get out of the buses when we would arrive at our hotels at 3 or 4 A.M. and shut down the bus generators. I could understand that he wanted to save money on diesel, but it was hard to get back to sleep after the move inside. Then Charlie was used to getting up early. So at 6 A.M., he'd get up and shower, waking me up in the process, and then go down to one of the guys' rooms to wake them up. No one got much rest when he was out on the road.

Larry Jones, who drove my bus, couldn't understand why Charlie was putting me in what Larry called "second or third class stuff" (buses) when he always bought himself brand-new four-wheel-drive vehicles just to feed cattle.

I knew some folks found Charlie distant and difficult to work with. At the time, I preferred to see his aloofness as a natural reserve, his occasional brusqueness with musicians as perfection-ism—after all, he wanted things to be just so for us. But, after a while, Larry says, he never had to ask if Charlie was coming to a show with us—all he had to do was look at me. Charlie caused that much tension. And Larry remembers that Charlie used to call me a "wench" right in front of me when he was talking to the band.

I tried hard not to let our professional problems affect the personal life we shared. Charlie and I did as much as we could together, realizing that our marriage deserved the time and care all relationships need. But what I had once admired and loved best about Charlie—his protectiveness—now revealed itself as a domineering nature, and was starting to cause trouble between us.

I'm not saying that I was perfect myself. I can recall, for instance, when we were newly married feeling impatient and hurt by some of Charlie's behavior after an afternoon performance at the rodeo in Louisville, Kentucky. We'd agreed to meet back at the trailer and I'd waited and waited and finally gone out to look for him—only to find him having a beer with the other cowboys and shooting the breeze. Maybe I should've been more under-standing about his needing time with the guys; maybe he shouldn't have broken our plans or left me to worry if he was laid up in some hospital somewhere with a broken neck. I do know that when I walked into that bar and spotted him there, my relief at seeing he was all right turned into anger fast and I came on to him like some crazed gunslinger out of the Old West. It didn't make either one of us look too good in front of his buddies, and I can't blame him for being upset about that.

But there was one incident that still stands out in my mind as pretty unforgivable, sadly showing the spirit and balance of our marriage.

Charlie loved to trade. He'd buy something he didn't need, and sell something he did, just to be trading. I'd come off the road and we'd have a new car. I'd come home a few days later and Charlie'd replaced the car with an orange Bronco. The next time I'd come in, he'd have traded that off too. Trading was his hobby, and sometimes I think it was an addiction. He enjoyed it, and usually I didn't really mind.

But I had one special possession, a gentle sorrel horse named Legs. I was on the road so much that I rarely got to ride him, but I loved to. He wasn't flighty, like a bulldogging or barrel-racing horse. I'd been around horses all my life, and Legs might have been my favorite horse of all.

He wasn't valuable to anyone but me—I thought!

One day when I came in off a tour, I went out to the barn. Legs was gone.

When I asked Charlie about my horse, his answer was brief and mumbled, the way he usually talked.

"I sold him," he said.

I was speechless.

"Why did you sell my horse?" I finally choked out, so mad I was almost crying.

"I got a good buy on him," Charlie said.

All Charlie had considered was the deal, not the fact that the horse was mine. He didn't even think that he had to talk to me before selling him. I was upset at losing Legs—I would never have willingly parted with him—but what really shocked and pained me was Charlie's failure even to think of my feelings.

CHAPTER 11

NINETEEN EIGHTY-FOUR BROUGHT ME THE TREMENDOUS honor of being named "Female Vocalist of the Year" by the Country Music Association (CMA), the first of four times I would receive the award. The CMA trophy is a beautiful crystal-looking, pointed globe. Before that, they were made out of wood. Barbara Mandrell approached the CMA board about changing it to clear glass. She said after they changed that she never won another one. Thanks, Barbara, they're beautiful!

Believe me, it is a tremendous thrill to receive the recognition of your peers. All artists have a certain amount of competitive drive—you have to, to keep touring and creating, to see your records fail yet keep the faith that they'll succeed someday—so it's especially meaningful to receive a sign of your fellow musicians' regard. I will always feel grateful for that.

Up to that point, I had been nominated for major awards, but I'd been the "always-a-bridesmaid" type. In 1981, for example, I had been nominated along with Terri Gibbs, Sylvia, Lacy J. Dalton, and Juice Newton for "New Female Vocalist" by the Academy of Country Music in Los Angeles. Terri won, and she deserved it for her huge hit "Somebody's Knocking."

In 1983, the CMA nominated me for "Female Vocalist of the Year." Janie Fricke won. Maybe the association made the same mistake as the woman who spotted me in the Dallas airport one time when I was standing with Charlie and George Strait. She ran up to me, pointing and shouting, "I know who you are. I know who you are."

I enjoyed the fact that she recognized me and not George Strait. I let it show.

Then she said, "You're Janie Fricke," and George and Charlie broke up laughing as I took an uncomfortable lesson in humility.

Now, Janie, I'm just kidding here. You earned that award fair and square! You know I'm still your biggest fan.

I did have one frustration with the awards process itself, though, that stirred up a lot of controversy—a frustration that I hope everyone involved understood reflected no lack of appreciation for the CMA's kind recognition. My trouble had to do with the way the ceremony was arranged back in 1984. The awards were presented at the Grand Ole Opry House, and after the show, the CMA would have all the winners go upstairs to meet the press. After all the interviews were finished there, we were shuttled to the Opryland Hotel, a mile away, where we would meet another flock of reporters in the ballroom. As you can imagine, all this moving around stretched the country music industry's biggest night of the year to 2 A.M. or so, and by then everyone was exhausted.

By contrast, at the Grammys, the American Music Awards, and the Academy of Country Music Awards shows, each winner talked to reporters backstage immediately after his or her award presentation.

In 1985, I suggested through my manager that the CMA do the same thing to make the night more of a celebration than a grueling marathon. But tradition doesn't break easily inside the Nashville music establishment, or anywhere else, I guess. People often do things a certain way because they've always done them that way—whether or not it's the best way. I repeated my suggestion in 1986 and was told by one CMA spokesperson, "You'll go where we tell you to go and do what we tell you. You're just lucky to be here."

"Okay," I said, "thank you very much."

That year, I was honored with two awards, "Female Vocalist of the Year" for the third time, and at the end of the evening, the greatest prize in the world of country music, "Entertainer of the Year."

I cried with joy, and then I returned to my seat in the audience. And when the show ended, Charlie and I headed out the side door to a waiting limousine.

Someone from the CMA rushed up to us saying, "Wait a minute! Where are you going? You have interviews to do!"

"I told you I wouldn't do any interviews under these circumstances," I said. And I left the building.

I wasn't trying to act like a star, though some in the CMA may have thought so. Instead, after repeatedly asking that the CMA consider the feelings of its artists, I was trying to maintain my dignity and joy on one of the most exciting nights of my life. But the uproar over my actions persisted until the 1987 CMA awards show the following October, when I was nominated in four categories: Entertainer of the Year, Female Vocalist of the Year, and Album and Video of the Year for "What Am I Gonna Do About You?"

To clarify my position, my manager, Bill Carter, issued a press release for me, which read in part: "While I respect the CMA's decision to maintain the current structure of the post-awards press conference, I must also abide by my own very strong feelings that this structure is not the most efficient for the media or the artist. I firmly believe that arranging media access to the winners and nominees backstage during the program would be more beneficial to all concerned, particularly those members of the media faced with an immediate deadline.

"The CMA awards are very special to me for many reasons, not the least of which being they present a rare opportunity to share an important evening with close friends, business associates and family."

I'm happy to say that I ended up winning my fourth "Female Vocalist of the Year" Award in 1987. But I'm almost as pleased to say that since then, the CMA has restructured its ceremony to help the artists face the press with all their wits about them—all the better to carry the banner of country music.

❧

BUT GETTING BACK TO THAT CMA AWARDS SHOW IN 1986: ABOUT A week after I was named "Entertainer of the Year," I had the most touching surprise. It came in the middle of the night.

I had been on tour and was riding through Atoka, about eighteen miles from home, when Larry Jones called me from the driver's seat of the bus.

"Reba," he said, "come up here."

I stumbled sleepily up to the front of the bus and peered out the windshield. There, on billboards and marquees—even trees —were signs made by my neighbors and friends welcoming me home as "Entertainer of the Year." My eyes filled with tears. The local folks had worked hard to make those signs and had made sure the signs stayed up until I came home seven days later. Thank you, friends.

❧

IN 1986, THE GRAND OLE OPRY CELEBRATED ITS FIFTIETH ANNIVERSARY.
It had begun as a radio program on WSM—the call letters stood
for "We Shield Millions," the slogan of its insurance company
sponsor—beaming out over a 1,000-watt "clear channel" from
Canada to Mexico and from the Rockies to the Atlantic Ocean. In
the days before TV, it had brought music and a sense of community into isolated rural homes, where it was often the only presence of the outside world. At that time, musicians would perform
live on the show, and people would travel miles and jam the halls
of the station to try to get a glimpse of the artists. Before long, it
took an auditorium to accommodate all those fans, and so the
Grand Ole Opry House was born. It was the cathedral of country
music, home to the artists who have shaped the music into what it
is today—alongside jazz and rhythm and blues, one of America's
great, native, unique musical languages. Now it is famous around
the world.

I got to sing on the Fiftieth Anniversary show in the company
of such country music greats as Dolly Parton, Loretta Lynn, and
Willie Nelson. The late Grant Turner, who brought me onstage,
had been at the Opry the night the great Hank Williams pre-
miered there, and had done many skits with such country music
legends as Roy Acuff and Minnie Pearl. After the show I took
pictures with almost everyone, which I have framed at home
now. They were some of my childhood heroes. I felt more like a
fan than a performer!

And then, three days after the Fiftieth Anniversary show, I
became a member of the Grand Ole Opry myself. For my part of
the show, I sang "Somebody Should Leave." It was a very special, highly emotional night because, since I was a kid, I'd always
wanted to be a member.

Ralph Emery, the host of "Nashville Now," had predicted
that 1986 was going to be a big year for me. Thank God, he had
been right.

R E B A   M c E n t i r e

❧

I HAD ANOTHER HIT SONG THAT YEAR, "WHOEVER'S IN NEW EN-
gland," one that did more to broaden my audience than any
record I'd made so far. It brought me to the attention of people
who'd never listened to country music and who had never heard
the name Reba McEntire. Songs like that are called "career
records," and this was my first one.

I never set out to record a "crossover" record. As I've said,
I've always considered myself a country artist and never wanted
to abandon my roots. I had simply come to the conclusion that it
would be better for me just to do good material, and if it happened to reach across the pop charts—well, fine—that would be
an unexpected little extra. But sometimes, the purest country
songs have crossed over to non-country charts, such as Merle
Haggard's "Okie From Muskogee" or Johnny Cash's "Folsom
Prison Blues" or Jeannie C. Riley's "Harper Valley P.T.A."

My first career song was about a woman whose husband
spends so much time working in New England, she suspects he's
having an affair. Don "Dirt" Laniere says that he heard the song a
year before he played it for me but thought it was so pop-sound-
ing that it would scare me to death. Still he wanted me to have it.
As he says, "She is the best natural singer I've ever heard, and
that song [would] really let her show her vocal aerobics."

Knowing that it wouldn't fit on the album I was recording at
the time, in any case, he asked the song's publisher to "stick it
under a rock" until he felt I was ready to hear it.

That wouldn't be for another eight months. I remember
hearing the song for the first time and getting chills! I even have
the sheet of paper where I wrote down *HIT!* beside the song's
title.

But as Jimmy Bowen remembers the story: "Dirt and I
schemed for two months to make sure she did that song. We did
everything we could to have her keep it in the final ten [songs

scheduled for recording] and we came in to record it, the last one we were going to do on that album. She was tired and didn't want to do it. I said, 'Let's just do it; we don't have to use it.' ''

He insists that even after I cut the song, its theme, adultery, made me leery about releasing it. Well, that may be so, but again, I remember the story differently. I used to believe that you can't sing songs that contradict your own personal lifestyle. But after a few years of maturing, I found that it's best to find the songs people can relate to—whether you can or not. There are a lot of people listening to country music who don't have perfect lives, who have the problems we sing about, whether it's wife abuse, drinking, cheating, or whatever. If it's a good song and people hear the message—the person in that song fixed his marriage and so can I, or the woman in this song walked out on a man who was beating up on her and so can I—well, you've used your music to make a statement and maybe to offer hope or another way.

So, whether Bowen and Dirt led me, tricked me—or if I went into "New England" with my eyes wide open—I'll always be glad we recorded that song.

ONE THING I'M SURE ABOUT IS THAT, SOON AFTER HEARING "NEW England," I began to think "music video." I had never done a music video before. And Bowen didn't believe in them a whole lot back then. He thought they didn't sell enough records to justify their production cost. But that song was meant to have a video with it. I could see the story unfolding as I heard the lyrics.

Bill Carter was nothing if not persistent. He kept arguing with Bowen about me doing a video, and Bowen finally agreed to it, *if* I would pay half of the production costs. So, off we went to Boston in the dead of winter. The city was covered with beautiful white snow.

Jon Small, the video producer and director, took one look at me and told me that my jeans were too long. He insisted I'd have to cut them off or get a shorter pair before we started shooting. "This is the way we wear them in Oklahoma," I told him. He fussed some more, but as you can see, long jeans made the video.

The video came off beautifully.

Weeks later, when I was staying at a Holiday Inn somewhere, I turned on Home Box Office. In between the movies, an Aretha Franklin video came on, followed by my "New England" video. I was not only amazed to see that I was on HBO, rather than Country Music Television or on The Nashville Network, which had been on the air for three years by then, but by the fact that being on HBO meant that I'd really hit the big time.

That video was such a success that in August 1986, I filmed my second one, "What Am I Gonna Do About You" Bill Carter got actor David Keith, who had gotten an Oscar nomination for his role in the Richard Gere/Debra Winger movie *An Officer and a Gentleman,* to play my love interest. Since David was shooting a film in Italy he could only spare one day to shoot my video, so I paid for him to fly round-trip from Milan to New York on the Concorde. It was worth it because his performance was terrific. We shot "What Am I Gonna Do About You" in New York City's Central Park.

Since then I've had some big stars on my videos with me: Huey Lewis, whom I loved working with on "Is There Life Out There" and Bruce Boxleitner on "Cathy's Clown." I consider videos as much a part of my work as the records themselves. I usually do two videos for every album I release.

꧁ꕥ꧂

BESIDES VIDEOS, WE KEPT TRYING OUT NEW WAYS TO PROMOTE MY albums. Thanks to Carter's negotiating skills, I had an unusual contract with MCA that gave me a certain amount of say in how my records were marketed. That kind of contract, Carter says, had never before been written in Nashville.

Bowen had strongly resisted my involvement in promotion at first. At the time, MCA didn't even have a marketing department in Nashville, and the last thing he wanted was some artist pressuring him with crazy ideas. So Charlie, Carter, and I had to go in and pitch him on our marketing game plan.

"Well, it looks like you know what you're doing here," Bowen finally said. "So I'll tell you what. We're going to eliminate all of your independent [promotional] efforts and you're going to do it within our system."

One of the first promotional ideas Bill Carter came up with was "Country in a Crate." It worked very well. People could buy my album in a crate that held space for ten other cassettes. There was also a drawing for a Jeep Wagoneer.

"That promotion sold a lot of records for us and really established Reba as maybe the first significant-selling female," Carter said. It also won a national retailing award for Carter.

We also found other ways to let retailers know who I was—I attended the Wal-Mart convention and others, and made dozens of promotional appearances in stores. My record sales began to explode.

☙❧

DESPITE THE SUCCESS WE SEEMED TO BE HAVING, CHARLIE AND BILL Carter seemed convinced that I had arrived, that I had done it, I had peaked. Their attitude depressed and confused me. It bothered Narvel too! As tour manager, he had to carry out all our conflicting directions. Years later he said it almost pulled him apart.

"In those days," Narvel says, "I was a driven tour manager. I was pushing myself to the max, determined to be the best. And I became the pawn because there were times on the road when it was just Reba and us (the band) and I would be semi in charge. Reba would tell me she wanted things done a certain way.

"Then we would go home and Charlie would come on our next trip and would say, 'No, it ain't going to happen like that. You need to do it this way.' And then we'd go into Nashville and Bill Carter would pull me aside and say, 'Is there any way you can pull this off? Try to make this happen? Try to get her to do this?'

"I was a diplomat. I got good at being a player between Reba, Charlie, and Bill Carter. The training at Prudential I had had years earlier helped a lot because it taught me to be a people person. I could hang out with Reba, I could hang out with Charlie, and I could hang out with Bill. But I couldn't get them together. And I have to say those were the most stressful days of my life."

I got so I couldn't always cope with the lack of harmony among my career planners. One time, Narvel, who was always scheming ways to improve the show, came to me with a new idea. "You know," he said, "we ought to find some little risers and get the band up on them, to make us look a little better."

I liked the plan, and as Narvel remembers it, I asked him to present the idea to Charlie and Carter in Nashville.

"I'll never forget this," Narvel says. "We went to Ruth Chris's Steak House and we sat down and everybody was in a good mood. It was like something you'd see in a movie. Then Reba says, 'Narvel has got something he wants to talk to you all about.' She left me hanging out there.

"The spotlight was on me," Narvel went on. "So I laid it out there, and Bill Carter and Charlie thought that risers was the most stupid, goofy thing one could ever come up with. Ultimately, Reba came to the rescue, and we finally got risers."

Narvel and the band had to set them up and take them down for each show, since at that point, we had no production crew.

But they didn't mind. After all, those guys had to set up the T-shirt concession and the bandstand and do all the rest of the manual labor anyway. The risers cost $1,700. I thought Charlie was gonna make the band pay for them but he didn't. Still, he never thought they were worth it.

Charlie's lack of enthusiasm for new ideas wasn't the only problem. For a long time, he had personally approved all of my personal engagements. George Mallard, my booking agent, would pick dates with concert promoters, then call Charlie to be sure I would play the dates for the agreed fee.

One time Charlie approved my being booked into a 17,000-seat auditorium in Daytona Beach, Florida, during spring break, a time when the town disappears and the college kids—who didn't want country music back then—come in. Both he and George should have known better. We sold only 1,700 tickets. The place was 90 percent empty! I could hear the echo of my voice floating across the hollow room.

How embarrassing!

So I called Charlie and told him that I didn't want him approving the dates anymore. He wasn't out on the road with me enough to understand the business. Needless to say, he wasn't happy at being cut out of the action.

It seemed like nothing was going right between the two of us, professionally or personally. It was clear that some kind of blowup was bound to come. One day in 1984, after Charlie and I had gone to Colorado to shoot the album cover for *My Kind of Country,* we drove back to Denver to catch our plane in near silence. It seemed that by then we didn't speak except to argue.

Suddenly, from out of nowhere, Charlie said, "What do you want, a divorce?"

It was the first time that word had been spoken between us.

"Absolutely not!" I snapped.

But I didn't know for sure if I meant that.

❀

Two YEARS LATER, WE SHOULD HAVE BEEN REJOICING OVER OUR tenth wedding anniversary—and would have been, if there'd been any joy left in our marriage. So, instead of having a celebration, Charlie and I went to Hawaii to try to repair our relationship. We came back after three days.

In 1987, there was an incident in Dallas, when we were there shooting the video for "The Last One to Know," that reveals just how estranged we had become. We were riding together on the bus between location shots—me back in the stateroom, and Charlie, Narvel, and Bill Carter up front.

The bus stopped for a red light at a corner where there were flower sellers, and Charlie said to the guys, "Watch this." Opening the door of the bus, he leaned out and bought a rose. "This will make it better," he told them. "This will fix everything." He smirked as he carried the rose to the back of the bus, setting it beside me on the bed.

The gesture was, as the saying goes, "too little too late," and Charlie's self-satisfaction about making it could only infuriate me. How could he behave as if our problems were so minor that one small gesture could fix everything? It's not that he didn't care— he did, a lot—but he was so bullheaded about seeing things his way, so unable to even try to understand my feelings, that he kept on making the trouble worse.

Years later, Carter remembered that time. "With Charlie, you had a tremendous male ego and with Reba you had this proud, strong woman growing. She was growing, just like a kid growing up. And he was from another world, another era. It was just that male thing, 'I got to be in charge.' I could just look at them and see this wasn't going to work."

Carter had in fact originally asked Charlie not to attend the shoot because he could see Charlie was interfering in my performance. I needed to be able to concentrate on my scenes, not on the problems that my marriage was having. Since Charlie had come anyway, I was an emotional wreck the whole time we were filming, though the video turned out okay. The next night I was booked for a show in Lubbock, Texas, and I knew that I just couldn't do it with Charlie along.

When I asked him not to come, telling him that I simply needed some time alone, Charlie got furious.

"I'll get my stuff out of the bus," he fumed.

Trying to calm him down a little, I asked, "Do you need any money?"

"No," Charlie said, "I got four hundred dollars out of your purse."

All I could say was: "You did what?"

That set him off. I'd never before confronted Charlie about money, even while I was clearly the breadwinner. That was a big no-no. One thing led to another and for the first time in our life together, I thought Charlie was going to hit me, as he reared back with his shaving kit in his hand. I didn't want to see what was gonna happen next, so I ran to the front of the bus. Carter started saying, "Charlie, stop! Stop it! Don't do anything you're going to regret later!"

"You get your ass out!" Charlie thundered to Carter.

As scared as I was of Charlie, I knew that Carter's presence would only provoke him more. So I said, "Bill, go ahead and leave the bus. He's not going to hit me."

And he didn't. Charlie had calmed down, and he just packed up all his things and left for Stringtown.

I felt relief that he was gone, and once again my gut feelings were reminding me it was time. Time to get out. His going through my purse without so much as telling me proved that, to him, my feelings didn't matter at all, that I didn't even deserve common courtesy. How could a man who was trying to save his marriage continue to abuse it so consistently?

I found it sort of fitting, I guess, that he'd threatened me with the shaving kit. I'd had it made for Charlie and wrapped it, lovingly and carefully, to give to him one Christmas. I'd meant it as a special gift, but when I'd set it on his lap, he'd let his two young sons tear the wrapping to shreds. They were just little kids, of course, who didn't know any better, but Charlie never tried to stop them; he just laughed. I was so hurt that he didn't seem to notice all the care I'd taken—and that he didn't seem to value a gift from his wife enough to want to open it himself.

That shaving kit was a symbol of all that had become unbearable to me about our marriage.

CHAPTER 12

THROUGHOUT ALL THESE CONFLICTS, CHARLIE, CARTER, AND I had been planning one of the most important shows of my career, a night at Carnegie Hall. Carnegie Hall is, of course, the foremost concert stage in America, the place that, when you play it, signals that you have "arrived" as a serious artist. At least that's what I thought! It was like the Grand Ole Opry of the North. Nearly every major classical, contemporary, or pop musician of the past one hundred years has played it, but not all that many country-music artists.

So when I got the chance to play Carnegie Hall, Bill Carter strongly recommended that I do it, even though he was pretty sure that we wouldn't make a profit on the show. As Carter says, at the time, "It could cost you up to $30,000. The expenses could exceed the ticket sales. I asked for Reba's and Charlie's approval and they gave it."

"When I went to Ron Delsener, the promoter," Carter continues, "he said something like, 'You're crazy.' But then he said, 'I'll help you with it.' So we fought it like a major battle. We postered the city, we did everything that you could possibly do, to put on that show.''

My debut at Carnegie Hall was set for October 28, 1987. At that time, the majority of people who attended country-music shows were "walk-ups," folks who waited until the night of the show to buy their tickets. That was the custom, and that was the case with the Carnegie Hall show, Carter remembers.

"Ten days before the show," he says, "we considered cancel-ing. We hadn't yet reached that point with our daily ticket counts where we were comfortable, so we were just freaking out." Not only did we stand to lose a lot of money, but it would be very embarrassing to have a poor turnout at Carnegie Hall. The big-gest press in the nation would be there, and as Carter says, "We made sure we had some important New York people there, such as the business manager for the Rolling Stones and the press."

I went to the sound check a couple of hours early. Carnegie Hall is the most acoustically perfect auditorium in the country, which means that any little glitch would really show.

Bill Carter had asked Allen Branton, who has worked with everyone from Michael Jackson to David Bowie, to come in and assist Gayle Hase with the lighting. That's how sure we wanted to be that the show would be spectacular. But Branton and Hase worked on the lights and the setup so long that I didn't even get a sound check. I would just have to hope for the best!

Before the show, Narvel and I went down the street to eat at the Carnegie Deli, where all the celebrities jam into the Formica tables to eat big sour pickles and corned beef sandwiches too huge to bite into. We were sitting there having some soup when I nearly shouted, "Oh, I forgot to take my Actifed!" Narvel liked to have jumped out of his seat.

Over the years, I had developed terrible allergies, due to dust and smoke from playing in clubs and the rodeo arenas, and so to clear my throat from the drainage, I always had to take an Actifed four hours before I sang. Nowadays, thanks to good nutrition, supplements, my chiropractor, and regular massage, I don't have to take them anymore. But then, not taking one long enough before a show just about threw me into a panic.

Finally it was time to get ready. That night I wore the first dress Sandi Spika, my costume designer, ever made for me. It was black suede with gold fringe. I wore my cowboy boots and my belt buckle that Gary Gist and John Smith had made for me after I had sung the National Anthem at the National Finals Rodeo in Oklahoma City for ten years. It wasn't what New York was used to, I'm sure, but I didn't want New York to see anyone up there other than Reba. So I went as myself. No airs—just me.

As I walked out onto the stage between two big partitions I was kind of in a trance.

I looked out past the spotlights to see the crowd. I couldn't believe it—they were all on their feet! I got a standing ovation before I ever sang a note.

That really choked me up, and because of that I had a little trouble singing the first song.

Our fears about ticket sales and all those months of worry had been totally in vain. Hundreds of people had to be turned away. Folks had ridden subways in from the outer boroughs, and businessmen from Midtown Manhattan had rushed in straight from work, their briefcases still in their hands. I had gone in the back way, so I hadn't seen them, but in Carnegie Hall tradition, posters announcing that the tickets were gone papered the outside of the building. A black SOLD OUT sign was streaked across my name. I wish I had one of those posters for a souvenir.

During my encore, "Sweet Dreams," I found myself amazed that the show was over. The whole show had passed like five minutes. I've never done a show that seemed to go by so fast.

I think the icing on the cake of the whole event was me being able to fly Mama and Daddy and Red and Gail Steagall to New York City to see me play Carnegie Hall. I couldn't have been there without all their support and love throughout the years. I'll never forget how Daddy walked into the swanky Parker Meridian Hotel and looked around the giant lobby. Daddy was never one to be overwhelmed by anything.

"A person sure could stack a lot of hay in here," he said.

❦

A LITTLE LATER, I HAD ANOTHER WONDERFUL SURPRISE, ONE THAT thrilled me as much as that sellout crowd at Carnegie Hall. At the 1987 Country Music Association Awards, I was named "Female Vocalist of the Year" for the fourth time in a row, a record number of awards for one artist. At the awards show in 1987, it was probably obvious to everyone how emotional the event was for me. At that time, I was being pulled to such extremes—my marriage had reached its lowest point and now my work was being recognized with a record-breaking award. I was completely overwhelmed with gratitude and affection. Standing in front of the television cameras, I delivered an impromptu speech that came straight from the heart.

Later, someone showed me what I said. "It's so sweet of you all," I began. "This is so sweet of you all. I appreciate it very much, being in the company of people like Tammy Wynette and Loretta Lynn. And this is the fourth time—you don't know what this means to me. I'm thrilled to pieces. And I'm just going to tell you something Mama said when we first came to Nashville. She said, 'We can go back, we can go back home, you don't have to do this if you don't want to. But you'll be doing something I never could have done.' It takes a lot of hard work, as Holly [Dunn] and all the other women that have been on this stage tonight can tell you. So any of you young ladies watching at home on TV, I got to tell you this is a great profession. There is a lot of love, lots of competition, and lots of rewards, even if you're not standing up here. Lots of love from the audience that you can get. So work hard and show 'em what you can do.''

When K. T. Oslin broke my streak by winning ''Female Vocalist of the Year'' in 1988, she acknowledged me from the stage, saying, ''You had a hell of a run, girl.''

The press tried to make something of her remark, like there was jealousy between us. There wasn't—and in fact I thought it was nice of her to remember me at a moment when almost anyone would be overcome with emotion and thrilled with their win. But not K.T. She took the time to acknowledge me. I took that as a huge compliment from a friend.

⚜

I HAD ONE EMBARRASSING BUSINESS FAILURE IN THE MIDST OF THAT BIG year. Some months before the Carnegie Hall show, Reba McEntire's Kitchen opened on Nashville's Music Valley Drive not far from the Opryland Complex, which thousands of people visit every year. I got 10 percent of the restaurant's revenues in exchange for letting the owners use my name. I had no involvement with the running of the place, the food, or the service. I think I learned enough to never enter into a deal like that again.

But of course, the failure that was preoccupying me the most that year was the final breakup of my marriage. Charlie and I split up right in the middle of the planning for my Carnegie Hall debut, and our divorce was final two weeks after the show, though the money questions weren't settled until after the first of the year of 1988.

After the shaving kit incident, Charlie had gone home to Stringtown and I'd gone on to Lubbock to do my show. When I got home on Sunday, it was our eleventh wedding anniversary. Charlie talked me into staying home that night, and the next morning we drove to Tulsa, where my Daddy was in St. John's hospital having some tests done on his heart. The tests would reveal that Daddy needed to have triple-bypass surgery right away.

I remember the date exactly—June 22, 1987.

On our drive Monday morning to see Daddy, we were crossing the lower railroad track at Stringtown, and I said to Charlie, "If I ever asked for a divorce, what would you do?" He said, "I'd ask for 10 percent of you for the rest of your life."

Charlie and I spent the night at the Hilton Inn, and we went back to see Daddy at the hospital the next morning. That's when I relieved Charlie of his co-management duties, telling him that I pretty much wanted him out of my career. From the hospital pay phone, Charlie called Narvel, who had been handling all of the tour managing, and who was now going to take over everything, all but Bill Carter's responsibilities.

"Well," Charlie told him, "Reba's going through a little thing here. Don't worry, I'll help you with things. She'll get over it in a bit, and I'll get back in there."

Charlie was just not getting it.

⚬⚬⚬

I TOLD CHARLIE TO GO ON HOME AND SAID I WOULD CATCH MY BUS there in Tulsa to go to my next show in Chattanooga. Then I went back up to Daddy's hospital room. Mama was there reading a book, so I took out my little white Bible.

The pages fell open to Ephesians and I started reading. I already knew what I was wanting to do because I had asked Bill Carter earlier to recommend a lawyer for me. And then I read a scripture that said something like "He is the fool that looks back while plowing the field." It seemed to be saying to me, "Don't look back, look forward," and I whispered, "Thank you, thank you very much." I felt as though God had sent me direction.

I closed my Bible and looked up at Daddy and asked Mama, "Do you want to go downtown with me?"

"What for?" she said.

"I'd like to file for divorce."

I thought my parents might try to argue with me but all Mama said was, "Sure." And Daddy said, "What took you so long?"

We visited Larry Leonard, the lawyer who had been recommended by Bill Carter. The divorce petition was written in Tulsa and filed in Atoka County, where Charlie and I lived.

Somehow Charlie found out about me filing for divorce before he was even served with the papers. He withdrew all the money we had deposited in a McAlester bank. It was later put back so the courts could decide how everything would be split. But on the day that Mama, Alice, and Suzy Wills, my former background singer, came with me to Stringtown to pack my personal belongings, Charlie showed me that he wanted more than money.

For example, I still had some copies of the very first album I had recorded for Mercury, *Reba McEntire,* which I was keeping for their sentimental value. Their cellophane seals weren't broken, and Charlie thought they might someday be collector's items. He said that half of them were his but he would only let me take the copies that had been opened. I thought Alice was gonna try to whip him over that.

I had a bed that Mama had given me for my sixteenth or seventeenth birthday. He insisted on keeping it, saying he needed a place to sleep.

"What about the brand-new bed I just bought?" I said.

"I want all the bedrooms to have beds in it," he said. I didn't fight him.

I wanted the grandfather clock that the band had given me for Christmas and little drinking glasses from the National Finals Rodeo Ladies' Luncheon that I got before I met him. He said okay on the grandfather clock but he kept the little glasses that meant nothing to anyone but me.

The hairsplitting went on. I had a habit then—and to this day
—of collecting all the toiletries hotels have in the rooms for their
guests. Like if I stayed at one hotel for a while, I'd always use the
same bar of soap for as long as it lasted, and when new ones,
along with shampoo, conditioner, and so on, would keep showing
up every day, I'd take the extras home and save them until I had a
bag full enough to send to the Red Cross or the Reba Ranch
House, or to churches at Christmas time. On that day, there
were two bags of collected toiletries under our bathroom sink.

Charlie said, "Leave one of those bags for me."

"What for?" I asked.

"I don't want to ever have to buy another bar of soap," he
said.

That spirit never left him. In 1993, I asked my collaborator
Tom Carter to give Charlie a chance to tell his side of the story
for this book. At first Charlie said he'd do it, but then he changed
his mind. He called Tom to say that I owed him $500 for a bed I
took when we split up; if I would pay him for the bed and give
him some additional money—he never said how much—he might
agree to an interview.

I told Tom not to call him back. Just to forget it. I had only
been trying to do right by Charlie, to give him a chance to tell his
side. But I guess he didn't want to accept that.

❧

I WANTED MY PARTING WITH CHARLIE TO BE FRIENDLY AND FAIR. THE
legal process wouldn't allow it. Funny how people can get married in the space of minutes, then spend months in court trying
to get out of it. Through his lawyers, Charlie asked for a share of
our assets that I didn't think was fair, for as my lawyer put it:
"The source of the income earned by the plaintiff is the plaintiff's
unique God-given talent which had already been discovered and

developed at the time the plaintiff and the defendant were married.''

And so the depositions began. A deposition is testimony, taken under sworn oath, that is admissible in a court of law. Depositions were taken from Charlie, my bookkeeper Linda Bowerman, Red Steagall, Bill Carter, and Jimmy Bowen, as well as me. I remember that I was interrogated as if I were on the witness stand, with a tape recorder and court reporter taking down every word.

I didn't like the personal questions, and didn't like having to answer them in front of relative strangers. None of those people had been on hand when Charlie and I had nearly frozen to death feeding cattle. Not one had helped me cook his meals or do his laundry. None of them had seen the inside of our bedroom or were witnesses to how cold our marriage had become. Yet they all would have something to say about what happened to us now.

For the trial, other people I knew were called in to testify, with some subpoenaed to Atoka County from as far away as Nashville. I hated it that people who worked with both Charlie and me—who were friends to both of us—were put in the position of having to take sides. But most didn't, and there wasn't any damaging testimony from anyone.

Finally, the divorce was granted in November 1987, by Atoka County District Court Judge Doug Gabbard II. Part of his ruling read: "When these two parties married in 1976, they moved into a house which they rented for $10.00 per month and to which they had to haul their own water. They had few possessions and the Defendant owed at least $40,000 in debts. Eleven years later the parties now have substantial assets, primarily due to Plaintiff's successful singing career . . . ."

Yet, while I'd agreed to give Charlie our 215-acre ranch and our house, the judge still awarded him what turned out to be $580,000. I was astounded at the inequity. Charlie had been a benefit to my career, and I had testified as much. But it was hard for me to see why he deserved so much of our net worth.

❧

AFTER THE DIVORCE WAS FINAL, THE ATOKA COUNTY NEWSPAPER RAN a front-page story about it, which was picked up on the AP wire and circulated all over the country. That story brought me a scolding letter from a fan, who wanted to know how I dared get a divorce when she had looked to me as a role model. That brought everything into perspective.

Certainly I believe that marriage should be for life, but things don't always work out according to our beliefs. Who of us can ever judge whether another person's troubles are really too much to bear? Like everyone else, I've made mistakes in my life, but I learn from my mistakes and go on with my life. Sure, I could say, I wish I'd never married Charlie Battles, but that's not true. I loved Charlie with all my heart, wanted to marry him, and for much of our marriage, I was happy. And when that changed, I changed my plans. I am very uncomfortable being seen as a role model in that way. No one is perfect but God, and that's what I told that fan when I answered her letter. That she should look to Him as a model. Not to me.

CHAPTER 13

I MOVED TO NASHVILLE AFTER THE DIVORCE.
Years earlier, I had told a newspaper in McAlester that I
would never leave my home state, and I meant that sincerely
at the time. Atoka County, Oklahoma, was the only home
I'd known for thirty-three years, and many of my neighbors
seemed to me like family. But Charlie had come from northeast-
ern Oklahoma as an outsider and, over the years, had won their
acceptance. Maybe I was reading more into it than I should have,
but I felt the community, or maybe it was just the court and the
judge, had taken Charlie's side in the divorce proceedings. That
left me feeling betrayed and very hurt.

So when I moved out of the ranch at Stringtown, I wasn't
looking to find a new place nearby. Instead, I moved to Nashville.

From my first day in Nashville, it was "Onward! Don't look
back!" A new era of my life had begun.

I found a large house in a very pretty part of town where all
of the transported "Okies" could stay. Sheri McCoy made the

move with me, and so did Cindy Owen, a friend from Jackson, Mississippi. Larry Jones, who was still my bus driver and pretty much acted as my bodyguard and protector, moved into the apartment over the garage.

We were not only living together, we were working together, so our lives were completely intertwined. Sheri kept on as my hairdresser until 1988, when she smashed her shoulder and right upper arm in a car wreck when she and her family were going to Wyoming to visit her sister Mary. Since she couldn't raise her arm to fix hair, she switched over to working in my office until she got the chance to start her own business. She and Ann Payne Rice, a good friend of all of ours, created a company that would advise performers on their wardrobes and get them ready for videos and photo shoots; and she also goes on the road quite a bit with Trisha Yearwood, who is also a super singer and a good friend of mine. Cindy Owen took over my fan club and correspondence; her duties have expanded to a gigantic degree but she's still in charge of the fan club today.

Larry is now the head of transportation for Starstruck, the company that I set up to manage my affairs in 1988.

Work became my refuge after the divorce. It's funny—I had grown so accustomed to the status quo, to the strain and the icy cold tension. But now touring got to be much more fun and much less pressured.

❧

I AM SO GRATEFUL THAT THE PEOPLE IN MY ORGANIZATION—SHERI, Cindy, Larry, Narvel, and others—rallied around me during those hard days of being on my own for the first time and making a home for myself in a new place. One of the ugly facts about divorce is that it always affects more than two people, and most members of our work family had been friendly with Charlie too. I know our split was uncomfortable for everyone, and I suppose it was inevitable that certain friends would drift away. I was saddened that one of those was Linda Bowerman.

Linda was the secretary and bookkeeper who ran my office at the Stringtown ranch. She took great care of me. Naturally, after I filed for divorce, she felt awkward conducting my business right under Charlie's nose. So I agreed to construct a small, freestanding building on her property in Centrahoma, Oklahoma, that would become the new offices of the Reba McEntire organization.

The building cost $15,000. I told Linda I'd split the cost of it with her since she'd get to own the building, and she agreed. But once I moved to Nashville, I saw very quickly that I had been naive in thinking that I could live there and still keep my headquarters in Oklahoma, 700 miles away. My record label, my manager, and everything else affiliated with my business were located within a few blocks' radius in Nashville; and it was clear that I needed to move my offices there too.

When Linda first came to work for me, Susie had just quit because of a falling out she and I had, and she decided not to come back and teach Linda her bookkeeping techniques. So Linda had had to hunt through all of my records and come up with her own systems of bookkeeping and business management. Those first few days were hard for her, I'm sure, and I appreciated the way she'd taken charge. Her skill and her friendship had kept me going in leaner times, and I fully expected her to share my more prosperous days.

When I played Norman, Oklahoma, in November 1987, Linda and her family came to see me, and I told her of my plans. The expression on her face told me what I didn't want to hear.

"What am I going to do?" she said.

"Linda," I said, "I'm sorry. I know I told you that this would never happen, but I'm going to have to go back on my word, and I apologize to you with all my heart. But it won't work this way, my business being in Oklahoma and me being in Nashville. Why don't you come to Nashville with me?''

"What about my family?" Linda said.

"Move them too," I told her, "you and your husband [Pee-Wee] and your whole family. There are great opportunities in Nashville.''

"I'll have to talk to Pee-Wee," she said.

After my sound check that day in Norman, I walked offstage and ran into Pee-Wee. His feet were spread apart and his arms were folded across his chest.

He stunned me by saying, "I'll give you until noon tomorrow to get your stuff out of that office or I'm burning it to the ground.''

"Now, Pee-Wee," I said. "Let's talk about this."

"I don't want to talk to you," he said. "You've lied to Linda. You've let her down and you're worthless.''

I made one attempt to reason with him, but he was in no mood to listen.

"Pee-Wee," I told him, "you've got this all wrong. The divorce, the move—everything happened way too quick. How was I to know how it was all going to wind up?''

"Shut up!" he said. "I'm talking."

"Go right ahead," I said.

When I could finally insert a word into his tirade, I asked why he and Linda didn't consider moving to Nashville.

"We don't want to move to Nashville if you're going to be there," he snapped.

If that was his attitude, there was nothing I could do. "We'll have the stuff out of the office by noon tomorrow," I said, and walked away.

Once again I was leaving someone who I had once thought would be a permanent fixture of my life. The Oklahoma of my young life was becoming a crumbling memory. I was also learning and maturing very quickly. I went to Narvel and told him what had happened.

He said, "I'll take care of it." And he did!

Larry Jones borrowed a truck and he, Jim Hammon, my tour concession manager, and his wife Debbie, Mama, Narvel, and I drove from Oklahoma City to Centrahoma and pulled onto Linda's place at nine the next morning.

Linda did what Susie had done. She told me nothing about her bookkeeping system, and I wasn't about to ask her anything. She didn't explain records of my fan club that would indicate who wanted to renew membership, who hadn't paid dues, and so on. My family, friends, and I got all of the office papers and dumped them into boxes. There wasn't any order to anything.

We finished loading by 11:30 A.M., thirty minutes ahead of Pee-Wee's deadline.

Larry drove the truck that contained my entire office from Centrahoma to Nashville. We met him there and unloaded all of the contents into my garage.

Fourteen months earlier I had been named "Entertainer of the Year." A month earlier I had made my Carnegie Hall debut. But in late November 1987, I was inside my garage trying to sift through records that looked like they had been arranged by a tornado.

It was there, sitting on the concrete floor, that I learned how to do my own payroll. I had no idea how to handle Social Security or income tax withholding or anything else. But I had employees who needed to be paid and so I figured it out, with the help of Mike Vaden, my accountant. All the checks went out right on time.

Linda was left with the building and a note for half of its cost, the way we'd agreed.

I didn't hear from Linda again until 1993, six years after I left Oklahoma. She wrote me a letter saying that though she'd paid off her half of the building's cost, she had decided that the deal we'd struck was unfair because she'd had to pay off the note. She now thought I should reimburse her for her share, plus pay her interest on the money.

I was understandably surprised at her request, considering that I'd already paid for half of a building that I couldn't use and which she owned outright, not to mention the unpleasantness of our final meeting and the length of time that had passed. Still, I wrote her a check for the total amount, interest and all.

"Here you go," I wrote, in a letter with the check. "I hope everything is fine in your life and I think this squares everything up between us."

It's been said that success changes people. But I've learned the hard way that it also changes the people around them.

꧁꧂

BESIDES LOSING LINDA, I HAD ANOTHER PARTING-OF-THE-WAYS TO deal with during that troubled time. I asked Bill Carter, my manager of four years, to let me go.

Carter recalls that he wasn't surprised. Once I had gotten rid of Charlie, he says, he expected to be next. He had never made a secret of his belief in Charlie's common sense and of his conviction that Charlie was good for me in many ways.

But that wasn't the reason I let Carter go. It wasn't that kind of personal thing at all. Perhaps Narvel's explanation says it best: "When Reba divorced Charlie, Bill Carter immediately said, 'Okay, Charlie is gone, I'll take control of everything.' What Bill didn't realize is that's exactly what Reba was running from. The move that Bill made at that particular time was the worst he could have. She was looking for space. That's where her head was. Instead of letting her grow and do some things she wanted, he came in and was domineering. And I can't say he would have done a bad job. But he smothered Reba."

Carter had been a tremendous help to me, getting me signed on MCA, where I have been recording for ten years now, guiding me through my first gold record, helping me broaden my audience, and, bringing off, among other milestones, my debut at Carnegie Hall. He taught me so much about how the music business works.

Most folks don't know that when I turned over my career management entirely to Carter he had never before managed anybody's career. He had been an immigration lawyer for the Rolling Stones and had represented guitarist Keith Richards and other entertainers in the United States. But I was his first management client. His skills helped me succeed, and my success helped his career. After our parting, many artists sought out Bill Carter for management, and I'm very glad.

But after the divorce, I felt like I was trying out my wings—living in a major city for the first time—and I wanted to feel that same spirit of exploration in my career, to fly higher, to try new things. I had gotten a new jolt of inspiration when I'd gone to Carter's management from Don Williams's and from Harold Shedd's record producing to Jimmy Bowen's. Now I wanted a new launch from another manager, and the person who I turned to was Narvel.

Once again I was turning to a person who didn't have any formal management experience, although he has told me often how much he learned at Prudential about managing and motivating people. In the eight years he'd been with my organization, he'd always impressed me with his drive. Like me, Narvel's a studier, soaking up everything Bill, Don, and all the rest of them could teach us. A real go-getter, Narvel was always coming up with ways to make the show bigger, better—our stage-lighting experiments, the risers for the band, and much more. He had big ambitions and excellent instincts, the kind of savvy that can't be learned in a classroom. He is one of the smartest men I have ever met.

In May of 1988 he accepted the job, and I've never regretted it. Almost immediately, he proved that he was the right choice. We were at rehearsals for the Academy of Country Music Awards Show, and the backdrop for my song was a country quilt—the show that year was working a traditional country theme into the set and staging. Trouble was, I didn't know about that and had brought along a beautiful pink evening dress with sequins and pearls to wear. I didn't notice the problem myself at first, but Narvel did! He met with Gene Weed, the producer, and asked him to get me another backdrop.

Gene wasn't used to being questioned by someone he didn't know that well or a person who didn't have a track record of being familiar with the world of television. But Narvel stuck to his guns. He kept explaining to Gene that the dress and backdrop would clash, and would he please put me on a different set. So finally, they swapped my backdrop with Tanya Tucker's. It all worked out fine, and today Narvel and Gene Weed are great friends.

WITH NARVEL TO HELP ME, I COULD REALLY BEGIN TO TAKE CHARGE of my career. From the time I signed with MCA, I realized how important it was to control as many aspects of my work as I possibly could, and today my organization's almost totally self-run and self-contained.

One of the first important decisions Narvel and I made together was to form our own booking and concert promotions agency. For twelve years I had worked for independent concert promoters who bought my shows from booking agents. On a lot of those bookings, I had to wonder whether my agents had any idea how far I had to travel between dates. Sometimes my band and I would arrive in a town barely in time for the show, without enough time to take a shower at a hotel. There is nothing worse

They say that clothes don't make the man, and the same is true of a woman. But if she's in show business, they sure do help. At left are some outfits I wore back in the early 1980s before I met Sandi Spika (with me below).

JANET L. STINGO

ng page, top left: The dress I wore to sing "Fancy" on my 1992 tour. *Center left:* Another Sandi creation for
same tour. *Bottom:* For my video "Does He Love You," Sandi found an elegant gown and put a fur stole with
ft) and made a beautiful dressing gown with a matching headdress to cover the Band-Aid over my left
·row where a skin cancer had recently been removed (*right*). *Top right:* Sandi also made the infamous lowcut
·dress I wore to the 1993 CMA Awards show; when she saw me onstage, my little sister, Susie, leaned over
·said, "Oh Mama!" But all Mama said was, "You need a few more sequins." *Above:* Sandi's dad helped her
· one of her most clever creations, the blue satin gown I wore to sing "For My Broken Heart." Anchored to
·et, the dress popped open so I could step out in different clothes for my next song. Shelby calls this "the
*·y dress."

feel honored to have been the recipient of some major awards over the course of my career. *Facing page, top left:* being presented with my first gold album, *Whoever's in New England,* in 1986 on TNN's *Nashville Now.* From left e Red Steagall, Bruce Hinton of MCA, me, my manager at the time Bill Carter, and *Nashville Now's* Ralph mery. *Top right:* The same year, the Country Music Association bestowed its highest award on me, Entertainer f the Year, along with my third award for Female Vocalist of the Year. *Center left:* I'm very proud of all three of y People's Choice Awards because they are voted by the fans themselves. *Center right:* At the American Music wards in 1991, I was thrilled to win both the Favorite Female Country Vocalist and the Favorite Country bum. *Bottom left:* I've been honored six times by TNN/*Music City News. Bottom right:* Accepting the sixth of my ght Academy of Country Music Awards; this is one of my favorite Sandi outfits. *Above:* In 1991, it was a thrill have President and Mrs. Bush attend the CMA awards when I hosted the show. During the closing seconds, e President made a spontaneous tribute onstage to the late Dottie West and I agree, we all miss her terribly.

Eight special people left us late one night. *Clockwise from left:* Kirk Cappello (musical director, keyboards), Joey Cigainero (synthesizer), our road manager Jim Hammon shown here with Narvel and me, Chris Austin (vocals, mandolin, guitar, and fiddle), Tony Saputo (drums), Paula Kaye Evans (vocals), Terry Jackson (bass guitar), and Michael Thomas (electric guitar). Almost everyday and at every show we think about them. They'll never be forgotten.

The real cops and killers behind SILENCE OF THE LAMBS

APRIL 1, 1991 $1.95

People weekly

EXCLUSIVE

Reba McEntire:

'THIS IS MY DARKEST HOUR'

The dramatic inside story of the night the country singer lost her band in a plane crash

The plane crash that took the lives of eight members of my band was the most profoundly senseless tragedy of my life, but I never questioned God—I know he's taking very good care of them. *Below:* One of the last portraits made of the band. Chris Austin and Jim Hammon were not there for this photo session. Suzy Wills (third from left), who had been with me for five years, had left the organization in December 1990, and Joe McGlohon (fourth from left), my saxophone player, was on the other plane that made it safely to Nashville.

LYNN BALDWIN

BETH GWINN

than going on stage wearing fresh clothes and yesterday's dirt. There were times in the early days that we had to unpack and set up our sound equipment all dressed up in our stage clothes.

Bill Carter was my manager then, and I talked to him about the prospect of handling my own bookings. Some other artists were already doing it. Bill said that if I hired enough people to do the bookings my overhead would be too high. But I just kept thinking to myself, "This system can be improved. This could be better."

Narvel and I always had a practice of studying and watching what other artists and companies were doing, learning not only from their accomplishments but also from their mistakes. Narvel began interviewing successful agents and promoters to run this new end of the business and finally narrowed the selection down to two candidates: Trey Turner, who had been an in-house promoter for Alabama and was then with Keith Fowler Promotions, and Mike Allen, who was working with C. K. Spurlock, who booked and promoted all of Kenny Rogers's dates.

"They both were coming from very powerful organizations," Narvel recalls. "I was really struggling, trying to decide which would be the best for Reba. And I was talking to Joe Gehl, another promoter friend of ours. He knew both of the guys real well. I told him I was really in a dilemma, and I asked him which one he would hire."

"Why don't you hire both of them?" Joe said. "What you're looking for is going to take more than one person anyhow."

So that's what we did. And I'm proud to say that our operation is one of the best in the business.

The secret in hiring people is to find folks who are ambitious, hardworking, creative, and loyal. Then you have to set a good example by working hard and giving 110 percent at everything you do. Larry Jones has worked for me since 1984. He said in August 1993 that the secret to working for Reba McEntire is to not get too comfortable.

"She and Narvel are always looking for ways to do their jobs better," he said, "and if you're going to last around here, you'd better do the same thing. One of the reasons I like working here is because it's like a book you can't put down. You never know what they'll come up with next. And whatever it is it's usually something better than they were doing before."

I'm someone in the music business who thinks the business is just as important as the music. I may sing for ninety minutes a night, but the singing is just a part of my sixteen-hour day.

A lot of people who have interviewed me insinuate that I oversee Starstruck Entertainment. That's not true. Basically, I'm the executive producer. In other words, because of the money I make, I can finance such an organization, but in no way could I have thought of all the things we're involved in. Nor could I run it.

Narvel is the director, producer, and overseer! But the most beautiful part is everyone runs their own department, whether it's publicity, publishing, fan club, the farm, jet service, construction, advertising, management, the house, or promotion. Narvel and the others at Starstruck keep me up-to-date on what's going on. I'm proud to have such a team.

❧

THAT'S NOT TO SUGGEST THAT WE NEVER RUN INTO ANY PROBLEMS. Sometimes we play what we in the business call "unusual dates," performing under low ceilings on small stages without enough room to set up our regular stage and all our production equipment. But these are usually private parties that pay very well.

Then there are dates that we call challenging! I just had one of those at the end of 1993. We were scheduled to perform at a Tropicana Twister, a sponsored show in Des Moines, which is a one-hour flight from where I live in Tennessee. Narvel, Sandi, and I left in plenty of time, bringing our friends Ken and Pam Keller and Leigh Reynolds to see our show.

But as we approached Des Moines, the airport tower told us we couldn't land because of the fog. We'd have to land at Ames, Iowa, some forty-five minutes from where we had to play.

It was already 8:15 P.M. and I was scheduled to go on no later than 9:50. So our pilot, Kevin McCutcheon, radioed Des Moines in advance so our limousine could hurry over to Ames to pick us up and take us to Des Moines. When we stepped off the plane, though, there was no limousine in sight.

Rather than waste time, while we waited for the car, Sandi and Pam helped me get ready in the tiny airport's ladies room. Sandi had my first outfit on the plane—usually she packs them in the wardrobe case, and the crew puts it on the truck. While Sandi heated the curlers, I changed into the outfit that I was going to wear for my first song. She had just rolled my hair up when the limousine arrived, and we had to run outside.

So there I was in curlers, wearing my pajama top to keep the hair spray off my costume, walking out of the bathroom to a small bunch of people who worked there at the airport. Our only delay was me signing autographs—in rollers.

Sandi did my hair by the interior lights, with me sitting in the floor board, as the limousine crept blindly through the fog. Once we arrived, I went straight to the Tropicana Twister meet-and-greet and stepped out on that stage exactly at the tick of 9:50.

DOING OUR OWN BOOKINGS HAS RELIEVED SOME OF THE NEEDLESS pressures my band and I used to endure on tour, but there's no getting around the fact that life on the road is grueling. So anything that brings a laugh is welcomed. I remember once being in Canada on a show with Steve Wariner, when he decided he wanted to show off his skills as a magician backstage after soundcheck.

"I'll need a volunteer," he said. "Do I have a volunteer?

"Thank you," he continued, and pulled me from my seat.

I hadn't raised my hand.

I got up there and he said, "Abracadabra." He pulled a brassiere out from behind me to make people think he had magically removed mine. Everybody broke up laughing. It was a simple joke, but typical of the kind of innocent humor that helps pass the time on tour.

But other jokes are much more elaborate and carefully planned. One of the most complicated and funniest tricks was the one Kix Brooks and Ronnie Dunn of Brooks and Dunn's band and mine played on each other.

As part of his act, lead singer Ronnie Dunn would throw his electric guitar offstage to his waiting road manager Eric Shinault. But one night Eric backed off the five-foot stage in the darkness and sprained his wrist. Galen Henson, my guitar tech, offered to stand in for Eric, and over the next month others from both organizations took turns. It got to be a game—each night's catcher would be judged by a panel of his peers, who would hold up scorecards rating him. Members of both organizations would cheer and boo the judges' decisions. I can't imagine what fans sitting close to the stage could have thought was going on.

Each night's score was entered into our road computer. My organization was beating the competition—until the night the guitar was stolen.

The catcher was robbed at gunpoint (fake, we later learned) by a man disguised in a long coat, sunglasses, and a black hood. For a few nights, there was no news of the missing instrument, and Dunn even had to do two or three shows with another guitar.

Of course, the robbery was all we could talk about. Someone said that Dunn had played that guitar for years and that it had sentimental value. Someone else thought it was the guitar that Dunn had brought with him when he moved from Tulsa to Nashville. Naturally, Brooks and Dunn's people blamed the theft on mine.

Soon Eric came to Graeme Lagden, my tour manager, and said it was time to cut off the silliness. "Where is that guitar?" he asked.

Graeme didn't know for sure, but he had heard rumors that the "thief" was John Markham, who ran the laser equipment for me. So Graeme approached Markham and suggested that he send Eric a ransom note along with one string from the guitar. Markham loved the idea and constructed several notes by cutting letters from magazine pages, in true kidnapper style, starting, "If you ever want to see your guitar again . . ." The notes were bolstered by midnight calls to Eric's hotel room, when an anonymous person would say, "We've got your guitar," and then hang up.

The first ransom demand was three of Brooks's expensive cowboy hats. Eric agreed to pay with hats but secretly went to Kmart and bought some cheap hats to pass off as the real thing. Then the guitarnapper upped the ante to include a batch of autographed pictures.

By the day of our next show, Eric was starting to think that his job was on the line. So he called Graeme, saying, "Hey, I've done my part. I've got the hats and the autographed pictures. I *want* that guitar."

"It will be there [at showtime]," Graeme insisted. "It will be there, don't worry."

But Eric did worry, and so, probably, did Dunn.

Graeme had made a secret arrangement with my rigger, Matt Jumper, the guy who oversees the hanging of the stage lights and other equipment. And so while Dunn was walking onto the stage barehanded, his lost guitar was dropping slowly from the front lighting truss, and it arrived at Dunn's microphone at the exact same time Dunn did. Ronnie reached up through the guitar strap, slipped the guitar on and hit his first note.

My guys made a videotape of Dunn's startled face as his guitar dropped from the sky. They still watch it a lot for laughs. The crowd that night probably thought the stunt was Brooks and Dunn's great opening, never suspecting that Dunn's dramatic opening was totally unplanned—unplanned by him, that is.

⚜

"THIS WAS THE ACTIVITY OF MEN WITHOUT REAL JOBS," ERIC SAYS.

CHAPTER 14

SOMETHING WAS SHIFTING INSIDE OF ME. MAYBE THE REASON was my new freedom as an unmarried woman—for the first time in my life, not having to answer to anyone but myself; or maybe it was the sense of confidence that came from restructuring my organization and putting some of my long-held pet ideas into practice. Whatever the reason, in 1988, I found myself drawn to the old Aretha Franklin hit "Respect." It just seemed to connect with my mental outlook at the time.

Jimmy Bowen, my producer, was surprised when I told him I was wanting to use the song as the opening number of my new 1988 show.

"Really," Bowen said, "I wouldn't have thought you'd like 'Respect.' "

"Oh shoot," I said, "I've been listening to Aretha Franklin, Frankie Valli, Fabian, Annette Funicello on 'American Bandstand' all of my life. It's nothing unusual for me to think that 'Respect' is a great song."

"Well, you know that we need some up-tempo songs for the album," he said. "Why don't you record it for the album?"

And so we did. It's on my 1988 LP *Reba*.

I was so pleased with the results that I decided to sing "Respect" on the 1988 CMA Awards show, one of country music's biggest events of the year. I knew it would be totally different from anything I'd ever done on the program. And since I was almost positive I wasn't going to win an award that night, I wanted to be sure I was mentioned in the next day's newspapers. I thought I could get publicity from performing "Respect."

To perform the song, I wore a tight, black leather outfit that was a dramatic change from the formal gowns that I'd always worn for the awards. But I wanted a different look because the song itself was so unusual for me. My backup singers, Yvonne Hodges and Suzy Wills, and I spent a lot of time on the choreography, under the direction of Chris Dunbar. We were extremely serious about pulling off the song well.

I knew that our performance would get a reaction, but I never expected that it would be so strong. I quickly learned that a lot of people in the music business disliked not only the production but even the idea of my doing "Respect." My collaborator, Tom Carter, was there that night, and remembers one of the old-timers saying, "Is this the CMA Awards or is this 'Soul Train'?"

But the day after the awards, there we were! A color picture in the Nashville newspaper. I didn't win an award, but I made the papers.

Many country fans tell me to my face what they like and dislike about my music and show. They send their opinions by mail if they can't see me personally. They can be so painfully honest. I remember that after I played in Vince Gill's golf tournament, two twelve-year-old girls told me that the shorts I wore made my legs look too scrawny.

There was nothing I could do about that, of course, but my

fans always know that I'll listen to their criticism. If I get a suggestion that's constructive, I use it. So I wasn't surprised to hear a lot of fan reaction to "Respect."

Shortly after my 1988 album containing "Respect" and the 1940s torch song "Sunday Kind of Love" was released, I played a show in Connecticut. Carol Scott, who had been a huge fan and good friend for a long time, was upset before she heard a note of my new material. When she came up to me before the show, she unhappily said, "Oh, you've left country [music]. You're leaving us."

I stayed very calm.

"Now, Carol, you watch the show," I told her. " 'Respect' is in it, and so is 'Sunday Kind of Love.' After the show, you tell me what you think."

We performed that night in a theater-in-the-round. Afterward, Carol came backstage and was kind enough to say, "I'll never doubt you again."

I hugged her neck and thanked her. But, honest to God, I never thought that my recording "Respect" and "Sunday Kind of Love" would upset some of my fans so much. I had never thought that anybody would accuse me, of all people, of leaving country music. Stretching out a little is good for any artist, and I appreciate my fans' open-mindedness and support when, now and then, I want to try new things.

⁓

THERE WAS AN EVEN STRONGER AND MORE CONFUSING SHIFT IN MY emotions during this time. Without ever expecting it or even wanting to feel that way, I had been finding myself drawing closer to Narvel. I had always trusted him and was excited to find our ideas so much in sync, especially now, during the renewal of my organization. But in the seven years we'd been working and traveling together, I had never before thought of him romantically.

Narvel is a very good-looking man. From the first night he played with us at that VFW hall in Nowata, Oklahoma, it was obvious that many women were staring at him. He used to sit over his steel guitar, concentrating, with his chin down. Then he'd raise his head, smile, make eye contact, and roll his shoulders to the music. The women loved it, which was just fine with me. My philosophy has always been, I don't care who the audience is looking at, just as long as they're looking at the stage.

Now, I had eyes, of course, and I could see what all those women were appreciating. But Narvel was married, and so was I. And even if I hadn't been, I was still Narvel's boss. He was the cornerstone of my organization, and it would have been crazy for me to jeopardize our business relationship.

Nor—to be fair—had Narvel ever taken the slightest interest in me. He saw me as his employer, not as a female, and worse, he always thought I was a country bumpkin and a hick.

Over the years of traveling together I'd listened to Narvel's stories of his road adventures as a teenage steel player, of his colorful ancestors, and of his fundamentalist upbringing. Although today his parents, Narvel Leroy and Gloria Alexander Blackstock, are more liberal, when he was growing up, their church's teachings were much more strict. They didn't believe in commercializing Christmas, so Narvel never had a Christmas tree. He was forbidden to participate in sports events, go to roller rinks and bowling alleys, and of course he was barred from anywhere alcohol was served. Since their church didn't believe in it, his parents never owned a television, so Narvel didn't have one until after he got married. At school, when the kids would say something like, "Did you see Andy Griffith last night on TV?" Narvel would say no, but he wouldn't say why. He didn't want his classmates to make fun of the beliefs of the parents he loved. So he kept quiet.

He was that sensitive and loyal, even then.

He never saw a motion picture until he was fourteen, when I

guess he got a sense of why the church objected to them! He was working one weekend with a gospel group. One of the guys, Ray Burdet, used to sing backup with Loretta Lynn. Well, Ray took Narvel to see *Carnal Knowledge,* the Jack Nicholson classic that was so controversial back then because it had a scene showing Ann-Margret's breasts. Telling about it, Narvel would laugh and say, "I knew this was the life for me."

And I loved to hear Narvel's mother tell the story about his great-great-grandfather Isaac Shelby Hurst, who must have been about as eccentric as my Pap McEntire. Back then, few people had insurance of any kind, so Isaac was insulted when his children took out a burial policy on him. To prove that he could afford his own funeral, he went to the bank and withdrew all of his money, and bought himself a casket. He hid the money that was left over, but he told no one where.

As he lay dying, he called for Marion, his son, promising to tell him where he had hidden his money. But when Marion arrived Isaac announced that he had changed his mind. He then went to sleep, eased into a coma, and died.

The family searched everywhere for that money, even inside the lining of his casket, without success.

So, Mama Blackstock, Narvel's great-grandmother, started seeking advice from fortune-tellers. One told her that the money was buried near a body of water, and the whole town set about combing the five bodies of water—a creek, a pond, and three wells—on the 200-acre farm.

Nothing.

A second fortune-teller told Mama Blackstock that the money was hidden inside the house and could be found in a wall so many boards up from the floor. Back home, Mama Blackstock checked the spot and spied a place where the boards were loose. Wedging her hand inside, sure enough, she touched paper. The money was hidden near a cistern, an aboveground well. So the first fortune-teller had been right after all.

Mama Blackstock pulled two grocery sacks full of cash out of that wall, then walked them across a field to the bank. She just told the banker to count the money and deposit it, not even asking the amount. Narvel's people were as trusting as they were trustworthy.

I could see where he got his traits.

❦

THROUGHOUT THE UNHAPPY UNRAVELING OF MY MARRIAGE AND INTO my early, unsure days of being alone, Narvel was my anchor, always there to say, "Don't worry about it, I'll take care of this." That dependability and devotion from him perhaps inevitably sparked some response in me. When you like and admire somebody like that, love starts growing in there too.

But it would take a long time for us to come together, and almost as long to recognize what was happening between us.

It's funny, thinking about it now. In some ways I believe we went out of our way to keep our distance. For example, I've never been much of a fan of public displays of affection. I'm a lot like Daddy in that respect. Unless I know a person pretty well, a handshake will do just fine. But I'll hug a buddy in a heartbeat. A lot of my old band members and I would give each other a hug, in greeting and good-bye, coming on and off the road, or maybe when a gig had gone especially well, but me and Narvel—never.

Narvel did hug me once, in 1986, when I won "Entertainer of the Year," but that was completely platonic. I was there with Charlie, he was there with his wife Lisa, Mama and Daddy were there, and Pake and Katy—we were all just hugging with joy. So except for that one time, Narvel and I were totally unaffectionate with each other.

When we did finally connect, it was with a kiss, nothing more, and it was totally unplanned. We were on tour. As Narvel recalls, "I think we kissed a couple times, and everybody came back on the bus, and everything went back to the way it was before. And when we all went to bed, Reba went to her stateroom and I went to my bunk. I was really nervous and confused. I was thinking, 'Wait a minute, what happened? Did that really happen?'

" 'Why did we do that?' I wondered first off. I was a very professional person, I didn't believe in mixing business and pleasure. I thought, 'Oh, God, I can't believe this.' And second of all, 'What is she thinking back there now in that stateroom and what is she going to be like tomorrow?' Is she going to be like, 'I regret what I did'? And how is she going to treat me?"

At the time, I was in the process of my drawn-out breakup with Charlie, a few months away from actually filing for divorce. But I want to say right now that Narvel Blackstock didn't break up my marriage and I didn't break up his. Both marriages had been in trouble for a long time. His situation was equally sad, and the timing of our troubles was so regrettably and uncomfortably close, it was awkward. And for this reason, in fact, I made it a point to keep Narvel from finding out that I intended to leave Charlie for good. I knew that Narvel was very unhappy at home, and had told Lisa that he wanted to separate. He had even told her that he was going to move to Nashville to work with Bill Carter.

"Lisa and I had a major, major confrontation," Narvel remembers. "I told her that I didn't feel like I loved her, and that I wanted to do something different. She cried all day long.

"It wasn't like I was leaving because of Reba, because in my mind the kissing was a thing that had happened for her because she was restless at home. I had been going through that for years, so I knew where my head was. But Reba had never gone through it. We had been on the road for three weeks, and it was such a little thing that happened. Once she got back home, she was going to get back to reality. Charlie always had such control over her. I just felt that's what would happen."

So in a telephone conversation the week after I played Lubbock, when Bill Carter told him that I had filed for divorce in Tulsa, Narvel was dumbfounded.

"It was a very difficult time for me from a couple of different standpoints," Narvel recalls. "Number one, at that point, I was way more involved in a professional career than I ever had been before, because Charlie was not there anymore. Even though Bill Carter was still the manager, I was the major input to him. And Bill didn't come out on the road, so Reba was my responsibility at that point, totally. And it was awkward because Charlie and I had been buddies."

So I had to tell Narvel straight out, "This is what I wanted to do in my life, for myself. I didn't divorce Charlie because of you."

I certainly didn't expect or want him to leave his wife for me. While some intense feelings had been ignited in us, if we were meant to get together, it would have to be a free choice, not some impossible rebound situation. And in the midst of my divorce, I could hardly imagine marrying again. Even if the thought of it had crossed my mind, I would never have considered marrying another man with children. I had already been through that with Charlie.

For his part, Narvel in turn recalls, "At first I thought that my plan was to get a divorce and I thought that mine and Reba's relationship would probably end. And I needed to be thinking in terms of going to Nashville and completely starting over with my own career. I felt real insecure about our relationship. I thought, 'This is a suicide mission.' That's the best description for how I was feeling."

So Narvel went to Lisa and told her he had changed his mind, that maybe they could work things out. But as he says, "I was living as an unhappy person," and so the effort to make up didn't work. Narvel wound up in divorce court himself four months later, in October 1987.

My own divorce was just about final, and there were folks who wanted to make something out of Narvel's timing. Even as recently as the summer of 1993, a tabloid newspaper carried a big interview with Lisa. The story strongly implied I was a home wrecker, something neither my heart nor the facts support. The truth is that once Narvel realized that he and Lisa weren't going to be able to work things out, he delayed filing for divorce as long as possible. He wanted to avoid giving the impression that our divorces were related, when in fact both marriages had been dying for years. Their funerals just happened to come a few months apart.

IT TOOK A FULL NINE MONTHS BEFORE NARVEL AND I DECIDED THAT we truly wanted to be a couple. Looking back, I'm not sure there was any one thing that decided it. Our whole relationship had been a growth process. I think Narvel and I became fans of each other.

As he says, "We were both fighting for a goal, and anybody who really knew me, including my ex-wife, knew how hard I'd worked and how badly I wanted it. I think Reba was the only other person who wanted it that bad. I think over a period of time Reba changed, I changed, and we became real good business buddies. We never had any romantic involvement at all, but when it happened, it happened."

We had a lot of great times together. One of those was on a trip to Wisconsin, when our whole group—band and crew—had some time off so we were gonna have a retreat in Oshkosh between dates. But on the way, Larry Jones started sweating and shaking so bad that I told Narvel to take over driving the bus. When Larry became delirious, we stopped and checked him into a hospital, where the doctors found that his appendix was inflamed and enlarged. He had to have emergency surgery. Sheri,

Narvel, and I checked in to a hotel so we could stay close and check on Larry daily.

Right outside the hospital, there was this beautiful little lake. So the next day Narvel and I packed a picnic basket, then drove the bus over and rented a small boat. We rowed across the lake—I was at one end of the boat and Narvel was at the other. I looked up and his face was just covered with sweat! It was about one hundred degrees that day, and here the sweat was running into his eyes. I just about died laughing —and Narvel just about died of heatstroke! Some little romantic moment that was!

But our romance did take off, and in May 1988, we bought a condominium together. It was there that we celebrated our first Christmas together, just the two of us, before we set off for our respective families' homes in Texas and Oklahoma.

Back home in Oklahoma, we had always gone to the pasture and cut a cedar for our Christmas tree, which my family and I decorated with the same Christmas ornaments we'd had since we were babies. But for our first Christmas, Narvel and I bought a beautiful blue spruce tree, which we had flocked. I had never had a flocked Christmas tree before. Narvel wrapped the branches with lights, and we tied bows to hang on its branches, along with beautiful, clear glass balls. It was the most glorious tree I had ever helped create.

The night we trimmed the tree was very special. We had a glass of wine, a fire, and soft Christmas music, and we took turns opening our gifts. I couldn't wait to give Narvel his presents, but he insisted, "You go first." He handed me a big box. Inside it was an Igloo ice chest, and at the bottom there were a couple of telephone books. I was pretty confused until I saw the note that read: "This one isn't it, go to the next one."

Narvel opened my first gift to him, a cellular telephone, and then it was my turn again. I got another large box—and another note! We kept taking turns, until finally I opened a box that had a smaller box inside. Within that one was a smaller box. Then another. And another.

The smallest box held a beautiful marquise diamond engagement ring.

What a romantic way to propose! When that man wants to do a production, he does a production!

❦

WE'D NEVER REALLY TALKED ABOUT GETTING MARRIED, AND I WASN'T sure that either of us even wanted to ever again. Still, we were certainly moving in the direction of permanence. By January 1989, we were talking about buying a house, perhaps a place on the water with some acreage. Linda DeMith was my hairdresser then, and since I figured hairdressers knew everyone and everything that was happening, I asked her about it. It only took her about half an hour to come up with a lead in Gallatin, a suburb of Nashville.

Narvel and I drove out late that afternoon to see the place. It was marked by two rock columns, which looked like somebody had started to build a fence. We drove between the columns across a cattle guard and kept going down an old road with chuckholes in it, hedged in by tall brush. Things didn't look promising—and then suddenly a four-story, red brick house rose up in front of us. It overlooked the Cumberland River and was ringed by giant oaks. It was impressive, but I was more taken by the geese that were swimming next to it in the cove.

When Narvel and I got inside, we noticed that the current owner used only three of the many rooms because she lived by herself. Most of the windows were covered with thick curtains that hid the river view. The decorating was not exactly my style —big, ornate swans for water faucets, velvet wallpaper flecked with gold, velvet and satin draperies. But as we walked around, Narvel got really inspired.

"We can take out this wall," he'd say. "We can add a window here."

By the time we finished looking, we were in love with the place. And when our realtor, Francis Almany, told us we could get the two adjoining tracts of land, we were sold. There was a lot of remodeling needed so we couldn't move in for a year. But that was the one and only house that Narvel and I ever looked at.

I guess you could say that I'm not a very romantic person, because on Valentine's Day in 1989 I bought Narvel a chain saw! He gave me a beautiful tennis bracelet. Narvel and I would go out to the place and help clear the land with the chain saw while the workers were on the bulldozers. At first we were working away but not getting very much done until we finally figured out that we had the chain on backward. But we had a lot of fun.

We totally gutted the house, rebuilding it from the inside out, with the help of an architect, Manuel Zietland. He designed a large bedroom for us, with two walls of windows overlooking the river, as well as specific rooms for Narvel's children, Brandon, Shawna, and Chassidy to stay in when they came to visit. Adjoining our suite was the room that would become Shelby's later on.

Anyone who's ever been through building or remodeling a house with someone else knows that it's a very tough thing to do. So, of course, Narvel and I argued through it all. For instance, we'd go into a paint and wallpaper store, look at the color chips and through the books, and before long we'd be out on the sidewalk, shouting at each other. Then we'd say, "Okay, we can do this, we're adults. Let's go back in." And so we would. Then I would ask, "What do you think of this?" And Narvel would make a face.

"You don't have to make a face," I would say. "If you don't like it, just say it."

"Okay, I don't like it," Narvel would say. And the fight would be back on.

We struggled to pick out doorknobs, windows, trims, faucets, bathtubs, doors, lighting fixtures—all of it. Having worked together for so long, we thought we knew each other. Yet we're still, to this day, very different people. Narvel says there's not an impractical bone in my body, and not a practical one in his. But we also both understand the importance of compromise in a relationship so we made an agreement. If I liked something and he didn't, we passed. If he liked something and I didn't, we passed. The only time we bought anything was when we both agreed on it.

Throughout the process I had always felt kind of "distant" to the house. But when I finally saw it with its red bricks painted the soft buttercup yellow we'd chosen, I cried. I just loved it.

Next we got to decorate it—which could have come close to setting off a reprise of our paint-and-wallpaper battles. Where I tend toward simplicity, Narvel wanted decorating schemes that I thought were just a little bit elaborate. But we worked it out.

While we were touring in 1989, Narvel and I shopped for furniture in almost every city we played. We'd finish our show, get on the bus, and Larry would drive us through the night to the next town for our performance. He would sleep during the day so Narvel would drive himself and me around town looking for the best furniture stores. He got pretty good at maneuvering that big, forty-foot bus around parking lots! We found pieces in Phoenix and Los Angeles, and got Chassidy's bedroom furniture in Dallas; Shawna's in Fresno, California. I did a live album in 1989 in Palm Desert, California, and sent home furniture from there too. And when we toured England (the bus stayed home) we bought a huge canopy bed that had to be shipped from London.

❧

AROUND THIS TIME, NARVEL CAME UP WITH ANOTHER GREAT IDEA. I had always toured the entire year, playing several dates every month. But now Narvel suggested that we put the show together and record in January, tour in February, March, April, and a little bit in May, take the rest of May and June off (except for Fan Fair), and then begin touring again in July and August. We would work the first week of September and then take the rest of September off. The tour schedule would then resume in October and November, and then about the first week of December, we would quit until we went back and put our new show together.

It was a great plan, one that would give us the chance to have more of a personal life and to enjoy our new home. But before we could put it into practice, taking our first break in May, I got the chance to live out one of my wildest dreams—to get a part in a movie. Of course, I'd been acting in my videos, for five years, and on a number of television specials, but this was my first shot at the big screen.

When I first signed with William Morris in 1982, I had hoped they'd be looking out for television and movie roles for me. But every script I was offered had me as a girl singer in a country band playing in a honky-tonk. I thought, why would I want to be in a movie playing a girl singer when that's what I do for a living?

If I'm going to be in a movie, I want to be in something different! Isn't Hollywood supposed to be about fantasy?

Other kinds of roles did come along. I read the script for *Field of Dreams,* but no one told me that Kevin Costner was going to be in it. While I'm not sorry I didn't do the picture, I think I would back down and play some girl singer if I was singing to him.

That's a joke, Narvel.

Now, finally, I'd gotten a shot at a likely script. John Gaines from the booking agency APA's motion picture department sent it to me. "Read it, you'll love it," he said.

Tremors was sort of a science-fiction/horror film, only funny.

As the press release later described it, "Kevin Bacon and Fred Ward star as two country handymen who lead a cast of zany characters to safety in this exciting sci-fi creature comedy. Just as they decide to leave Perfection, Nevada, strange rumblings prevent their departure. They discover their desolate town is infested with gigantic man-eating creatures that live below the ground.

"The race is on to overcome these slimy subterraneans and find a way to higher ground in this enjoyable thriller . . ."

John was right. I did love it and I really wanted to read for the director, Ron Underwood, so the next day I called John back. He had already set it up.

Auditioning is hard. You have to read for a group of people who just sit around listening silently. You can't tell what they're thinking, and it makes you self-conscious to have all that attention on you.

When I finished, Ron said to me, "Now, you know this picture is going to be shot in the desert."

"I figured that, that's what the script said," I answered.

"Well," he continued, "you're going to get dirty, you won't have any makeup on. You'll have your hair pulled back."

"Yeah, I know," I said.

"Well, isn't that going to bother you?" he asked.

"No," I said, wondering if he was trying to talk me out of the part.

I guess he didn't know how I was brought up! All he knew were my publicity pictures with the makeup and big hairdos.

I wound up having to read a couple more times, once for the executive producer, Gale Ann Hurd, before I was told I had the part. Filming began in May 1989.

It was pretty rough! It was so cold on the set in the mornings that I needed a heater in my trailer and hot enough for an air conditioner in the afternoons. I had neither. My trailer was a little room that had a tiny table for my makeup. There was a couch and a partition that hid a toilet that smelled. At night, we all stayed in motels in Long Pine, California.

But the movie itself had a great story, and the cast was *great.* Besides Kevin Bacon and Fred Ward, it featured Finn Carter and Michael Gross, who played my husband. As Richard Schickel said in *Time* magazine, "It's in the tradition of the 50's horror movies. *Tremors* is bound to become a classic!"

Not a bad way to launch a movie career. . . .

CHAPTER 15

I DON'T KNOW THAT NARVEL AND I REALLY WOULD HAVE EVER gotten married if I didn't have such a strong urge to have a baby. Up until then I had reconciled to myself that I would never have a child. That was because of Charlie. Charlie had his two boys from a previous marriage, and he wasn't about to go to any extra trouble to make a place for kids in our life. "If you have children, you don't sing," Charlie had told me. "I'm not going to be cleaning shitty diapers while you're off on the road."

And Charlie didn't want to share me with a child. When I was in love with him I took his attitude as a compliment. Later, I was so thankful that I never had a baby with him.

But my relationship with Narvel was so different, and I found myself longing to have a baby with him. And so finally Narvel and I began to talk seriously about marriage.

After my first week shooting *Tremors,* he came out to meet me in Southern California. I toured on weekends throughout the shooting, and he planned to accompany me to our concert date. So we were sitting in the Los Angeles airport when Narvel asked, "What do you think about us getting married in Lake Tahoe?"

I loved the idea but wondered how we could get both of our families to Lake Tahoe. Then I got a brainstorm: "Let's figure out how many American Airlines Advantage miles we have between us," I said.

We called our travel agent and, sure enough, we had enough mileage credit between us to send almost all of our family members round-trip to Reno, where our bus would pick them up and take them to Lake Tahoe. Our list included: Narvel's children, Brandon, Chassidy, Shawna and her boyfriend, Jeff; Narvel's mom and dad; his sister, Patricia, and her husband, Dan Law, and their three kids, Jeff, Jan, and Kim; my parents; Pake's wife, Katie, and their three children, Autumn, Calamity, and Chism; and my sister, Alice, and her husband, Robert, with their children, Trevor, Garett, and Vince. Susie and Pake were working and couldn't come.

The week before the wedding, Mama flew out to be with me on the set of *Tremors* in Lone Pine, California. After filming that week, we left together on Thursday and drove to Lake Tahoe. On the way, we stopped at Yosemite National Park, which I had always wanted to see. We had a great time. It was so special to get to do that with her. It wasn't until I had Shelby that I understood the depth of Mama's love for me. It wasn't measurable!

Then Mama and I went on to Lake Tahoe to meet Narvel, while our families arrived later that night, having flown in to Reno. I had been booked to perform at Caesars Palace, and they all came to watch the show. Then the next afternoon at two o'clock, we all boarded two of our buses and went to Zephyr Cove, loaded onto a catamaran, and crossed the lake to Emerald Bay.

Although it was June 3, it was so cold you would have thought it was the middle of November. I wore a simple white cotton, long-sleeved summer dress. Everyone else had worn thin summer clothing too, which offered little warmth against the wind coming off the lake. Some of us huddled in blankets and others stayed below. The sun came out as Narvel and I said our wedding vows on Lake Tahoe's beautiful Emerald Bay. If you ever get the chance, go see it! Dan Collier, from Nashville, performed our simple ceremony, and his wife, Kathy, was there as well.

Afterward, we had a wedding toast and ate the wonderful food provided by Caesars. Then we headed back across the lake to the hotel.

I did my first show and later we had our reception, catered by Caesars Palace and attended by my band, crew, and both families. I did a second show and then Narvel and I put our families back on the bus for Reno. They flew out of Nevada about six o'clock in the morning.

That much activity would kill me if I had to do it today—but I was young back then.

After the wedding, we returned to Nashville and to the annual "Music City News" awards show, televised over The Nashville Network. I won "Female Vocalist of the Year," and when I went to the press conference after the show, I held up my wedding ring. That was my first official announcement that Narvel and I had gotten married.

Our honeymoon had to be postponed until I finished shooting *Tremors,* and Narvel joined me on the set for the last few days.

On the final day of filming, we were just winding up our dinner break when someone walked onto the set, waving at me. I waved back, and as the person got closer I was thinking, "Man, that guy looks like Narvel." Well, it was Narvel! I hadn't recognized my own husband!

"What have you done?" I asked.

"I was bored in the room," he said, "so I shaved off my beard. We'll be gone for a week on our honeymoon and I just wanted to see how I would look without it. How do you like it?"

"Put it back!" I said.

He started growing it back the next day, and he hasn't shaved it since.

꧁꧂

THEN WE WERE OFF TO CANCÚN, MEXICO, FOR OUR HONEYMOON. I had always heard that you shouldn't drink the water south of the border. We wanted to be very careful so Narvel drank Diet Coke and I drank bottled water. But one night when we went out to a show—a very nice theatrical production with mariachi bands and dancers—I drank a margarita. Later that night I started feeling queasy; and I figured that the ice in the margarita was to blame. Even the thought of food made me ill, which was very unusual for me. I'm almost always hungry!

By the next day I was sicker, and Narvel was feeling queasy too, so we had to put off our planned drive to see some ruins a couple of hours away. We just didn't think we could risk not having a bathroom close by. When my stomach trouble persisted, we decided it would be best to cut short our trip and return to the States.

Back home in Nashville, I discovered that I wasn't suffering from Montezuma's Revenge after all. I'll never forget the excitement of the moment when, sitting on the edge of the bathtub in our condominium, I saw the white dot on the home pregnancy tester turn bright pink.

I was pregnant deader than a hammer! There was no doubt about it.

Narvel was at the sink, grooming his new beard, when I cried out to him, "Narvel—I'm going to have a baby!"

He came over, looked at the pink dot, and leaned down and hugged my neck. I was so touched that I cried.

That afternoon, as we were flying out to do a show, I called Mama from a pay phone at the Nashville airport to tell her I was pregnant. She was thrilled, of course, and Gloria, Narvel's mother, was too. Both mothers agreed not to spread the news for a while so we could have the chance to tell the people in our band and our organization personally. Also, I wanted to make sure everything was okay before we announced my pregnancy. I was thirty-four at the time.

I didn't have a doctor in Nashville then. Dr. Darius Maggi, my gynecologist, who had also delivered most of the children of my sisters Alice and Susie, was in Denison, Texas, too far away to allow for regular prenatal visits. So once again I turned to my hairdresser, Breon Reynolds, and also to Kathy Collier, the wife of the minister who had married us, to ask for advice. It was through Kathy that I got an appointment with Dr. John Van Hooydonk.

At my first appointment, he said to me, "Now, Reba, you're thirty-four years old. If you had an amniocentesis and found out that something was wrong with this baby, would you have an abortion?"

"No," I said instantly.

"Okay," he said. "I'll be your doctor."

"You wouldn't be my doctor if I had said I was going to have an abortion?" I asked.

"No," he said. "I couldn't do that."

"Okay," I said. "I'll be your patient."

Not everyone would agree with the doctor's point of view or with mine, and they're entitled to their opinion. But I felt glad to have a doctor who stuck to his beliefs and had the integrity to come right out and tell me where he stood. I respected that.

That integrity made me feel sure that it wasn't Dr. Van Hooydonk who leaked the fact of my pregnancy to the press. That very same night, I was shocked to see my picture on the ten o'clock news, and to hear the broadcaster say that I was going to have a baby. I didn't like the invasion of privacy, of course, but I mostly resented losing the chance to announce the upcoming birth of my first child myself. Still, the news leak was just a small cloud on our joy.

I loved being pregnant! Every bit of it!

I continued to tour for the rest of 1989 and finished on December 3 in Orlando, Florida, where Alice and Mama joined us for the weekend. It was Alice's birthday, so Jim Hammon, our tour manager, and the band joined Narvel, Alice, Mama, and me in my beautiful green dressing room, where I presented Alice with her birthday cake. At one point, I looked over at my band leader, Kirk Capello, and he was laughing.

"What are you laughing at?" I said mischievously.

Then I smeared cake all over his face.

The next thing I knew, we were in a food fight. Cake wound up all over the carpet and walls! We were having a blast! It had been a great year, with a great bunch of people to work with! Something like that might not happen in one of our homes, but when you're on the road, the kid comes out in all of us.

I had to apologize to the proprietor, and I was asked to pay rent on the room, probably for cleanup. I haven't been allowed to use that dressing room since! I really can't blame them.

When I got back to Nashville on December 4 and went in for my regular prenatal exam, Dr. Van Hooydonk told me my cervix had thinned considerably. Although my due date was March 8, Narvel's dad's birthday, more than three months away, I was already having minor contractions.

"You'll have to take it easy or we'll have to take more drastic measures," he said.

Of course, I got worried. "Can I go to Oklahoma to spend Christmas with my family?" I asked. "Or would that be too risky?"

Dr. Van Hooydonk said that I could go, but only if I promised to lie flat on my back in the bus all the way from Nashville to Oklahoma. So I did that for the entire 1,400 miles round-trip and stayed off my feet the whole time I was home too.

Larry Jones drove us out there, since his family lived in Duncan, Oklahoma. I hadn't been on my bus for a while because we had leased a plane to get to my November and December dates. As I lay in the stateroom relaxing and listening to some demo tapes, I told Narvel how much I had missed my bus. After a few hours of talking and listening to tapes, I headed up front, thinking as I walked through the front curtains that surely we'd be almost to Little Rock.

"We just passed Jackson, Tennessee," Larry said.

"Good Lord," I said. "We'd already be asleep in the hotel if we had flown!"

So much for missing the bus!

But for all my precautions, when I returned to Nashville I was put in the hospital twice, since I was still having contractions. After my second admission they sent me home with a little syringe, activated by a pump I carried in my shirt pocket, which was attached to a tube that ran to my stomach. It would pump a small amount of medicine into my stomach to stop the contractions. Then, every three days, I had to go to the doctor's office where nurses would change the needle in my stomach.

It was a painful ritual. But I would have hung by my toes from the ceiling if it meant having a healthy baby.

Staying in bed all that time did have two positive effects: one, it gave me the chance to listen to my intuition. I had been having that "feeling" again, that sixth sense that has exhibited more wisdom to me than anyone's mind, including my own. I still think that small feeling I get is really the whisper of God.

What I was getting the feeling about was Jimmy Bowen. I was scheduled to record with him January 16, 1990, but I was in the hospital with pregnancy problems at the time. And what the feeling was telling me was that I had to find a "logical" reason to tell Bowen, the president of my record label, with whom I'd had the biggest recording successes of my career, that I wanted another producer.

I called Bowen and asked him to come by my condominium on Hillsboro Road. When he arrived we made small talk about my size and about how the baby would be a boy. And then, since I hadn't come up with my reason, I just decided to blurt it out, without explanation: "I think we have been together long enough," I said. "I think I need to get someone different to produce me."

"I agree with you one hundred percent," he said, "and I'll work to find you another producer."

That's all the discussion we had—it was that quick and that easy.

I called him later and told him I'd interview Randy Scruggs, Garth Fundis, and Tony Brown. I eventually settled on Tony Brown, with whom I would record *Rumor Has It* in 1990, *For My Broken Heart* and *It's Your Call* in 1991 and 1992, and *Greatest Hits Vol. II* in 1993. Each album, as of this writing, has sold more than two million copies, and each continues to sell.

The "feeling" had steered me right, once again.

Two, I couldn't do much of anything except lay in bed, read, watch TV and listen to demo tapes. The latter is what I did most. I found some wonderful songs for the next recording session. We would later call that album *Rumor Has It*.

❧

IT WASN'T UNTIL FEBRUARY 1990 THAT MY DOCTOR TOLD ME I COULD start going back to a more normal routine. "If you have the baby now, it will be fine," he assured me. Although I still had fourteen days before my due date, the baby's lungs were developed and he would be strong even if he came a little early. I was so relieved! And after spending most of two months flat on my back, I was definitely ready for a change. During this whole time, I had only left our condominium to go to the clinic for my treatment, except for Saturdays when I got to go out to the new house.

So on Thursday, February 23, I went out shopping, but I got so tired that I had to go back to the condo and lay down. I remember calling Mama to tell her how tired I was. She said, "That's how it is, close to the birth of a baby." Little did we know how close I was!

Later that day, Narvel and I went out to the new house, which was fast becoming filled with our new furniture. While Narvel, Tom, and Gretta, our groundskeeper and housekeeper, were trying to lay down a beautiful Persian rug under the dining room table, someone said something funny; and when I laughed I kind of felt I might have had a little accident.

I went, "Oops! Excuse me," and waddled into the kitchen bathroom, and when I got up, I noticed that the water in the toilet looked sort of milky. Could that mean that my water had broken?

Excitedly, I called out to Narvel. "Look at this!" I said. "What is it?"

He came in and looked but he was no help.

"I don't know."

Three children, and he still didn't know what was happening? Narvel's excuse was that all of them had been delivered by cesarean section.

I called the doctor and described the milky liquid. He confirmed that my water *had* broken.

"Come to the hospital now," he said.

I'm amazed that I stayed so calm as I said, "Okay."

As Narvel and I set out on the thirty-five-mile trip to Nashville's West Side Hospital, I started getting really strong contractions.

I was banging on the window while holding a pencil and paper so I could time the contractions and how long they lasted. Later on I tried to read my notes, but my handwriting was pretty bad. When we hit the interstate, Narvel was driving more than 100 miles per hour, while talking on the car phone to my Mama, telling her that we were on our way to the hospital. Then he called his mother and his children, Chassidy, Brandon, and Shawna.

I was admitted to the hospital at 10 P.M., forty minutes after my water broke. For security reasons, I checked in as Mrs. Narvel Blackstock, with no mention of Reba McEntire. I was shaking real bad as I got out of the car and into the wheelchair. The nurses said I was in shock.

They wheeled me up to the labor and delivery floor, where I exchanged my long maternity sweater, white maternity pants, and tennis shoes for a hospital gown. Then I was put into bed. I had my baby in that same bed, in the same room, and didn't leave it for two days.

It was wonderful to have a private birthing room so Narvel could stay with me when the baby came. I had insisted that once he was born, my baby was never to leave my sight without my permission. You've got to understand this was my first baby, and I guess I was pretty overprotective about everything. Everyone was real nice and indulged me.

Dr. Van Hooydonk arrived and began an examination that included placing a prenatal monitor on top of the baby's head. He also put one on my stomach. "This is it," he said. "You're really pretty far along."

Then he turned to Narvel and said, "Let's go have a Coke." "Wow," Narvel thought to himself. "What are we going to get a drink for at a time like this?" When they got downstairs to the cafeteria, Narvel confronted the doctor. "Shouldn't we be upstairs?" he asked. "It could happen any minute."

"Oh no," said the doctor. "It will be at least five hours before the baby is born."

That's the first time Narvel realized it wasn't going to be quick.

But I'd known the whole time that it was going to be painful too, and had agreed earlier to have an epidural. Right before he

Daniel Law

June 3, 1989. Our wedding day.
Top: From left, Narvel's parents,
Narvel Leroy and Gloria Alexander
Blackstock, join Narvel and me
and Mama and Daddy on board a
catamaran. *Second:* My sister Alice
and me down in the hull of the
catamaran. Alice is the rock of us
kids, always there when you need
her. I hope I'm always there for
her too. *Third:* The first shot of
the new family I gained—Narvel
and me with his children. From
left are Brandon, Shawna, and
Chassidy. *Bottom:* The newly-
weds—Mr. and Mrs. Narvel
Blackstock.

Daniel Law

Daniel Law

These are some of my favorite pictures of my son, Shelby, including one in which he isn't pictured—I was seven and a half months pregnant (*left*) with Shelby Steven McEntire Blackstock. *Below:* On Shelby's arrival, February 23, 1990, with Narvel and our doctor John E. Van Hooydonk. *Facing page, top:* The first portrait of Shelby and me. *Bottom right:* I loved giving him his baths. *Bottom left:* Shelby's first time backstage at my show in Houston in 1990.

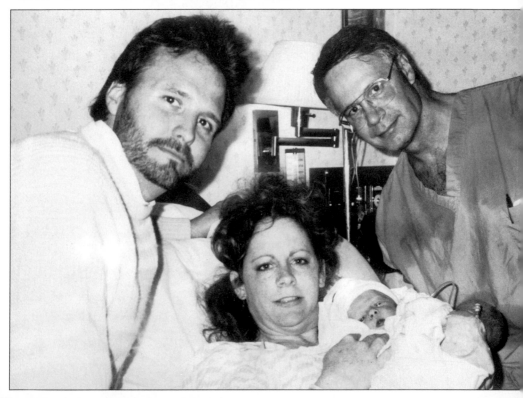

MICAEL-RENEE LIFESTYLES PORTRAITURE

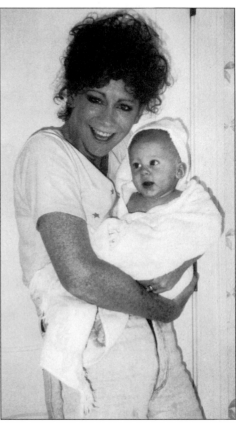

Above: In 1988, Narvel and I formed our own company, Starstruck Entertainment. Today it handles artist management, business management, booking, promotion, advertising, art, publicity, fan clubs, and other businesses we started including construction, jet service, and horse farm. Pictured here are, from left, Trey Turner (management/promotion), Narvel and me, and Mike Allen (management/booking). *Left:* I've always loved horses, and for Christmas 1990 Narvel gave me a beautiful quarterhorse (*left*), which I named Little Bit. *Below:* In 1992, we were totally surprised to find that the jockey of one of our race horses, Western Gentlemen, was one of my high school boyfriends, Rick Wilson. We won that day too! *Facing page, top:* I do at least two videos for each of my albums. Here I'm being "aged" by Jon Cagloine for our 1992 video "The Night the Lights Went Out in Georgia." *Below:* Jon Small, the director of most of my videos, gives me a camera lesson.

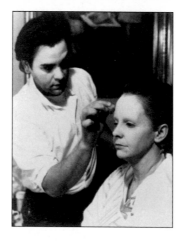

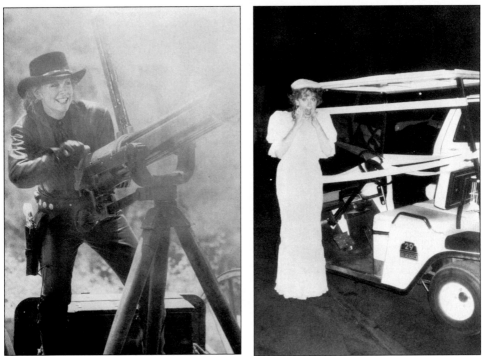

Above left: Right after the crash in 1991, Ken Kragen offered me a part in Kenny Rogers's movie *The Gambler*. I needed the work to get my mind off the tragedy. *Above right:* During filming, I had to take cuts in the food line at dinner so I could be ready for the next scene. Other cast members retaliated (jokingly) by wrapping my golf cart, our means of transportation on the set, with duct tape. *Below right:* I kept Shelby with me a lot of the time during the shooting of *The Gambler*. You can see we're both a little tired. My other films so far include: *Tremors,* 1989 *(below left)*; *The Man from Left Field,* 1993 *(facing page, top)*; and *North, 1993. Facing page, center:* Here I'm on the set of *North* with, from left, Jeff Nicks, my co-pilot, Linda Davis, Kevin McCutcheon, my pilot, Sandi Spika, and a calf that was a gift from Dan Ackroyd and me, in the movie, to *North's* star Elijah Woods's character. *Bottom:* From left, Narvel, Tony Brown, president of MCA, me, and Bruce Hinton, chairman of the board of MCA. In December 1993, Bruce and Tony presented me with my platinum and gold CDs and videos for that year.

LISA SMITH

CINDY OWEN

I've been very fortunate in my life, and I always try to give something back. *Center:* The Reba Ranch House is a home away from home for those with family members hospitalized in the Texoma Medical Center in Denison, Texas. *Left:* Here I am at the groundbreaking ceremony. *Below left:* On the proud day that I cut the ribbon, I was joined by (from left) Darius Maggi, who started the whole thing, Bill Wilcox of the TMC Foundation, and Narvel. *Below right:* I sponsored the first all-women Habitat for Humanity home-building project. From left, Ruth T. Raines, volunteer chairperson, Dianne Baber, senior business development representative of the First American National Bank in Nashville, Jim Crowley, executive director of the Nashville office of Habitat for Humanity, Gayle Kinzer, homeowner, and me.

QUINN STUDIO

took Narvel down for a Coke, Dr. Van Hooydonk tapped my foot. "Hold off on the drugs as long as you can," he said.

Just then another hard contraction hit, and I'm not the least bit ashamed to report that I said, "Ladies, bring on the drugs!" just as the door closed behind them.

In my years growing up I had been thrown, fallen off, and been stepped on by horses, and I kept right on riding. I never let getting hurt affect me. But the pain of childbirth was something else! I figure every woman has her own threshold for pain and mine is pretty high. But this was no time to be a martyr.

Once the drug kicked in, I was like "Hey, no problem!"—I was suddenly having a good time. I couldn't feel the contractions, so the labor nurses had to tell me when I was having them. They knew because of the monitors I was hooked up to. They were just wonderful to me, getting me ice chips and rubbing my shoulders. They never left my side. When Narvel got back, he called his parents again, and I was feeling good enough to casually tell them how far I was dilated. When I handed the telephone back to Narvel, his dad told him I wasn't ready to deliver because I wasn't hurting enough.

He wasn't far wrong. I wouldn't be ready to give birth until 4 A.M. Then the room was filled with nurses, and it was getting really serious. Shelby wouldn't come out. So I said, "Let me roll over." I'd try to move him around. I'd get up on my hands and knees and back on my back, and I'd push some more and still he wouldn't come out. His shoulders were hung on my pelvis bone.

Even though he was a veteran father, Narvel's previous births-by-appointment didn't quite prepare him for the excitement of natural childbirth.

Exactly at 5:04 A.M. on Friday, February 23, my baby son was born. They cut the umbilical cord, and the nurse handed him to Narvel, who carried him to me. I was overcome with joy and began praising and thanking God for my beautiful baby boy. Dr. Van Hooydonk, a very spiritual man, understood perfectly. The birth was a miracle; the most profound spiritual experience I've ever had. I was crying and kissing my baby at the same time.

I've seen my name in letters as tall as a house. I've been toasted by audiences who've seen me on international television. I've won virtually every major award my career offers. I say all of that simply to say this: I've never been as fulfilled as I was when my son was born.

We named him Shelby Steven McEntire Blackstock—Shelby after Narvel's paternal grandpa, Shelby Hershel Blackstock, Steven after my paternal great-grandfather Clark Steven McEntire, McEntire after me, and Blackstock after Narvel.

By 6 A.M., Narvel and I were both exhausted, as much from the emotional as the physical strain of those long hours of labor. So while I had been determined never to allow Shelby out of my sight after he was born, we both said, "You're on your own kid! Take him to the nursery." And we immediately fell fast asleep.

As soon as I woke up, I had them bring him back to me. It's funny, but as every mother knows, what people call "maternal instincts" are real. I knew his cry instinctively. I'd hear other babies and knew they weren't Shelby.

Mama flew in Friday morning to be with me, and Narvel's Dad, Narvel and Mother, Gloria, drove in Saturday. I slept and held Shelby all that day. On Saturday night, the nurses gave us a lovely surprise—they prepared a romantic steak dinner for Narvel and me! We ate by candlelight—blue candlelight actually, in honor of our new baby boy. Narvel drank some wine, and I had grape juice in a wineglass. The next day, I checked out at noon and then Narvel and Mama brought Shelby and me to our semi-settled new house while pictures were taken for a family album.

The three of us were home—grandparents and all! What a lucky little boy.

CHAPTER 16

EVER SINCE THE FIRST MOMENT OF SHELBY'S LIFE, I'VE HATED to be separated from him. I enjoy motherhood. It was something brand new for me, and I'm so glad I waited until I was mature enough to cope with the huge responsibility.

But as much as I enjoyed staying home, I knew I'd have to go back to work pretty soon. I'd taken off December, January, February, and March, then in April I recorded my first LP with Tony Brown and put the 1990 show together. We went back out on the road in May.

Shelby was too tiny and fragile to come along then, so we found a wonderful nanny, Cindy Bailey, with the help of Don Schlitz, who wrote "The Gambler." She was a good-natured, down-to-earth Kentucky girl with a great, loving family background. She stayed with us until December 1993, when she married her one-and-only, Dean "Bud" Gillihan. Now Shelby has Michelle Nunn to take care of him, another fun-loving Kentucky girl with a degree in preschool K-4. He loves both of them to pieces.

The same week I hired Cindy, we also found a great husband/wife team, Rose and Jimmy Carter, to be our house- and groundskeeper. They're wonderful with Shelby too—Rose would breathe for him if he'd let her! So I know Shelby's always in good hands.

I'd been pregnant during our last days of touring in 1989, so the bus became too rough for me to travel on. When I told Narvel we might have to cancel our last two weekends, he found a way to make our dates. We started flying. We loved it so much that, after Shelby was born, we decided to sell my bus to Patty Loveless and to continue flying. We've been flying ever since.

In 1990, I was flying to all of my dates. I could leave for a show around 6 P.M., along with Sandi Spika and Narvel, and be home by around 2 A.M. to spend the night in my own bed. I could be there when Shelby woke up in the morning and spend the day with him, instead of spending it in a hotel room somewhere or staring out the window of the bus as the miles between our jobs went by.

The band continued, for the majority of our dates, to travel by bus, along with our stage sets, costumes, and equipment. And since Narvel and I weren't along on most of those trips, the job of tour manager took on a new significance. The tour manager was the one who had to make it all happen, to see that all our gear made it to its destination and that our musicians got there too, in good shape and ready to play. He also had to handle any crisis with personnel, paraphernalia, or transportation that might arise along the way.

Jim Hammon was the consummate pro. I had met him in Fort Worth, Texas, in the late 1970s, and then in 1980, he sold me my first public-address system, the one that none of us could figure out how to work on the night Narvel first played with us in Nowata, Oklahoma. Jim later went on the road with Red Steagall, and then started selling concessions for me. He printed the T-shirts himself. I remember that one night in New York, Jim sold more than $10,000 worth of T-shirts. He was as proud as a new father.

In 1988, when Narvel became my manager and the overseer of my entire organization Jim took over as tour manager. From then on, he and Narvel had kind of friendly competition, always trying to outthink each other on ways to improve the show.

Perhaps more than anybody else in the organization, Jim lived rather than worked his job. He was a benevolent "control freak," who always wanted to know what was going on with everybody, usually for their own good. One night when we played in Switzerland, for example, my publicity director Jennifer Bohler had too much to drink at a bar; so her friend Hugh Waddel, who played drums for Johnny Cash, escorted her back to her hotel. Hugh had barely gotten Jenny inside when Jim burst into her room, demanding to know who he was and making sure that Hugh wasn't trying to take advantage of Jenny. After Hugh left, Jenny stuck her head under the covers, sick as a dog, but thirty minutes later Jim popped back into the room—just checking to see that Hugh hadn't snuck back inside. By that time, understandably, Jenny was pretty fed up with Jim's protectiveness, much as she appreciated his diligence.

I benefited by Jim's protectiveness too, and I relied on it. I felt totally secure as he led me on- and offstage through the dark and through twisting hallways that opened in front of thousands of people. Many times, I'd walk to the back of the stage at the end of a show after having the spotlight blinding me. From out of nowhere, Jim's hand would grab me right above the elbow, and he'd steer me safely through the noise, crowds, and confusion.

Larry Jones remembers seeing Jim get angry only one time. I was somewhere signing at the head of an autograph line, and I could hear a voice in the line yelling the four-letter word I hate. Jim was on the scene instantly, yanking the young man out of line without creating a commotion. Jim handed the kid over to the cops before he knew what was going on, and the signing went on as if nothing had happened.

A big part of Jim's job was supervising the musicians, and it's hard to be liked if you're the guy who's enforcing the rules. But Jim managed to retain the musicians' goodwill while gaining their respect. One way he did it was by keeping his sense of humor about him at all times. Musicians are always going to poke fun at the tour manager, and Jim could take it.

I still can't believe what Sandi, who is normally quiet and reserved in new situations, did to Jim on the second day she knew him. She had just joined the show and had barely met anyone, but she got up the nerve to play one of those inevitable road jokes on Jim. He was snoring on the couch in the middle of the day, when she snuck into her makeup bag and carefully pulled out fuchsia nail polish and applied it to Jim's beefy fingernails. Sandi remembers that it wasn't until it was time to eat that Jim noticed his bright fingernails. She said he had the most confused look on his face!

Sandi went after Jim another time too, when they were standing in the dark backstage. She walked up real close and began to whisper in his ear to distract him, then she started shooting at his crotch with a water gun. When he entered the lighted, crowded dressing room after the show, everyone thought he had wet his pants. He just shrugged off everybody's laughs.

Jim looked like a grizzly, but he had the soft heart of a teddy bear.

⁂

LET ME INTRODUCE THE OTHER MEMBERS OF MY MUSICAL FAMILY AT that time, as we began touring after our break in early 1991.

Kirk Capello was my band leader and musical director, a genius I had hired away from the Barbara Mandrell Show in 1989.

Of all the musicians I've ever worked with, he had the most potential to become a record producer—the keen ear, the ability to juggle different layers of sound at once. He could play his keyboard while directing the other players and the singers without missing anything else happening onstage. He was my personal Paul Schaffer.

He also composed music. Suzy Wills had been inspired by a Bible class she took entitled "Undivided Heart" and wrote the lyrics for a gospel song of the same name. She tried to get Kirk to write the music for two years. He kept putting her off, finally finishing the song the day before what would become the last leg of our early-1991 tour.

It wasn't surprising that Suzy couldn't push Kirk. He was one of the most hardheaded members of my organization, a real individualist. When we toured, I liked to sight-see in the cities where we played, and usually the band would come with me. But not Kirk. Larry Jones used to say that trying to get Kirk to do things with me, his boss, was as hard as trying to get a teenager to do something with his parents.

Sandi remembers that when I wanted to stop to see Niagara Falls, Kirk refused to get off the bus, and that in Los Angeles, he snuck out halfway through the Universal Studios tour. Kirk was bored by that kind of stuff, and Jim used to fuss at him, telling him he was too cool for his own good.

But I didn't mind Kirk's ways. I realized that while I was the musicians' friend, I was also their employer, so I didn't take it personally if someone didn't want to spend his time off hanging around with me.

Paula Kaye Evans was just the opposite of Kirk. She was like a tourist at almost every stop, running around sight-seeing and taking pictures. On one trip she waded into snow that was as deep as she was tall. There were many times they'd get into a town real tired from the road and the routine. Everybody wanted to lie around until it was time for the show—but not Paula Kaye.

I met her in 1990 when she auditioned to become my second background singer, alongside Suzy Wills. Her husband, Larry Wallace, was running the sound for Pink Floyd and occasionally taught techniques to my sound man, Ricky Moeller. When Ricky mentioned to Larry that I was trying out background singers, Wallace suggested that I listen to his wife.

Paula Kaye was one of six girls remaining who auditioned that day, and she wasn't one bit nervous. I liked her confidence, her ability to move onstage, and obviously, her captivating personality. And so I hired her.

On one tour, the backup singers and I used to do a choreographed routine that involved moving our arms a lot. Paula Kaye hated that bit, and nicknaming it the "air traffic control" part of the show, would do spoofs of it when we were offstage. She not only loved to make fun of our theatrics, but she could also do a super imitation of fashion models strutting down runways. She would suck in her cheeks and tummy and prance. No matter how many miles or hours had gone into a bus trip, Paula Kaye could break into her air traffic control or her model routine and crack everybody up.

Another source of amusement, to everyone but them, was Paula's running conflict with Jim Hammon about her luggage. He always thought she brought too much, and just couldn't understand why a girl who might be away from home for three straight weeks needed to pack more than a toothbrush and change of clothes. At one point Jim grew tired of arguing and resorted to the silent treatment, just staring at Paula's bags as the two of them rode a hotel elevator and hoping that would get to her. But he usually couldn't keep up the war of nerves, and by the time they reached her floor, he'd have launched into the thousandth verse of the same song about how she could have left some bags at home.

Paula also loved to paint. I have two tiny watercolors that she gave me of vases and flowers, which I cherish.

Guitarist Michael Thomas came to me after working for T. Graham Brown. He was simply one of the best guitar players around, an artist with as much stage presence as talent. From the first time we played together, he'd always look directly into my eyes as he took a guitar "ride," as if he was trying to stare me down. Since he was new to the show, I was surprised he had that much gall, but then I figured maybe he wasn't wearing his contact lenses and so he wasn't really staring. Then I asked him. No, he told me, he always wore them onstage. He could see me fine. He just had the guts to play the fire out of his guitar while looking me squarely in the eye. I really liked that.

Michael's wit was extremely dry, and naturally, his special target was often Jim Hammon. Now, Jim was a heavy eater himself, but he just hated having to wait for slowpokes when they would all stop to eat. Then came the night in Texas when Jim was the last to finish dinner and get back on the bus.

"Where is Hammon? Where is Hammon?" the band was chanting.

"He's still inside," Michael said without emotion, "waiting on his deep-fried Shetland pony."

When Michael was with T. Graham, he pulled a famous stunt on his roommate, a guy who always enjoyed a party. Most nights Michael would go to sleep after the show, only to be awakened by the clatter of his party-animal friend. So one night, in his ever-present prankster fashion, Michael took the television remote control with him to bed and hid it under his covers. He pretended to be asleep when his roommate stumbled in and turned the TV on low before sliding into bed. The minute he laid down, Michael pushed the volume button, and the television slowly began to get louder and louder. Michael's buddy jumped from under the covers and ran to turn it down, then tiptoed back to the bed. Michael let him tuck himself in before he pushed the volume control again. Once again, the guy rolled and wrestled himself out of bed to slam down the volume before it woke up

Michael. No telling how many times that happened before Michael got caught.

Michael caught Jim Hammon in a similar trap of his own making. Jim had laid down a rule that everyone had to sleep in his or her own bunk on the bus. But being such a big man, Jim hated his own bunk because it felt too cramped. So he would wait for everyone to fall asleep, then he'd sneak to the front of the bus and *he'd* sleep on the couch. No one might have noticed except that Jim snored so loud—I mean, like a freight train. Larry Jones would be driving maybe ten feet away, on the other side of a closed curtain, yet he claimed he could hear Jim plainly over the crackle of the citizens band radio and above the whine of the diesel engine at sixty-five miles per hour!

So one night, when Jim's snoring was waking everyone up, Michael tiptoed up to Jim and laid a tape recorder by his side. The next morning he slipped the tape into the bus's tape player and turned up the volume. Jim's snoring sounded like a cross between a chain saw and an outboard motor. Jim didn't like that at all!

My drummer, Tony Saputo, was one of the other jokemasters in the band. Jennifer Bohler remembers a time when the bus broke down about an hour outside of Nashville. Nothing is more frustrating to a road musician than having a breakdown when he is almost home after a tour. So, as everyone else sat fuming, waiting for its repair, Tony suddenly came bounding from the back of the bus dressed as a mummy. He had wrapped himself in toilet paper from head to foot.

Tony had a loving, almost childlike nature, and so no one found it unusual that he enjoyed children's toys. After all, there are lots of worse kinds of eccentricities in the music business! He would stash his collection of toys in the cupboards above the table and sometimes play with his toy dinosaurs or whatever to pass the time.

His stash included some packages of stick-on facial features—

eyes, noses, teeth, and more. He would plaster them on in the right and wrong places, and get everyone rolling in the aisles. Once he talked Suzy Wills into putting fake eyeballs on her eyelids. It looked pretty funny—with her eyes closed, she had eyes, and with her eyes open, she had eyes. But when it was time for all of this to be over, Suzy couldn't get her stickers off! She went nuts! She thought she was stuck with them for life. When she finally succeeded in removing her fake eyes, they yanked out her real eyelashes too. By that time she was hysterical with worry, and Tony and the band were hysterical with laughter.

Bass guitar player Terry Jackson, who had moved to Nashville with Tony, claimed that he liked touring because of his apartment. He'd signed a six-month lease on a place in a "hip" apartment complex overlooking the Cumberland River, wondering a little why no one else had grabbed it. Well, he soon learned that it was directly across the river from the city's sewage plant. He said the odor was so foul he could taste it. No wonder his rent was so cheap. Terry was as easygoing as his friend Tony was outgoing—the target rather than the initiator of jokes. But he never seemed to get angry. Maybe that was his way of fighting back.

Terry was one of the most sought-after bass players in Los Angeles. He had even played on some Michael Jackson sessions, and I could see why. His sense of showmanship was wonderful, for one thing. I used to sing "Little Rock" while walking up some portable stairs. Terry would come bouncing down from the top to meet me halfway for a jamming standoff. I loved it and so did the crowds.

He was one of the few black musicians in the country music business, and he was making a name for himself.

Chris Austin was a new addition to the band, and he showed up for work on his first day carrying a Bible and his guitar. A veteran of the Ricky Skaggs Show, he was a born-again Christian who was also a talented secular and Christian songwriter. I hired him to sing harmony after Suzy Wills quit my organization in December 1990. His high voice blended beautifully with Paula Kaye's.

Chris took a genuine interest in others: Sandi Spika remembers sitting next to him on a commercial flight to Alaska in January 1991, and how he deflected questions about himself to learn more about her and the rest of the band. Eventually we found out that he was married and that he and his wife, Trish, were in the process of buying a house. Chris was sure they'd get the financing, so he decided to paint the place before they were approved to move in. As Larry Jones recalls, Chris disappeared into the bedroom with a bucket of paint but when his wife walked in, she saw that he wasn't covering the walls. Instead, he had only painted "I love you" in giant letters. He was a gentle, romantic man.

Keyboard player Joey Cigainero was kind of the baby of the group. Kirk had thought that a second keyboard player would enhance our sound, and so Narvel approved the hire.

Joey was an innocent boy in that he hadn't been on the road all that long, and he was truly a gentleman as well as a real professional: No matter how far we had to travel between restaurants or motels or show venues, no matter if we were playing in 100-degree heat or in Canada in January, he never complained. He was always on time and prepared to play.

If all the players had been like Joey, I might not have needed a tour manager.

The reason I'm going into so much detail about these eight people, I'm sure you already know. We lost the "Crazy Eight," as Garth Brooks called them, in late 1991.

Rounding out our band were Joe McGlohon and Pete Finney. Joe, my saxophone player, also came from T. Graham Brown and started working for me in 1989. He was one of the passengers on the second airplane, which landed safely in Nashville. After the crash, Joe took over guidance of the band and today he is my band leader.

Pete Finney played steel guitar in the band. He had been with Foster & Lloyd before he joined our group in October 1990. He also flew on the second plane.

As we began the early-1991 leg of the tour, our performance schedule was heavy, so heavy that sometimes we had to move our entire organization by plane. In January, we did two shows in Alaska, and so of course we had to fly.

Then came a week, beginning March 11, 1991, when we were booked into four different cities spread across the country over six days. We had a show in Saginaw, Michigan, on Thursday, March 14; then a private show for IBM in San Diego on Friday, March 15; and then we had to make it to Fort Wayne, Indiana, on the sixteenth and then to Evansville, Indiana, on the seventeenth. We'd fly back to San Diego for another private show on Tuesday, March 19.

There was no way we could move all of my people that far and that fast without flying.

We'd been leasing our planes from Roger Woolsey, and for that week he'd promised us a Gulfstream I. It would seat seventeen people and cruise at about 280 miles per hour—that was a lot faster than our bus, of course, but it would still mean a lot of time in the air. But a day before the Saginaw show, Roger called and said the Gulfstream would not be available. He said he had worked out another plan for our transportation. He would lease us two small jet planes, a Sabreliner and a Hawker, for the same price as the Gulfstream. We'd have to split the band between the two planes, but they'd be faster. Narvel and I had flown in a Sabreliner and felt very comfortable and familiar with it, and so we agreed to the plan.

For the Saginaw show, Narvel, Sandi, and I flew up and back home in the Sabreliner. The band and crew had traveled to Saginaw by bus. After Roger dropped us off in Nashville, he flew back to Saginaw where the planes were scheduled to leave for San Diego early the next morning. We wanted to fly the Hawker because we'd never flown in one before and it was a good time to try it out. So the band took our Sabreliner that we usually flew in with the other leased plane. Narvel, Sandi, and I flew out that afternoon in the Hawker, and by the time we touched down at San Diego's Lindbergh Field the band was already in town and getting ready for the show.

Jim Hammon stood on the runway to meet us in the drizzling rain, walking us one at a time under an umbrella to our waiting limousine. Later Narvel and I would recount all the little details of that trip.

As soon as Jim got into the limousine beside us, the talk turned to airplanes. "The Hawker is a little bit bigger than the Sabreliner," Jim said. "Do you all mind if we take the Hawker to Fort Wayne and you all take the Sabreliner when you fly back?"

That was fine with us—we didn't need the extra space. Our only other passenger on the way home would be Sandi. Then, as Jim, Narvel, Sandi, and I rode to the Harbor Island Sheraton Inn, where we would do our show and Narvel, Sandi, and I would spend the night, Jim brought up another problem.

"We got a dilemma here," Jim said. "The show is at nine o'clock. That means Reba is going to come off at about ten-fifteen. But there is an eleven-o'clock curfew at the airport. Still, I think we [the band] can make it to the airport before eleven."

"Man," Narvel said, "that's only forty-five minutes after she walks offstage. You'll have to load up the equipment and get over to Lindbergh Field. I don't think you can make it, Jim. That's too close."

So Narvel told Jim to have the pilots fly the Sabreliner and the Hawker over to nearby Brown Field. It had no curfew, and the band members could take their time getting to their planes after the concert.

We did our show, but when it was over, Jim heard my voice still singing "Sunday Kind of Love." He realized that someone had made a videotape recording, which was forbidden by our contract with the promoter, and so Narvel sent Jim to get that tape. It amounted to the last recording of the last show I ever did with that band.

The band did not play on "Sweet Dreams," my encore song. I always sang it a cappella. Instead they went to their rooms to pack up, and because of the change in airports, many had the time to call home and to take showers before heading out.

After the show, Jim walked Narvel and me back to our suite. The three of us stood on a twenty-foot-long balcony overlooking the Pacific. The first hint of spring was in the air, and we laughed in the ocean breeze that swept over our faces.

That's when Narvel told Jim to plan a party for the band, crew, and us when we played the same hotel the following week. We all said our good-byes.

❧

NARVEL WAS WATCHING TELEVISION AND I WAS ASLEEP WHEN I WAS jolted awake by a ringing telephone. "Who would be calling at this time of night?" I wondered. For an instant, I thought an enthusiastic fan had gotten my room number or that it was a wrong number. But it was Roger Woolsey, our pilot.

"Can you come to my room?" Roger asked Narvel. "I think something bad has happened."

"I'll be right there," I heard my husband say, and he hung up.

He dressed quickly while I asked questions he couldn't answer. I sat upright in bed. I wouldn't lie down again until the next night at my home in Tennessee.

Later, Narvel would describe Roger as being white as a sheet when he walked into his room. "I watched everybody get on both planes," Roger said to Narvel. "Both planes taxied to the end of the runway and I got in my car to come back to the hotel. I looked in my rearview mirror and I saw this huge ball of fire. And I don't know if it was them or not."

Roger couldn't return to the airport that night because it was closed; our planes had been the last two to take off that night. So when Narvel got to his room, he found Roger dialing madly to get information. Narvel later said it was easier for him to maintain hope because he didn't have the sight of a fireball branded in his mind like Roger did. Roger's brother Wayne was a copilot on one of the planes.

Finally, Roger hung up the telephone and turned to Narvel. "Yes," he said, "a plane did go down."

I remember that I was sitting up in bed when Narvel came back. He told me what Roger had learned, and I asked, "Is everybody okay?"

"No," Narvel said, "they're not. Reba—it's a possibility that everybody is dead."

"Oh, Narvel, surely not!" I said.

"Yeah," Narvel almost whispered. "Roger thinks from what he saw, he thinks everybody is dead."

I burst into tears.

Mike Allen, who booked the date, and Sandi Spika had stayed behind to fly home the next day, Sandi with us and Mike on a commercial airline. Narvel telephoned them both and asked them to come to our room.

At that point, we still didn't know much. It was a while before we would receive confirmation that it was one of our planes that had gone down. And even then, there was no word about survivors.

Through radio contact, the pilot of our aircraft still in the air had supplied his passenger list, so we could figure out who was on the fallen plane. It was now approaching 6 A.M. in Texas and Oklahoma, where Narvel's and my parents lived. We didn't want them to hear the news on television or the radio before we talked to them, so Narvel called his parents and I called mine.

After I heard my Daddy say, "Hello," I lost it again. Like a fast dream it all went through my mind—they'll never hear their daddies' voices again. Narvel was in the other room getting ready to call the band members' mamas, daddies, wives, and husbands.

"Hello, Daddy," I said, "this is Reba. I'm okay, but something terrible has happened."

"Okay," he said. I could tell he had been sound asleep.

"We're in San Diego and the band and crew flew out on two planes and one of them went down and we're pretty sure everyone is dead."

That was the first time I'd heard myself say it.

I called out the list of names to Daddy of people who'd been confirmed as passengers on the crashed plane. He kept asking me about others he knew in my group, although I had already told him everyone who I knew was on board.

Mama later told me he hung up and walked into his and Mama's bedroom, where Mama said, "Clark, what is it?"

He stood there trying to breathe and couldn't speak. "Wait just a minute," he said.

"It's Reba, isn't it?" she asked.

"No," Daddy said, "she's okay. It's her bunch. Their plane went down, and they're all dead."

Narvel called nine families, including his parents, during the next two hours. The rest of us—Sandi, Mike, and I—were still in total shock. I would follow Narvel pacing from room to room in our suite, crying, but Narvel kept a level head, and he later said that staying busy kept him from breaking up. Many times that night I saw him silently hold a telephone while I could hear someone screaming at the other end of the line. It was worse than any nightmare I could imagine.

The Cable News Network and other channels were updating the reports. Narvel moved back and forth between our suite and Roger's room, where they were receiving information from the various airport workers and rescue teams. Narvel kept getting conflicting stories, which he'd piece together as best he could and then pass along to the families. Later, we'd learn that it was one of the worst private aviation disasters in the history of San Diego County.

In the tense confusion, Narvel forgot to call his children, Chassidy and Brandon, who were living with their mother in Texas. Cindy Bailey, my son's nanny, had contacted Shawna, Narvel's daughter, who was living in Tennessee. And so the very thing that Narvel had struggled to prevent from happening to the other families had happened to his own children. They heard on the news that seven unidentified band members and their manager—the report didn't distinguish between tour and career manager—in the Reba McEntire Show had been killed. They thought their daddy was dead until they got the facts from Narvel's Mom and Dad.

I called Barbara Mandrell in the hours after the incident, because Kirk Capello, my musical director, had worked for her before he joined me, and I thought she should know. Barbara is also my closest girlfriend in the music business. I respect her a lot. Barbara had seen tragedy up close, barely surviving a two-car collision that also took a man's life. And so in this darkest hour of my life I called her because I wanted to talk to someone who knew the Lord as I did. I needed that strength. We cried and prayed over the long-distance telephone.

By now the sun was up, and still there was no official confirmation of the deaths that Narvel and I had reported to loved ones. But aviation officials and rescue workers knew from their calculations what we knew in our hearts—that it was impossible for anyone to survive a headlong plane crash into the side of a mountain.

It would not be till late in the morning that we finally got definite word: I had lost Kirk Capello, my musical director and keyboard player; Terry Jackson, my bass guitarist; Tony Saputo, my drummer; Paula Kaye Evans, my background singer; Chris Austin, who had just joined us and played mandolin, fiddle, and guitar; Michael Thomas, my guitarist; keyboard player Joey Cigainero; and Jim Hammon, my tour manager, as well as the pilots, Donald Holmes and Chris Hollinger.

A LOT OF RUMORS AND MISINFORMATION HAVE BEEN PRINTED ABOUT the early-morning events of March 16, 1991. There was speculation, for instance, that the pilots had earlier been drinking inside a bar at Brown Field. They had—they'd been drinking coffee, according to Teresa Sharp, the bartender who served them. There have been rumblings about the last-minute switch in aircraft and airfield, and questions as to whether the plane was under the guidance of an air traffic controller.

So I asked Tom Carter, my collaborator, to go on a fact-finding mission on my behalf, to pull together all the reports on the crash so we could get as close as possible to the truth. Tom went through documents and official reports from the Federal Aviation Administration, the National Transportation Safety Board, and the medical examiner who performed the autopsies. He examined newspaper accounts and magazine articles, and interviewed Kathleen Tucker, a volunteer rescue worker with the sheriff's department, who was one of the first five at the crash site. Tom went to Brown Field to interview people who saw the fatal flight depart and who visited with members of my band and their pilots shortly before takeoff. I asked him to visit San Diego's Otay Mountain, where the plane went down, and to record everything he saw, heard, and felt at the death scene. That's the only way I could get through the reenactment of the crash. Someday, I also might climb that mountain. But I'm not ready yet.

What follows is, I hope, the most complete account yet that anyone has been able to construct of what happened that night.

The twin-engine Hawker jet left San Diego at 1:41 A.M. The National Weather Service reported conditions as clear with a calm wind. Official documents place the crash time at roughly three minutes after departure and about eight nautical miles from Brown Field.

According to the NTSB report, released months after the tragedy, the crash occurred on the western slope of Otay Mountain, at about 3,300 feet mean sea level, or about 172 feet from the summit. The mountain is rocky, with vegetation and brush ranging up to eight feet in height. It is steeper in places, according to the report, with "an upslope of about 30 degrees." It continues: "The aircraft's left wing first contacted a rock outcropping or small ridge. Scars at this location were consistent with an airplane being in shallow left bank." An early account suggests that the plane was no longer ascending, but had leveled off, causing investigators to believe that the pilot thought he was flying high enough to be safe. Even though later reports found that the plane was still climbing when it crashed, the pilot obviously had no idea that a killing peak lay in his path. There were no lights on the rural mountain.

Had the aircraft been 200 feet higher, or slightly to the right or left of the peak, it would have cleared the mountain. Instead, the plane clipped the mountain and began to cartwheel before exploding on impact about twenty-five feet away from the second contact point. Mechanical and human remains were scattered for the length of three football fields in grass that was eight feet high. Later on, the firemen, who somehow managed to pull their heavy and awkward trucks up the mountain to put out the fire, spoke of the odor of the jet fuel that hung in the early morning smog more than three hours after the blaze.

The pilot in command of the plane that went down, Donald T. Holmes, 43, was instrument rated and a certified airline transport pilot. The copilot, Christopher D. Hollinger, was also instrument rated and a certified commercial pilot.

How could two such well-credentialed pilots fly into the side of a mountain? Fans and family have asked me that question, but not more than I have asked it myself.

The records of the medical examiner, Dr. Mark A. Super, M.D., show that the autopsies of the pilot and copilot, performed twenty-four hours after the crash, "revealed no evidence of physical incapacitation or impairment that would have been causal to the accident."

Instead, the National Transportation Safety Board reports trace a fatal series of mishaps leading up to the crash. First, before the pilot could take off, he had to file a flight plan based on instrument flight rules (called IFR), meaning that he would be under the direct supervision and guidance of an air traffic control tower. He called an FAA flight service specialist at nearby Montgomery Field to file his plan, wondering how long it would take to go through and hoping he could avoid a long wait. During their conversation, it was suggested the pilot could take off whenever he wanted if he used visual flight rules (called VFR)—meaning he would not be guided by the tower but instead would be responsible for knowing about and avoiding any obstacles in the terrain that were in his flight path—and then obtain his IFR clearance while in the air. The pilot elected to go that route, a decision not all that unusual for a private airplane pilot.

Second, until the pilot came under the supervision of the tower, he would be forbidden to fly into San Diego's Terminal Control Area (called a TCA). TCAs, in theory at least, make flying safer by separating faster aircraft like his jet from smaller, slower ones. So, apparently trying to avoid entering this TCA before he received his clearance from the tower, the pilot radioed the flight service specialist twice more. According to the transcript of the third conversation, the specialist confirmed that the pilot's proposed plan would put the plane into the TCA without clearance.

The pilot then said, "So, I would be better off if I headed right northeast and stayed down, say, down below three thousand [feet]?"

"Uh huh," said the specialist.

"Do you agree?" the pilot asked him.

"Yeah, sure, that'll be fine."

Later, Jim Miller, supervisor of the FAA's Effectiveness System, suggested that when the pilot mentioned 3,000, he might have meant 3,000 feet above sea level. The specialist apparently thought the pilot meant 3,000 feet altitude—that is, 3,000 feet above ground level—which would have put him several hundred feet higher.

That miscommunication would be deadly.

There was another cruel irony in the situation. The plane had left more than an hour and a half after its original departure time. Long before takeoff the pilot had filed a flight plan based on a departure time of midnight, which he could have updated at any point. He must not have, for at 1:30 A.M. his plan was automatically canceled by the tower's computer. So, about a minute after taking off on VFR, when the pilot radioed to be hooked into the tower, he was told that his clearance had "clocked out" and that it would be "put . . . right back in." But when the controller called back to ask for his position, all he got was silence.

Another problem may have been the nature of the airspace around San Diego. On July 8, 1991, the *San Diego Union and Tribune* carried an article headlined "Local air map can baffle private pilots. Prohibited space rules called most complex in nation." The story, which was a follow-up on the crash, began by stating that "airspace restrictions over San Diego County are needlessly complex, some pilots complain."

The paper quoted Steve Elleson, a veteran flight instructor and former assistant dean of National University's School of Aerospace Studies, who said that San Diego's TCA, one of twenty-nine nationwide, is especially difficult. "It's probably the most complex TCA in the country. There are all these little extensions and legs and strange little corridors that go through it."

Dick Russel, an aviation consultant and retired airline pilot with thirty years' worth of experience, confirmed what Elleson had said about the complexity of the San Diego TCA. "It's ridiculous," the newspaper quoted him as saying. "It makes no sense."

The newspaper also reported that the NTSB had yet to complete its investigation but would likely blame the crash at least partly on pilot error. It cited Donald Norman, chairman of the University of California at San Diego's Department of Cognitive Science, who had studied pilots and cockpit interaction for three years and found that while TCAs were put in for safety reasons, coping with them is the hardest part of a pilot's job. According to the paper, Norman said, "Read the TCA map, go spend a couple of hours trying to learn it and you won't be able to in a couple of hours. And then when someone violates it, you call it pilot error. Come on."

❦

AT 2:40 A.M., A GOVERNMENT HELICOPTER PILOT SPOTTED THE FLAMES of the fallen plane in the darkness. He radioed the fire's exact location to officials waiting on the ground. Fifty-four rescue workers would eventually turn out to comb the mountaintop, including members of the San Diego Mountain Rescue Team, members of the Chula Vista Mounted Police, sheriff's deputies, and county medical personnel.

One of them was Kathleen Tucker. She was told that there were no survivors of the crash, and as she recalls, "There were three or four of us who were selected to go to the mountain and recover the remains, and any personal items we could find—anything that we felt was significant to try to return to the families."

Daylight hadn't broken when they began to ascend the mountain. "It actually took a moment to realize what I was looking for," she says. "I had been to other emergencies but never to a plane crash—what I saw was debris everywhere. Paper, pieces of metal, small airplane parts . . . Most of the plane was in pieces the size of a half-dollar."

It would take days for the workers to sift through it all and to bag and tag the personal effects for the families, who had provided lists of what they thought their loved ones had carried. "We sent back leather jackets, drum cymbals, books, jewelry, and broken pieces of guitars, that I remember," Kathleen says.

In Spring 1993, two years and three months after the air crash, Kathleen returned to Otay Mountain with Tom Carter. The mountainside was totally quiet. A significant rainfall had broken a long Southern California drought, and it washed up debris that was driven into the ground on the night of the crash. Kathleen and Tom found a crumpled piece of the plane's fuselage about the size of a large orange at the site. Someone had built a fence to keep the area secure from trespassers, and Kathleen and Tom found the trees that she and someone else had planted there shortly after the crash. Not far away, two tiny homemade crosses stand firm.

Anyone seeing those crosses for the first time would wonder why they were built more than 3,000 feet in the sky on an isolated mountaintop. Brown and green have returned to the grass, bushes, and weeds that were scorched in the crash. The growth is stirred only by the wind. There are no telltale signs that anything tragic had ever happened there.

But those of us—family members, colleagues, friends—who lost people in the crash will be marked by it forever.

CHAPTER 17

BACK AT THE HOTEL, WE WERE PACKING TO LEAVE SAN Diego. There was nothing left for us to do there, and a tremendous amount of work lay ahead of us in Nashville. By noon, the hotel lobby was swarming with reporters and cameramen, so security personnel escorted us out of the building through a back way exit, and we were able to evade the press.

For most of the night, people from my organization who had flown on the second plane—band members Joe McGlohon and Pete Finney and crew members Gayle Hase, Ricky Moeller, Galen Henson, Brian Leedham, and Robert Kosloskie—were unaware of their colleagues' fate. Narvel had telephoned instructions to their pilot to fly straight to Nashville, rather than to Fort Wayne. When the plane stopped for refueling in Memphis, Brian Leedham looked out his window and recognized the Federal Express corporate headquarters. The passengers instantly knew where they were and wondered why.

Copilot Wayne Woolsey, Roger's brother, turned to the group and made the announcement. "Guys," he said, "the other plane went down. I don't know if there were any survivors."

Joe McGlohon thought that Wayne was trying to be funny, and got on him for kidding about something so serious.

"No," said Wayne, "I'm serious. The other plane went down."

Joe, Brian, and the others hurried off the plane. They walked with Wayne into an airport waiting room where he used the telephone. Minutes later he confirmed that their friends and colleagues were dead. It was approximately 10 A.M. in Tennessee.

Gayle Hase at first refused to get back on the plane for the forty-minute flight to Nashville. He said he was going to lease a car, and Joe briefly thought about riding with him.

"I can't ride in a car for two and a half hours," Joe said. "I need to get home now," adding that he needed to be with his wife and children.

"Look," Joe told Gayle, "you can do what you want. But we got to go. We got to get home as soon as we can."

The group, including Gayle, reluctantly climbed back on the aircraft. Boarding must have been especially difficult for Brian. The crash marked the third time he had been in the "other" plane.

In all the confusion of those hours, we forgot to call and inform our bus driver, Larry Jones, who was waiting for his passengers in Fort Wayne. He had planned to do what he had done hundreds of times—pick them up at the airport, drive them to their hotel, and later to our show.

There is an intense bonding between band members and their bus driver. He's not only the guy who takes the band on long overnight hauls between shows when most members get their sleep, but the driver is also the guy who at three o'clock in the morning will have a musician approach him and sit on the steps beside him and pour his heart out. Being a bus driver is kind of like being a lay psychiatrist to the band. Those players trusted Larry as much as he loved them.

So he was shocked when another bus driver said to him, "Man, that's terrible about the band, isn't it?"

"What about the band?" Larry asked.

"Well, their plane crashed."

"What do you mean their plane crashed?" Larry pressed. "Is everybody okay?"

"No," the driver said. "I think everybody is dead."

"I totally freaked out," Larry recalled. "In those two airplanes were the most important people in the world to me, except for my mother and brother."

Not wanting to believe it, he went back to the motel, turned on CNN, and fought back the tears. Seconds later, he walked across the hall and knocked on the door of Larry Wallace, Paula Kaye's husband.

"What has happened?" Larry said.

"Every one of them is dead," Wallace said, and said nothing else.

Acting on reflex, Larry went to work. He walked to the front desk to turn in the keys for rooms that wouldn't be used. "That's the hardest thing I've ever done, tell them people we didn't need their keys," he remembers. "I had to look at everybody's names on those envelopes. Nobody at the motel seemed to care. I got mad. It was like, 'You don't need them, so what?' "

I'm glad that no one at the motel, who might not have known about the fatalities, confronted Larry about turning in so many keys. "You know how everybody wants to pass pain along," Larry says. "I was definitely wanting to pass some pain along."

NARVEL AND I WERE RUNNING ON ADRENALINE WHEN OUR PLANE touched down in Gallatin. We drove straight home. Cindy, our nanny, and Shelby were waiting on the front porch. I got out of the car and immediately took Shelby into my arms. He had just turned one. Holding his warm little body was such an affirmation of life, a comfort I really needed right then.

Cindy took Shelby back so that Narvel and I could go see the families, starting with Jim's wife, Debbie Hammon. Her place was filled with family and friends. As we sat thrashing out the situation, over and over, she told us a couple of stories. The first was about Jim, who on the day he was to leave for Saginaw, could not seem to get packed. This was so unlike Jim, who was accustomed to organizing a band and crew and moving them 1,000 miles a day. Debbie said that as he tried to pack he kept saying, "Man, I just wish I didn't have to go."

"He never said that before," Debbie told me. "He was always so ready to get on the road with everybody."

Then she told me a story about Jason, her older son. He had been at home in Nashville by himself. Debbie was in Gatlinburg with her youngest son Jeremiah, when Narvel had called, and Jason had given him her number.

Debbie told us that on Saturday morning right before Narvel phoned, Jason had been asleep and woke up because he thought he heard somebody walking through the house. He got out of bed and looked around. He found nothing and went back to bed. Shortly after, the telephone rang with Narvel's call.

I still wonder about that. Could it have been Jim, his spirit, coming back to look in on his family one last time?

From Debbie's we went to see Dana McVickers, Michael Thomas's wife. Before he'd left on that last trip, they'd played and wrestled on the couch, laughing together. When Michael called her that night after the band got to Saginaw he said he'd been late getting to the bus. Dana said she was terribly sorry she'd made him late, but Michael told her he wouldn't have missed that for the world.

It was late when Narvel and I got back to our house. We went from home to home again the next day. By the time that long, terrible weekend was over, we were emotionally and physically exhausted.

⟡

ON MONDAY, MARCH 18, MY STARSTRUCK ENTERTAINMENT OFFICES opened for the first time since the accident. The telephones were ringing as my people walked in at 9 A.M. The answering service was jammed with calls that had come into the office over the weekend.

Our staff set to work, returning calls, fielding press requests, communicating with the coroner's office and sheriff's department in San Diego, and talking with the families about funeral arrangements. The families were scattered all over the country, and we quickly realized that there was no way that we and the victims' friends in the music community would be able to attend each funeral. So Narvel and I decided that we would organize a memorial service in Nashville to honor all eight of our friends as well as the two pilots. We set about finding a church for the service and arranging for round-trip transportation and lodging for ten sets of surviving parents or spouses. Nashville's Ramada Inn on Spence Lane, the Holiday Inn Crowne Plaza, the Doubletree and Opryland Hotels were good enough to offer us complimentary rooms.

On Monday morning, Narvel provided the leadership he's always been famous for and outlined our intentions to the staff. He said that none of them, except for my publicist, Jennifer Bohler, was authorized to talk to the media, and that Starstruck would make a counselor available to anyone in the organization who wanted one. He was very supportive of everyone's needs.

Then he began to cry before the whole group. Some cried with him, and others sat silently. Many of us began to hug.

I am so proud of how tirelessly everyone worked for our loved ones. The word "overtime" was never mentioned. People in my office would be hurrying and planning one minute, and then someone would fall into tears the next. And all of us pressed on.

One of the saddest tasks had fallen to Deborah Carlen. She had been hired by the Starstruck Publishing Group three days after Shelby was born, and was working there at the time of the accident. She became our liaison to San Diego, educating herself, literally overnight, in the legal procedures necessary to recover the victims' remains. By Saturday, Deborah had single-handedly arranged for the return of all the remains to the various families; none of the funerals—scheduled to take place in each hometown immediately after the memorial service—had to be postponed.

Debbie Hammon had mistakenly processed the wrong paper-work to recover Jim, and Deborah tracked down the correct forms that would authorize the transportation of her husband's remains.

Some families were desperate for specifics on the condition of their loved ones. They insisted that Deborah tell them which body parts had been found, and some even wanted to know the sizes of the parts. Deborah tried to discourage these requests, and eventually, troubled, she came to me. I told her to give them what they wanted. I treat people like I want to be treated, and I would have wanted to know too.

Deborah also received from officials in San Diego all she could of the victims' personal property, and worked with their survivors to identify it. Most of the personal effects arrived smelling like jet fuel. They were temporarily placed in Deborah's office, and the scent lingered for weeks afterward. Then, to make the return of the personal effects easier, they were moved into our conference room. Narvel met each family inside that room as

Our 1993 pictures. *Left:* Narvel and I at a concert. *Bottom right:* Shelby and Narvel in a picture they gave me for Christmas. *Bottom left:* One of my favorite photos of Shelby and me.

I'm blessed with a loving family and a lot of precious friends. *Facing page, top:* My first family, from left, Pake, Susie, Alice, and me flanking Daddy and Mama at their home in Stringtown on Thanksgiving Day 1993. *Center:* At Christmas in 1989, I was pregnant with Shelby and just thrilled by Susie's present—my old high school basketball shoes. *Bottom:* I'm still in touch with some friends I've known since first grade. From left: Joni Winslett Patton, Melia Echelle Rose, Sherry Stiles Fields, and me. *Left:* My second family is Narvel and Shelby. Here Shelby and I relax in the backyard at our home in Tennessee. *Below:* My third family is made up of Narvel's children. From left are Shawna, Narvel, Brandon, me, Shelby, and Chassidy.

JIM MCGUIRE

MICAEL-RENEE LIFESTYLES PORTRAITURE

I've gotten the biggest kick out of watching Shelby grow. *Above left:* This is a portrait of Shelby that was our birthday gift to Narvel. *Above right and center:* Playing the piano at home and the drums that Scotty Hawkins, my drummer, and Larry Jones, our head of transportation, gave him. *Below:* Shelby made his stage debut in 1992; he brought a rose out to me. *Facing page, top:* A future outfielder? *Bottom:* A visit to a blacksmith on the Ponderosa Ranch near Lake Tahoe in June 1993.

VINCE BUZZEO

JIM McGUIRE

Holidays are special times for us. *Facing page, top:* Shelby and I coloring Easter eggs in 1993. *Bottom right:* Shelby dressed up as Barney the dinosaur for Halloween. *Bottom left:* From our Christmas card photo shoot in 1992. Harry Vickery made the rocking horse. *Right:* He's only two, but look how much Shelby (right) resembles Narvel at age four in this picture Narvel's mom and dad had made for us for Christmas 1993. *Below right:* I love to ride when I can find the time. Here I am on Little Bit, with Shelby on Ole Jay and Brandon on Bobby. *Below left:* My little boy wants to ride Ole Jay and have his rope, but around naptime he has to have his "blankie" too.

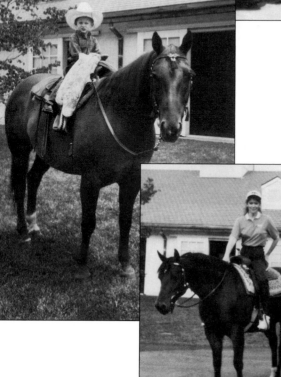

It would be easy to let our work take over our lives, so Narvel and I are careful to plan time for fun. *Above left:* Brandon (left) and Chassidy (right) joined me, Narvel, and Shelby in Aspen in 1992. *Center left:* Shelby took to the slopes at Christmas time in Aspen, Colorado, 1993. *Center right:* In 1988 Narvel and I took a helicopter ride to a glacier in Juneau, Alaska. *Left:* The three of us in New Orleans in 1992 after my show. *Above:* After I took up golf, Vince Gill asked me to play in his Vinney Golf tournament for charity. I hope I didn't hit anyone!

they came to claim their loved ones' property. Families again wept openly, and Narvel was wonderful at comforting them.

In the meantime, preparations for the memorial service were going on. We met with the police department. We met with the church staff. We talked about who would handle the music, and who would handle security. We arranged to release pictures of the deceased to the press—ironically, Jenny had coordinated a photo session for the band just days before the accident.

And then, Narvel and I wanted to find someone in the entertainment industry to speak at the service. I called Waylon Jennings.

Waylon had been through a similar tragedy in his life. In the late 1950s, he had been the bass guitar player for the Crickets, Buddy Holly's band. Waylon and Buddy were on tour in Iowa, and Waylon had given up his seat on a small airplane so someone else could fly with Buddy.

The plane crashed and Buddy, the Big Bopper, Ritchie Valens, and others were killed. Waylon's life was spared.

Waylon had had to come to a tough reckoning with himself about that, and I was greatly comforted by his words. "Don't you feel guilty because of the plane crash," he told me. "It wasn't meant for you to be on that plane or you would have been. So don't blame yourself and don't feel guilty."

But when he told me that he couldn't speak at the memorial service, I could understand his feelings. Not all that long ago, I spoke at Conway Twitty's memorial service. That's all I could do —talk. The Oak Ridge Boys, Tammy Wynette, and Connie Smith all sang, and I admire them for it.

So I thought for a long time about who could relate to our tragedy—someone who had been through all kinds of rough times. Then it came to me: The Man in Black, Johnny Cash, who has virtually seen it all. I didn't know he had buried his mother a week before, to the day. But, God bless him, he said he would do it.

❧

ON WEDNESDAY, MARCH 20, SHORTLY AFTER NOON, A CONVOY OF
twelve limousines carrying the families, Narvel and me, Narvel's
parents, and my Starstruck family made the long journey to
Christ Church in Brentwood. We had asked that the press be
barred from the service, but cameramen were stationed everywhere behind the barricades, shooting video and photographs
with telephoto lenses. One tabloid reporter nearly slipped the
police cordon by pretending to be a family member or friend.

A crowd of about 2,000 people had gathered at the church,
and my eyes were drawn to two of my dearest buddies, Vince Gill
and Larry Gatlin. It really made me feel good to see them there.
Back in San Diego, four days before, as Narvel and I were getting
ready to check out of the hotel, the phone rang. We hadn't
received many phone calls because Narvel had kept the line tied
up, calling the families and piecing together information from the
authorities. I picked up the bathroom extension when Mike Allen
said the call was for me.

"Hey, little buddy." It was Vince. I began to cry when I
heard his voice, and he began to cry with me.

"Vince," I said, "what am I going to do when I'm onstage
and turn around and they're not there?"

"If you want me to," he answered, "I'll be on your stage.
I'll be there for you."

I'll never forget that.

The Reverend Dan Scott, one of the pastors at Christ
Church, read from Psalm 91, my favorite chapter in the Bible.
Then a ninety-member choir, standing on steps behind a white-
ribboned wreath that almost covered the pulpit, raised their
voices in song.

In his sermon, Reverend Scott called music the breath of
God. He said that no other group of musicians would ever be
that band, would ever be able to make their extraordinary mu-

sic. He also offered the traditional Christian words of comfort, that death is the entry to eternal life for those who have accepted Jesus Christ as their personal savior—such welcomed words.

When it was Johnny Cash's turn to speak, he sang "Jim, I Wore a Tie Today," about a musician attending another musician's funeral, and inserting the names of the band members into the verses. He could not have chosen anything more appropriate or more uplifting.

Some of the lyrics were: ". . . the preacher said a lot of things but I didn't hear a word he said . . ." They reflected my own feelings all too well. I felt that I was moving through the service in a daze, at times completely out of touch with what was going on around me. I had brought my body to the service. It hurt too much to bring my mind.

At the end of the service, Narvel and I walked up the center aisle, and he decided to check out front before we walked to the limousine. He told me to stay inside the church. As people passed by, my eyes fell on members of my organization. I was shocked again by the realization that some members of my group were missing and that their faces would never be seen again.

I took a few steps with Narvel to the car, and once inside, the dam finally broke. I think that keeping incredibly busy had been my mental leaning post for days. Now, for the first time, I could finally let those days' worth of suppressed emotion free. I cried during most of the twenty-mile ride back to my office. That helped—it released a lot of the stress and pressure. It was easier to meet with the families at the dinner we had planned for them.

꧁꧂

MEANWHILE, WE'D BEEN GETTING A LOT OF HEAT FROM THE PRESS. I probably had two dozen requests for interviews within forty-eight hours of the crash. Jennifer Bohler, my publicist, turned them all down. I hadn't come to terms with the tragedy myself, and besides, there were families, friends, band members, crew members, and fans that hurt so bad each time the crash was brought up. I didn't want to increase their agony.

But my silence didn't stop the flood of news stories compiled without the input of anyone from my organization. The tabloid accounts were especially cruel: one ran a photograph of each band member with a banner reading "DEAD" over each shot. The tabloid was on display at supermarket and convenience-store cash registers for seven days. Debbie Hammon was going through the checkout line at the grocery store with her son, Jeremiah. When she saw the paper, she left her shopping cart on the spot and took her son home.

It was clear that I couldn't escape the press completely, so Jennifer Bohler, Narvel, and I decided to talk to Jane Sanderson, a reporter I trusted with *People* magazine. I appeared on the April 1 cover of *People*. The cover copy said: "Reba McEntire: 'This is my darkest hour.' The dramatic inside story of the night the country singer lost her band in a plane crash." Beneath my picture was one of an investigator standing by a piece of the destroyed plane's fuselage.

Jane later said that after interviewing me, she sat up all night to weave together the story. It was such a private and painful period for me, but I had hoped that the interview would satisfy the public's need to know and that I could retreat back into my life and all of us, the families too, could begin the painful process of healing.

After that, when I did press interviews again, it was always with the stipulation that reporters not bring up the crash. Jenny Bohler or Stacey Harrison-Boyd sat in on almost every interview. The reporters would ask their normal questions about my latest album, or Shelby, or a concert, or whatever. Things would be going fine, and then from left field the reporter would say, "Where were you when you heard about the plane crash—"

"That's it!" Jennifer would snap. "End of interview," and it would be.

I feel sorry for people such as Michael Jordan, whose father was murdered during the time I was writing this book. Michael was hurting but wasn't left to suffer in privacy. Certainly he shouldn't have been hounded by strangers with notepads and cameras who wanted to plaster his grief across the fronts of newspapers and magazines to make money. Only someone who has been through that can realize how hard it can be on them. After you've given all you can to support friends, loved ones, and yourself, you have nothing left for the millions of strangers who read or watch the mass media. You just have nothing left.

❧

I LOOKED FOR SOLACE IN THE PLACES WHERE I'D ALWAYS FOUND IT before—in the Lord and in my music. A couple of days after the memorial service I stunned the music community, and myself, by announcing I would be returning to work.

The question, inevitably, had come up even before we left San Diego, and I was not prepared to confront it. Mike Allen, our booking agent, didn't know what to do about our dates. "Cancel everything," I remember saying. "Cancel everything until July, and we'll decide later."

One of the dates was an appearance on March 25, nine days after the crash, at the annual Academy Awards, the Oscars. I couldn't imagine how I could pull myself back together in time.

I remember thinking about it as I sat in front of the makeup mirror in my bedroom dressing room. It was Sunday morning, the day after. Narvel was in our sitting room watching TV while I was getting ready for that second day of visits with the families.

The song I'd been scheduled to perform was "I'm Checking Out," which Meryl Streep had sung in *Postcards from the Edge.* "I'm checking out of this old heartbreak hotel," it went, and I tried to imagine myself singing it.

Before the crash, the band, Jim, and I had talked about me singing at the Oscars. They'd been thrilled for me. And I got to thinking that that heartbreak hotel was the world, that "We're checking out" was the band's way of saying, "We're not here hurting, we're okay." And I just knew in my heart that if I could have discussed it with them, the band would have told me to go on and do it. It was a gut feeling, a sign of their approval.

A peaceful feeling swept over me as I went into our sitting room and said, "Narvel, I'm going to do the Oscars."

"Are you sure?" he asked.

"Yes," I said. I would do that show for the band.

Narvel called Sandy Brokaw, my West Coast publicist. Sandy called the Academy the first thing Monday morning and told them I would appear. He found out my name had never been taken off the list; another sign, I thought.

When I sang at the Oscars the following week, I think most of the audience knew what had happened to my band and Jim. The song took on new meaning for them, like it had for me. I sang it with all my heart.

Then, after the Oscars, I went back on the road. Needless to say, not everybody agreed with my decision. Some people accused me of being disrespectful, and others said I was money hungry. But I believed I was returning to work with full respect for the dead, and that money had nothing to do with it. I would have done no one any good by lying around; there were many people depending on me—the surviving band members, my stage and production crew, many of whom had families to support. And then too I feared that if I allowed myself to hurt that hard for that long (July was four months away), I might never return to work.

We had to put a band together in one week. That was barely enough time to meet, much less rehearse, six musicians and a vocalist.

Dolly Parton had called me at the office when she heard of the crash. She said if I needed anything to tell her and that I could use her band and her whole organization if necessary. No wonder I've been a huge fan of hers from the beginning. I thanked her and asked if we could use the services of Gary Smith, her band leader and record producer who'd also played with Ricky Skaggs and Barbara Mandrell. He knew every good musician in Nashville. We asked him to form a band for us. No promises were made to the new musicians that they would have a job with me indefinitely. After what we'd been through, it was inappropriate to even pretend to think anything could ever again be definite.

I rehearsed with the new group and immediately realized how much pressure was on them. They knew that some fans would compare them to the old band. Narvel tried to reassure them by pointing out that these fans could not be objective, that their attachment was sentimental and understandable, under the circumstances. We all had to try to do the best job we could—it would be hard for all of us.

I mentally prepared myself for that first show in Columbus, Ohio. I knew that I would turn around and see Andre Reese instead of Michael Thomas playing lead guitar or Charlie Anderson on bass guitar instead of Terry Jackson. I knew that the sound would be the same but different. I knew that the new players' body language would be new.

And I was pulling for them. Those guys held up like troupers, totally applying themselves to their playing and performing. I respect them for taking the job and respect them more for pulling it off so magnificently.

Vince Gill opened the show, then sat offstage with Sandi on instrument cases while watching my set. She had been so incredibly close to my former players, and she cried through the entire show. Vince put his arm around her and never took it down until I sang my last note.

❧

THERE WOULD STILL BE MANY DIFFICULT DAYS AHEAD FOR US ALL. Early on, before the Columbus date Narvel had told Joe Mc-Glohon that he didn't have to go back on the road with me. But he wanted to, and was one of the most understanding people about my reasons for going back to work so soon. So Narvel named Joe McGlohon band leader, and as part of his new role, Joe was to help teach our sound to the new players. But he missed his buddies greatly, and he began to bury his distress in alcohol.

Although Joe was never drunk onstage, he'd head for the nearest bar immediately after the shows, and often went down the road drunk with the band that was looking to him for leadership. As Joe recalls, "I didn't know which end was up."

Narvel told Joe he understood the tremendous strain he was under and sympathized, but that he could no longer drink heavily on the bus. Then, not long after he was named band leader, we went on an extended tour of Canada. "And I left a swath of empty whiskey bottles in many bars," Joe said in 1993. "I tried dealing with it that way."

His behavior was also changing in ways that made us all concerned. He didn't talk much to the new guys and seemed to be making an unconscious effort to recover the past. He began to wear his hair like Tony. Then he'd do his hair like Kirk's. He had kept a lot of the guys' clothes from the bus. "I wore some of Michael's clothes," Joe said. "I wore all of those guys' clothes. I did that for about a year. A shirt here, something else there. I wore Tony's hat for a while. I don't know, it was just some tangible piece of them I was trying to hold on to. I definitely hung on to bits and pieces.''

Throughout his trauma, Joe always thought about the band members' families. He called them regularly and talked to them for a long time whenever they came to recover personal property. The goodness he showed was helping him, but not enough.

I had lost too many friends to death. I didn't want to lose another to grief. So it came to the point where Narvel told Joe to straighten up or leave.

That probably saved Joe's life. He finally came around and is still my band leader to this day. Joe is a terrific father and a very happily married man. We're very proud of him.

❦

AT THE END OF 1991, NARVEL AND I HAD TO CONSIDER WHAT WE WERE going to do about a band for 1992. My musical organization has a history of changing each year. It's common knowledge in Nashville that I—and other entertainers—add and subtract players at the beginning of each year. I think that change helps maintain a band's freshness; I even go so far as to change my entire show every year—costumes, choreography, videos, and, of course, songs.

We asked a number of the new band members—Joe, Charlie "Chopper" Anderson, and Andre Reese—to return with us in January. The others, six altogether, were given ample notice, along with our heartfelt appreciation for all they'd done for us. That was on December 4, 1991. As most Nashville entertainers hire their bands at the beginning of each year, we wanted these people to have plenty of time to find new employment. We also invited them to play my New Year's Eve show at double salary.

All but one member of the band took a professional attitude. The disgruntled musician talked to a reporter and a big story followed. It said I had fired my band two weeks before Christmas and suggested that I didn't care about the players or their families. It made no mention of my considerations.

The story was a distortion and an embarrassment for me. It was an unfortunate end to a painful, difficult year. I had to wonder at the time if the fallout from the tragedy we'd suffered would ever stop.

❧

BUT THROUGHOUT THIS SAD TIME, THE OUTPOURING OF SUPPORT from my fans was overwhelming. Let me tell you how much I appreciated your kindness in helping me get through it. I love each and every one of you for your love and support, as well as for your financial help to the victims' families.

I'm very grateful to members of the country music community too—for the flowers, letters, donations to the families, phone calls, for coming by, for being at the memorial service, and for being my friends, I thank you.

And I owe a special expression of gratitude to C. K. Spurlock, Kenny Rogers's international promoter. C.K., who was very close to Michael Thomas, was the one who organized the benefit to provide financial help to the crash victims' families.

C.K. staged the benefit at Nashville's Municipal Auditorium, which is where I hold my annual Fan Fair party each June. In addition, a second benefit starring Merle Haggard was held at Pheasant Run Theater in Chicago. All the proceeds, including contributions mailed in by fans, went directly to the survivors.

To organize the Nashville show, C.K. got on the telephone and simply asked entertainers to appear. Word of mouth about the program spread like wildfire on Music Row, and artists began calling him asking if they could perform too. Eventually, there was more talent than time to present it, and a few acts had to be turned down.

Entertainers on the show included Ricky Van Shelton, T.

Graham Brown, Gary Morris, Patty Loveless, K. T. Oslin, Eddie Rabbitt, Willie Nelson, Exile, the Oak Ridge Boys, and Kenny Rogers. Ralph Emery, the former "Nashville Now" host, was the master of ceremonies.

Each performer donated his or her time, and a few passed up paying engagements so they could be at the benefit concert. Willie Nelson was in the middle of a recording session, left to do his set, and then returned to the studio.

Many singers used a house band that C.K. had put together and the rest paid for their own bands' time, as well as transportation and lodging. Monies from ticket sales and fan donations were deposited in Nashville's Third National Bank a few days in advance, so there would be checks ready to present to the families at the show.

The evening was bittersweet. The sellout crowd seemed a little confused at first, C.K. remembers, because they didn't know if they were meant to let go and have a good time at a concert memorializing such a sad event. Eventually, the overall mood was happiness.

The evening was a difficult one for me—it was gratifying to be a part of this great tribute to my people, but deeply emotional too. Narvel and I had reached that stage of mourning where you think you're beginning to recover but you're not. So at first we weren't even sure that we should even go. The previous weeks had drained us, spiritually and physically. I wasn't scheduled to entertain, and we weren't certain what our function would be.

But I realized that some of the entertainers were reaching out to me as well as the families. And I decided my place was with them, I belonged there.

I used to end all of my shows with "Sweet Dreams." It had been the last song the band had ever heard me sing. So in the middle of the benefit program, I walked onstage and sang it a cappella, just as I had done that night in San Diego.

❦

IN MAY 1991, I WENT INTO THE STUDIO TO RECORD *FOR MY BROKEN Heart,* the album that was my commemoration of the band and of other lost loved ones. Some of the session musicians, among others, remarked on how sad the songs were, but as I wrote for the liner notes:

> It seems your current emotional status determines what music you'd like to hear. That's what happened on the song selection for this album. If for any reason you can relate to the emotion packed inside these songs, I hope it's a form of healing for all our broken hearts.

FOR MY BROKEN HEART MEANS THE MOST TO ME OF ALL THE ALBUMS I've recorded. It clearly expresses my feelings of hurt and my hope for healing. In the time after the tragedy, my thoughts were really reflected in the words of the title song, ". . . I guess the world didn't stop for my broken heart."

I heard that song, written by Liz Hengber and Keith Palmer, for the first time in early 1991 and I remember how it gave me chills. Originally, I planned to record it with Clint Black. But the crash and other things prevented Clint and me from getting together. I never recorded it as a duet.

The final song on the album is called "If I Had Only Known," obviously dedicated to my band and Jim. Matt Rollings and John Jarvis played for me on it. I recorded that song last intentionally. I thought that once the musicians were through laying down the instrumental tracks on the other songs, they'd leave the building. So if I did happen to lose it when I sang the song, at least I wouldn't have an audience. One of the few who stayed was Larry Londin, the greatest drummer I've ever worked with. We lost Larry in the summer of 1992; I miss him terribly.

I ran through the song once with John and Matt and then recorded it. "That's it," I told Tony Brown, my producer. "That's all I can do." He understood. There was so much of my heart in that song it tore me up to sing it. Listening to it later, I realized that the song isn't in perfect meter, but that didn't seem to matter.

It is a song about living for the moment, the only moment we know for sure we have:

If I Had Only Known

If I had only known it was our last walk in the rain
I'd keep you out for hours in the storm.
I would hold your hand like a lifeline to my heart
Underneath the thunder we'd be warm.
If I had only known it was our last walk in the rain

If I had only known I'd never hear your voice again . . .

THERE HAVE ONLY BEEN A FEW TIMES THAT I HAVE SUNG "IF I HAD Only Known." For a while I wasn't sure that I could perform it publicly at all. I tried it at one of my shows as an encore, and it left people walking out of the auditorium very sedate and quiet. I performed it on an AIDS benefit television special, which seemed appropriate. I also performed that song in a video for the St. Jude's Hospital in Memphis, Tennessee, and it's on the sound track for the movie *8 Seconds,* the Lane Frost story. I also sang it on "Oprah Winfrey," where some of the audience cried through the whole song.

I was caught off guard on that show. Right after I was introduced, the first thing I was hit with was film footage of the crash, while a camera stayed on my face to register my reaction. I was shocked, but now I see that Oprah is a very wise woman. She recognized how, when you're a public figure, folks look to you for leadership. They want to see how you handle a tragedy that might be similar to one they once went through or might go through. But for a while, I was too brokenhearted to assume the role.

⚜

MUSIC IS SO WEIRD SOMETIMES, SO THERAPEUTIC AND HEALING. IT'S almost like it's waiting to be there for you when you need it— just like a good friend with open arms. In 1992, when I went into the studio to record my new album, *It's Your Call,* the first song I chose was Skip Ewing's "Lighter Shade of Blue." I had found it just before we left on that fateful trip to San Diego and it had really moved me. Then, when we returned to Nashville after the crash, on the night of March 16, I had gone back down to my office in the house and played that song again. It gave me hope in those dark days that my sorrow would eventually subside.

When the new album came out in 1993 with "Lighter Shade of Blue" on it, people would ask me if I was "over" the crash. I could only say, "It's just like the song . . . 'I've only turned a lighter shade of blue.' "

CHAPTER 18

I N THE AFTERMATH OF THE CRASH, WE WERE TOURING A LOT BUT I found myself wishing for something different to do to get my mind off the accident. The answer to my prayer came from Ken Kragen, Kenny Rogers's manager. Kenny was making a two-part television miniseries, *The Gambler IV: The Gambler Returns,* and he wanted me to be in it. I had thought that *Tremors* would be my first and last movie, but I really needed a distraction and I knew it would be a lot of fun to work with Kenny. I've always been a huge fan of his. I got to play a madam back at the turn of the century. It was a western so I rode a horse and wore beautiful full dresses.

Dick Lowry, the director, helped me a great deal with my acting technique. One of the most important tips he gave me was to slow down and lower my pitch when I was talking before a camera. Kenny always talks so fast that he had me rattling like an auctioneer to keep up with him! I've used Dick's advice in every movie I've made since.

My next role came in 1993, in the made-for-TV movie *Man from Left Field,* in which I co-starred with Burt Reynolds. Burt is not only a great actor, but he's also a great director. Part of the reason I accepted the role was that Burt had directed me earlier in an episode of his hit television series "Evening Shade." Burt is also great with the folks around Jupiter, Florida, where we filmed the movie. He has given so much back to his community. They all think the world of him—just like I do.

In the movie, Burt unintentionally helped me moderate my speech because he talks so slowly himself—enough so that I sometimes wondered if he had forgotten his lines. He'd look down at the tablecloth or stare into space when I thought he should be talking. But that was just the timing that makes him Burt Reynolds.

In one scene, where Burt and I were lying in the sand, he had about three pages of dialogue to do. If I'd thought about it, I would have wondered how in the world he could memorize all of that. Suddenly, I heard a tiny, muffled voice.

"Where is that coming from?" I said to myself. But I stayed in character, as you're supposed to do until someone yells, "Cut."

I heard Burt say his line, then the little electronic voice again. Finally I noticed a wire running from inside Burt's shirt to an earpiece. Someone off camera was feeding him his lines! I thought that was clever, and had I known that could be done, I might have asked for the assistance myself.

Man from Left Field was a fun movie to do. All the kids in it were local kids, and they did a marvelous job! Look out Hollywood! Shelby was with me part of the time on the movie so it was a lot more vacation than work. Sandi did my hair for the movie and I did my own makeup. Thanks, Burt, for the opportunity.

That same spring, I got the part of Ma Tex in the movie *North,* which had a cast accomplished enough to intimidate any fairly green actor: Bruce Willis, Dan Ackroyd, Kathy Bates, and many more! I learned a lot by watching them work. The film's star was Elijah Woods, the child actor star of *Huckleberry Finn*. It was produced and directed by Rob Reiner, who treated me as nicely as I could have ever asked for.

None of the actors were allowed to drive their cars onto one of the locations outside of L.A. We all had to drive to a certain point and then be shuttled in—except for Bruce. But his idea of a car was an eighteen-wheel semitrailer truck that carried his private gymnasium. I sure got a kick out of that!

And I really enjoyed Dan Ackroyd. On the first day, after Dan and I had rehearsed our dance routine a couple of times, I thought I was making a joke when I said to Rob, "I think he could have a career in dancing someday."

"Uh, he's already had a pretty good career there," Rob said.

I had forgotten that Dan and the late John Belushi had developed the characters the Blues Brothers, who sang and danced in their hit motion picture, on "Saturday Night Live" for years, and even opened for the Rolling Stones. I felt like I had my foot in my mouth plumb up to my ankle.

Dan entertained us on the set with stories about his actual ghostbusting service, which he and his brother had set up and which may have inspired Dan's hit movie *Ghostbusters*. The service is very serious and scientific. They literally go into houses that are supposed to be haunted and rid the places of the presences. His great-grandfather conducted séances so Dan kinda came by his ghostbusting honestly.

And in 1994, I got a small cameo part in the movie *The Little Rascals*. That came about after I had met the director and producer, Penelope Spheeris, when I was auditioning for a part in *The Beverly Hillbillies*. I didn't get that part, but Penelope remembered me and I got to work with her in her next movie. It was great. She's a super director and I loved working with her.

I'm also releasing my own made-for-TV movie, based on my video *Is There Life Out There?* It's the story of a woman who's made a good life—marriage, children, a home—but she can't help but wonder if she's missing out on something. The video ends with the woman (me) receiving a college diploma and a chance to make her good life better.

Nothing I've ever done has touched so many women's hearts. I can't count the number of letters I've gotten from women who said they went back to school after watching that video. I even received a letter from a guy who said that he was working two jobs, and came home from work one night to find his wife crying on the couch. He looked at the television screen and saw my character getting her diploma. He vowed then and there that he was going to put his wife through school, no matter what it took from him.

She's a lucky woman to have a man like that.

It's responses like these that make me feel so blessed and lucky at what I get to do for a living—that I have the chance to give people a message that can inspire their lives. The songwriters, Rick Giles and Susan Longacre, did a lot of good for people by creating and writing that song, and it's one that I'm proud to sing. I hope that the movie will help spread the word that yes, girls—and guys too—there is life out there; and you can reach out for your dreams.

❧

I'VE HAD A GOOD LIFE MYSELF, AND IT MAKES ME FEEL GOOD TO GIVE something back, not only through my music but also through social involvement.

One way I'm doing that is through the Reba Ranch House. It's connected to the Texoma Medical Center in Denison, Texas, about sixty miles away from the town where I grew up. It's a home away from home for families whose loved ones are hospitalized at the Center, so they can be nearby to care for and comfort them. Ranch House Director Barbara Potter takes care of the house along with Billie Jennings, the housekeeper. It has eight bedrooms with a living room, library, playroom, and kitchen.

The lighted walkway through the woods from the ranch house to the hospital center is dedicated to the memory of my band.

It's a project I'm very proud of. My heart goes out to the folks who stay there. The Development Committee, Barbara, Billie, Narvel, and I all hope you never have to come back again. But if you do the Reba Ranch House is there for you.

Recently I've gotten involved with another wonderful organization, Habitat for Humanity. It's a group that builds new houses or restores abandoned ones for, as their slogan goes, "God's People in Need" around the world. Volunteers work side-by-side with the homeowners, who contribute five hundred hours of "sweat equity" and then get zero-interest mortgages to buy the property. So I helped select Gail Kinzer, who is a data-entry operator with two children, to be a homeowner. I underwrote the construction costs of her new Nashville home. And here's a nice twist: That home was the first one in the entire worldwide Habitat for Humanity program ever to be sponsored and built entirely by women!

⁓⁓⁓

SINCE WE FIRST STARTED IN 1988, STARSTRUCK ENTERTAINMENT HAS been expanding to include three music publishing companies, a publicity agency, a concert booking and promotions agency, a construction company, a racing stable, a jet service company, my fan club, an advertising company, and an artist management company that includes four managers and their assistants.

The music publishing companies were formed after I had been a contract writer for several years in the 1980s for the Welk Music Group in Nashville. The songs I wrote before that went into Red Steagall's publishing company. My biggest hit—in fact the only single ever released of a song I've written—is "Only in My Mind." In it, after being asked if he or she ever cheated, the person answers, "Only in my mind." I wrote it in my dressing room one night on tour, with my eyeliner pencil on a paper towel. I recorded it, and it went to number five on the *Billboard* charts. I'm very proud of that.

But while I do write songs myself, most of the material my companies publish comes from eight to ten staff writers. They've produced some terrific work, including "For My Broken Heart" and "It's Your Call," both title songs from my platinum-selling albums. Their primary job isn't necessarily to create songs for me. Our song pitchers, as we call them, make sure as many producers and artists as possible hear Starstruck songs.

As for me, no matter who writes them, or publishes them, I'll only record songs that I love, that touch my heart. I almost hate to tell you some of the songs that I've turned down, including "Does Fort Worth Ever Cross Your Mind?" which was a big hit for George Strait. I really toyed with that one, but I could never get used to that line in it about "cold Fort Worth beer." I'd never sung a song with beer in it, so I just decided it wasn't right. And I also passed on "Learning to Live Again," a great song, which Garth Brooks picked up. When I saw him singing it on the Jay Leno show, I said, "Hey Narvel, I turned that song down," and he said, *"You did what?"* But I thought it was better for a man to sing, and I'm just really glad for Garth that he did it.

I'm not sick about turning those songs down—again, I just had to go with my gut feelings.

So, while I believe in my writers, of course, I'm also very honest with them. If I don't like a song, even if it's a good song, it's just not for me. I think that is one of the reasons my career has stayed strong for seventeen years—because I've learned that the song is the foundation of it all. The song has to be the best.

As of February 1994, our aviation company has expanded to owning two jets and managing three. We lease them to anyone who has a need—corporate people as well as entertainers. I feel it's a business that has lots of room to grow. We deal in sales, management, leasing, and charter.

Our construction company started after we completed all the building at our place in Gallatin, Tennessee. The next big under-

taking will be our new headquarters for Starstruck Entertainment, which will cover five lots on Nashville's world-famous
Music Row. Construction began in February 1994.

Starstruck Farms, our horse racing division, is expanding too:
We handle horses all the way from breeding to watching them
run on the track. Since I've always been a fan of horses and
racing, it thrills me to watch horses race down the homestretch,
and even more so if one of them belongs to me.

At the beginning of 1994, Starstruck Farms has twenty-nine
horses, with three babies on the way. Three of them are quarter
horses and the rest are thoroughbreds. We also have three horses
in partnership with Joe Gehl. We have horses in New York,
Florida, Arkansas, Louisiana, Kentucky, Oklahoma, and Texas, as
well as at our place in Gallatin, Tennessee. They have run at such
major tracks as Saratoga, Belmont, Aqueduct, the Meadowlands,
Gulfstream, and Oaklawn. We've had a few letdown-losings, but
also some exciting wins!

Patricia Lounsbury-Lagden, our Starstruck Farms manager,
breaks the horses we buy and gets them jockey-ready. The horses
are then sent to Kindergarten Farms in Ocala, Florida, where
Jimmy Gladwell prepares them for the track.

These horses are beautiful, temperamental, calm, flighty, and
fun. The hardest thing about having stables is seeing one of the
horses get so sick or injured that it has to be destroyed. We've
lost three horses so far, and it's been heartbreaking.

One of them was Kiowa Cowboy. Narvel and I had gotten
that horse as a yearling at the Keeneland Sales in Lexington,
Kentucky. Before you give a horse a name, you have to check by
computer to be sure that it hasn't been used before. But I very
much doubted that anyone else would pick "Kiowa Cowboy,"
which was the name of my high school mascot back in Kiowa,
Oklahoma. Narvel thought the name was goofy and suggested, "Well, why don't we call the next one 'Burleson
Elk'?"—referring to his Burleson, Texas, hometown.

But I won out.

Kiowa Cowboy was a three-year-old who won three of his seven races. His specialty was racing up from last place to a contender's position. I'll never forget his fifth race on March 5, 1993, at Aqueduct. It was snowing and the track was muddy. Kiowa Cowboy was last coming out of the starting gate and was never mentioned again until the homestretch. Then suddenly the announcer was shouting, ''And they're making the turn, coming down the homestretch, and it's Go Cuervo, Cinco Roy, followed by Kiowa Cowboy. But dashing through the snow, through the sleet, here comes Kiowa Cowboy!''

He won by three lengths.

Kiowa Cowboy quickly rose from a $25,000 claiming horse to a stakes horse, and I just know that, had he lived, he would have been a potential Kentucky Derby competitor. That horse had a lot of heart. It was during a Kentucky Derby ''prep race'' at Aqueduct on April 16, 1993, that he suffered his fatal injury. He was coming from eighth place to within a nose of taking the lead, but when he changed leads he put his foot down wrong and broke it. When he went down, he threw jockey Herb McCauley free from the saddle; Herb fortunately escaped injuries except for a broken collarbone.

Kiowa Cowboy had to be put to sleep immediately. It wasn't our decision to make. The track veterinarian just had to do what was humane.

We lost a second horse at Belmont to a viral infection. And on October 16, 1993, we lost a three-year-old stud colt to colic, which is a twisted intestine. He was in intense pain and he had to be put down.

Narvel and I have a few other horses now, A Firm Mister, Red McFly, and Chockie Mountain, who are as promising as Kiowa Cowboy. We can't wait to see what 1994 holds for all of our horses.

As for the music end of things, *FOR MY BROKEN HEART*, as of this writing, is headed for triple platinum. It won "Country Album of the Year" at the American Music Awards in 1992. Its follow-up, *It's Your Call,* also went double platinum in record time.

And in 1993, I got the chance to celebrate the success of someone especially close to me, one of my best friends in the business, Vince Gill, whom the Country Music Association named "Entertainer of the Year." His song, "When I Call Your Name," which had been out only two years, had become the second bestselling country music song of all time. It was with Vince that I did the fourth and fifth duets of my career, "Oklahoma Swing" and "The Heart Won't Lie." I'd done my first two with Jacky Ward, "Three Sheets in the Wind" and "That Makes Two of Us" and my third with Hank Williams Jr., "Mind Your Own Business."

"The Heart Won't Lie" was a big hit for Vince and me. In 1992, he toured with me, and we did "The Heart Won't Lie" together onstage. But now when I perform it alone in my live show, we project a videotape of Vince on a video wall and on the video screens. I stand next to Vince's video image so that it looks like we're singing together. I once had a fan ask me who I got to stand in for Vince Gill. That's when I knew our optical illusion was working well. The crowds love it.

One night in 1993, Vince opened my show at the Greek Theatre in Los Angeles during the last game of the 1993 World Series. An avid sports fan, he set up a small television onstage, right between his sound monitors. During his instrumental breaks, he kept stepping back to look at the game, and then he would ease forward when it was time to sing again. You know what? He never missed a note!

It was funny how I met another person who, like Vince, I became a huge fan of.

Back in December 1989, when I was pregnant with Shelby

and, on doctor's orders, flat on my back in bed, I had lots of time to listen to demo tapes, to get ready for my 1990 LP, *Rumor Has It*. One night, when Narvel came home from the office, he asked, "Did you find any good songs today?"

I said, "I don't know about the songs, but there's one girl singing on a lot of these tapes, and *she's great!*"

Her voice was so believable, so personable—it touched me. When I played Narvel the tapes, he agreed with me. Checking up, Narvel found out that her name was Linda Davis and that she was on Sony Records and was represented by Irv Woolsey, George Strait's manager.

Before long, Linda left Irv and asked Narvel to be her manager, and after asking for her release from Sony, he got her a deal on Liberty Records. Then, after two albums and not much success, Narvel asked Jimmy Bowen to release her from her contract.

Linda decided to take a break from recording and get refocused. So Narvel asked me if I'd be interested in having Linda sing backup for me on the road. I thought it was a great idea and said, "How about getting Lang"—her husband, Lang Scott, who has a great voice and also plays acoustic guitar—"to join us too?"

That brought us up to six husband-and-wife teams in my organization: Linda Davis and Lang Scott in the band; Rose and Jimmy Carter, our house- and groundskeepers; Frances and Paul Voorhees, our truck drivers; Patricia Lounsbury-Lagden and Graeme Lagden, our horse farm and tour managers, respectively; Kim and Bill Nash, both writers in my publishing company; and, of course, Narvel and me. And it works out very well!

It was in the early part of 1993 that I came across the song "Does He Love You." I thought it was the perfect song for me and Linda to do as a duet. It's a strange story about that song. I knew from the very beginning that "Does He Love You" was a song just waiting for Linda Davis to sing it. At the time, Billy Stritch, who co-wrote it with Sandy Knox, was in a trio in which he sang and played the piano. The other two members of the trio, both female, needed a song to do, so Sandy and Billy got together and finished "Does He Love You" in 1982. It was later played for Liza Minnelli, Frank Sinatra, and Barbara Mandrell, but no one grabbed it until I did in 1993. That's destiny!

Narvel flipped over the tune too, but he sat me down for a serious talk. "I think MCA would rather you record this with somebody who's more established," he said.

"Well, who?" I asked.

Since Trisha Yearwood and Wynonna were both on MCA, it was easy to say they would be MCA's choices.

So I called Tony Brown, my producer, who told me that Wynonna would probably record the song if I asked her personally. He added that Wynonna didn't like to sing songs about marital problems, the theme of "Does He Love You." Still, I packaged the demo tape with a personal note to Wynonna and sent it to her via Larry Strictland, her stepfather, a former background singer for Elvis Presley. I never heard from Wynonna.

So during Fan Fair week in June 1993, I recorded the song with Linda.

It was one of the two new songs we put on my 1993 *Greatest Hits* album along with eight of my greatest hits. The first week it was released, that album shot to number eight on *Billboard*'s pop chart. And as a result, after we performed "Does He Love You" on the 1993 CMA Awards Show, Linda got a deal on Arista Records, the Clive Davis company whose Nashville division includes Alan Jackson, Pam Tillis, and Brooks and Dunn. And in 1994, "Does He Love You" won a Grammy for "Country Vocal Collaboration." I just know Linda's going to be a mega-star.

And I'll say it again: No matter what other people tell me, I've almost never gone wrong when I've followed my heart.

I'll give you one more example: From 1984 on, I wanted to record "Fancy," the 1968 hit that Bobby Gentry wrote and recorded. My producer at the time, Jimmy Bowen, was against it because he thought the song was strongly associated with Bobby and had probably seen all the popularity it ever would.

It wasn't until I changed producers in 1990, from Bowen to Tony Brown, that I was given the green light for "Fancy." Tony liked it as much as I did. The song only went to number seven on the charts, but the album it came from, *Rumor Has It,* sold more than any album I'd ever had up to then, mainly because of "Fancy." Again, I attribute that to my personal feeling about myself and my career, and the chills I got the first time I heard that song years ago.

In my stage show, I show parts of the music video of "Fancy" and I arrive onstage in the same costume, a coat, that I wear in the video. When the song builds to just the right place, I remove the coat to show a floor-length evening gown. It indicates how the once poor little girl grew up to become a mature and "successful" woman—a "rags to riches" type story.

I performed the song that way on the Music City News Awards Show during Fan Fair in 1993. As I looked over the bottom floor of the Grand Ole Opry House, I saw a lot of music industry people with funny looks on their faces. They had no idea I use that kind of theatrics when I'm onstage. The balcony was filled with fans, many of whom had seen my show, and they were just about going nuclear. They knew what to expect and were cheering me on.

I have become a firm believer in showmanship. I believe people come to my concerts to get something more than they can hear on their records at home. I want them to thoroughly enjoy my show, and I want them to leave that night wanting more.

But my showmanship wasn't the main thing that people were talking about that year. In September 1993, I had foot surgery and was supposed to lie in bed with my feet above my heart for five days. During that time, Sandi Spika came over to my house with some new dress designs, along with fabric swatches and pretty beads and sequins that she could use for the dresses she had drawn. We both wanted to come up with a dress that was really special for that year's CMA Awards Show, where I was scheduled to sing "Does He Love You," with Linda Davis. I selected a crimson fabric with blood-red beads and rhinestones, and Sandi and her mother, Alice Spika, made the dress for me.

It was spectacular. From the minute I walked onstage to sing, I was hearing "o-o-o-o-os" and "a-a-h-h-hs." But I soon realized that some of those sounds from the audience were actually gasps —at the lowness of my neckline.

Even Narvel had raised his eyebrows when he'd seen me in the dressing room. I had asked Sandi earlier to add on a few more beads in the right places, and she had. But I never tried the dress on again until the night of the show, and I have to admit that it was still a little—well, daring.

I think that dress shocked even more people than my singing "Respect" had on the CMA Awards Show. Photos went out over the news wire services to virtually every newspaper in America. Outraged letters immediately appeared in Nashville's two daily newspapers. Jerry House, a popular morning disc jockey on Nashville's WSIX, got such a strong protest from one woman he felt he had to defend me. When I called the next day to thank him for his help, he taped our conversation and played it on the air so the fans could hear my side. He was my knight in shining armor.

Two weeks later, I went on "The Tonight Show" and that dress was the first thing Jay Leno asked about. And during the whole uproar, I was performing at Caesars Palace, where I thought I'd better address the situation. I told the audience that I was not up to par because I had recently had foot surgery, then said, "So if I'm not doing all of my dance steps, be patient with me. Some guys in the back said that if I'd worn that red dress from the CMA Awards Show nobody would care if I danced or not."

Then I told the crowd that Sandi Spika had made the dress and had done a great job. "I just wish she had told me that I had it on backwards," I said.

They went wild.

This might be a good place to thank Sandi for all that she's done to help me further my career. She is an extremely talented and creative person, not only with material but also with hair. She's also a workaholic—I mean that as a compliment. She worked so many hours on my clothes for the CMA Awards Show one year that she fell asleep while sitting on the toilet in the middle of the night. When she woke up, both her legs had fallen asleep, and when she tried to get up, she fell over and almost knocked herself out on the bathtub.

And once, I discovered for myself just how big a part of her life her work actually is. I was at her house, and when I headed into her upstairs bathroom, she yelled for me to use the one downstairs.

"I'm already up here," I said. "I'll use this one."

"No," she insisted, "come downstairs."

"Sandi, why on earth don't you want me to use your upstairs bathroom?" I asked, and then I walked in and sat down.

Her shower curtain was the same fabric as one of the dresses she'd made for me! I guess she just loved that material. Either that or she didn't want to waste the leftovers.

But getting back to that infamous dress. The tabloids, of course, went crazy over it. On October 19, 1993, the *National Enquirer* ran a screaming headline: "OH REBA! MOM OUTRAGED BY SEXY DRESS THAT SHOCKED MILLIONS." The story inside called me a "hillbilly Madonna" and said that my Mama had called to scold me from her Oklahoma home.

The whole story was "a story," naturally. The truth is that Mama attended the awards show in Nashville along with my sister Susie and her husband Paul. And all she said to me at my office after the show was, "You need a few more sequins on that dress, girlie.'' Pake said he thought the dress was beautiful—and would look great on anybody other than his sister.

I never bothered to respond to the *Enquirer* story. Everyone knows that the tabloids invent things just to create a sensation, and the inaccuracies are sometimes comical. But there was one tabloid story that bothered me, and so because many of my fans ask about it, I thought I should set the record straight.

The story claimed that I had stripped off my clothes in front of Shawna, Narvel's oldest daughter, while he was in the room, embarrassing her and shocking Lisa, her mother, after Shawna told her the story. It said that the incident took place in my home.

That story was malicious, dishonest, and sick. Here is the truth:

One night in 1988, I was in my stateroom on my bus with the door closed, getting ready for a show. I was wearing pantyhose and a brassiere. Shawna was lying on the bed watching Breon Reynolds (then my hairdresser), who is female, by the way, help get me ready. There was no real reason for Shawna to be in there, but I saw no reason to kick her out. It was merely a friendly visit during get-ready time.

At one point, Narvel came into my stateroom to say that it was fifteen minutes until show time. Then he left.

That's the whole story—a perfectly innocent, thirty-second event. I know the tabloids and sensational TV shows give the public what they want, but I think it's sad that people's lives are invaded so others can make money off of it.

꧁꧂

BUT WHILE THE *STAR*'S VERSION BOTHERED ME BOTH BECAUSE IT was so preposterously false and because it violated the privacy of Narvel's children, who are not public figures like I am, I have to look on the bright side. Dolly Parton calls herself, with some humorous pride, ''the queen of the tabloids'' because she's been featured in so many of their wild tales. She must have felt hurt and mistreated dozens of times. So the fact that the tabloids would consider me anywhere near her league —worth picking on regularly—sort of means that I've arrived, I guess. It's a positive way of saying that I'm making it in my profession.

I didn't think so positively back in 1977, when I was just starting out in the music business. One or two of my songs had been released on Polygram-Mercury Records, and Mama and Daddy had driven me to Fan Fair. Mama stayed there with me inside the Polygram autograph booth, and as it turned out, she was about the only company I had.

I was supposed to sit there for two hours, and I spent about one hour, fifty-nine minutes, and forty-five seconds watching celebrities in all the other booths sign their names for happy fans. I might as well have been invisible.

Finally, an elderly man and his wife walked up to my booth.

"Oh, great!" I thought, "Somebody wants my autograph." My spirits lifted, I sat up straight, and got my pen ready.

As the couple came closer, I saw the man raise his eyes to read my name on a cardboard sign above my head.

"Pardon me," the man said. "Can you tell me where the bathroom is?"

So today I'm flattered when fans recognize me and ask for autographs or want to have their pictures taken with me. Sometimes I wish they would simply ask and not feel the need to apologize. "I know you're busy," one might say, "I hate to bother you, and I know you have a lot to do, but may I have my picture made with you?"

But I'm as guilty of doing that as anyone else. One time I was in my dressing room getting ready for a television special with Bob Hope in San Diego when somebody said Jimmy Stewart had just entered the building. No fan has ever been more excited than I was at that news.

"Take these rollers out of my hair," I said, and I took off to see Jimmy Stewart.

As I timidly walked up to him, do you know what I said?

"I know you're busy and I know you have a lot to do, but may I have my picture made with you?"

He kindly granted my wish.

We all have many experiences that seem designed to keep us humble. Once I was invited to the White House by President George Bush. When Narvel, Shelby, and I were escorted into the President's chambers, we stood in awe—but Shelby, less than a year old, grabbed the President's thumb and started slobbering on it. I apologized, but he told me not to worry about it—he was used to that from his own grandchildren.

Mrs. Bush was very welcoming and gracious, and even showed us where they lived and the rooms where other Presidents had slept. I stood in one of the rooms that Jackie Kennedy had redecorated and in the Lincoln Room where Michael Jackson had stood at the window and waved to fans. A girl who never had her own room as a child walked among the private chambers of the most powerful men in history.

On another visit to Washington, I performed on the same stage as Aretha Franklin, the First Lady of Soul, on a Christmas special from Constitution Hall, hosted by John Denver. Narvel, Sandi, and I had flown to Washington that night from an engagement in Las Vegas, and I remember worrying so much about how I looked that I put on fresh makeup and changed clothes on the plane. Then Aretha arrived and set my mind at ease—she was wearing a bathrobe embroidered with an "A" and a midlength mink over that!

When it was time for her to rehearse her song, she only mouthed her words. The conductor stopped the song and asked why she wasn't singing. She told him that she didn't sing during rehearsals, but that she would when it was her time on the show. And you can be sure that, later that night, her performance was outstanding, rehearsal or no rehearsal.

After the show, Mrs. Bush invited us all to the White House, where she had twenty-one spruce trees beautifully decorated in different themes. She showed Aretha to the piano that had been a gift to one of the Presidents many years ago. Aretha played and sang "Amazing Grace." It was a very memorable moment.

◈

STILL, MEETING SOME OF THESE FAMOUS FOLKS HASN'T IMPRESSED ME as much as meeting some of my everyday fans. So many of them have followed my career from the very beginning, and I appreciate their loyalty tremendously.

I have wonderfully devoted fans who travel for hundreds of miles behind one of my buses. They'll follow it from the Midwest to Florida where I might be doing four days' worth of shows.

I've heard that fans skip school or work to stand in line to buy concert tickets. I've heard that they camp out for several nights in the freezing weather and snow so they could get a good seat.

I've seen fans come to my concession table and say they were spending their rent money to buy a cassette. I used to sit at that table after shows, signing autographs, and whenever a fan said that to me, I'd give him or her the cassette free of charge. The guys running the concession table got on to me for that.

I have fans who come to my shows in wheelchairs or on crutches.

No one could be more loyal or loving than my fans. They have put groceries on my table for years.

I hope that in some way I have brought a little joy into their lives.

CHAPTER 19

HAPPINESS TO ME IS BEING ABLE TO HAVE YOUR FAMILY around you, and knowing that they want to be.

When I've had a long day of photo shoots, recording sessions, or television shows, and I walk in tired and Shelby's little voice says, "Weba, is that you?" and then he runs down the stairs and wraps his little arms around me, that's the greatest feeling in the world.

And when I tuck Shelby into bed, we say our prayers together and he asks for blessings upon his mama and daddy and others among our friends and family. If he isn't sleepy, and if he doesn't want me to leave, he'll ask for blessings for everybody he knows, as well as for the curtains, the chairs, the pillows, and all of his stuffed animals. And afterward we say, "Thank you, Jesus, you live in our hearts."

I thank the Lord daily for Shelby, and for putting Narvel and me together so we could have him. Family unity is priceless. So I want Shelby with me a lot, and I often take him along on personal appearance tours. He and I might go swimming or just play during the day and then I leave him with Michelle, his nanny, while I do my show. Sometimes, he goes to my after-show visits with members of my fan club.

At my annual fan club party in June 1993, Shelby came onstage with me. He looked the crowd right in the eye, and he talked to me and he talked to them. I know it thrilled him to be in front of an audience. He already has quite a bit of show biz in him.

In October of that same year, I was playing Las Vegas and Shelby flew out with Cindy Bailey, who was then his nanny. On the second night he asked if he could go to my show with me.

"Shelby, do you want to come out on the stage tonight and bring me a towel because I sure do get sweaty?"

"Yeah, Mama," he said. "I do that."

So I told Graeme Lagden, my tour manager, "When I say, 'I've been worried about how to introduce Shelby into the workplace, especially since this is the music business,' send him out."

So Shelby came out right on cue, carrying a towel. Instead of bringing me a rose or something, he was bringing me something that meant he was really working. The crowd loved it.

I played Phoenix the next night and asked Shelby if he'd like to repeat his performance.

"No, Mom," he said. "I'm too tired of that. Let Graeme do it."

I have a million cute stories about him, like any mother has!

One has to do with Shelby's potty training and the honesty of a child.

Shelby learned to use the bathroom by coming to me and saying, "Pee-pee, Mama, pee-pee." We'd run to the bathroom, Shelby would do his business, and I'd say, "Good boy, Shelby, good boy."

One day when we were on vacation, in 1992, Narvel, Shelby, and I were in the bathroom getting ready to go out to eat. Shelby still carries a security blanket, and was carrying it inside the bathroom with Narvel and me. When Narvel stepped over to the toilet to use it, Shelby walked over to him, took his blankey out of his mouth, and said, "Good boy, Dad, good boy."

That was one for the baby book.

Shelby has owned two dogs. Red Steagall gave him a beautiful golden Labrador retriever, which we named Chockie after my old hometown. Chockie had a bad habit of going across the road to see other dogs and also across the highway to a convenience store. So one day when Chockie went over there, Mark Garrison, one of our groundskeepers, rode over on the golf cart to pick him up. He loaded Chockie up in the cart and started back across the highway, but Chockie jumped out. He was killed by a semitrailer truck.

That was the first dog that Shelby lost, and it took me a long time to tell Red, because I felt so bad about the whole thing.

Shelby's next dog came on his second birthday. Dixie Stephens, who handles the itinerary for Starstruck, had a litter of cocker spaniel puppies, so we bought one and named him Freckles.

About fifty people, including twelve children, were at Shelby's birthday party when Narvel came in with Freckles. I took the dog from Narvel and handed him to Shelby, whose little face lit up when he saw him. I just bawled, it was so moving and cute. All the kids gathered around Shelby and Freckles. I thought I was gonna have to rescue the dog.

Freckles lasted until the spring of 1993 when he ran across a road by our house and a lady accidentally hit him. Mark put Freckles on the floor of his truck to take him to the veterinarian, but by the time he came and told me and got back to his truck, Freckles was dead. Mark had to bury both of Shelby's dogs.

One day Shelby and I were in my Explorer truck, and Brandon, Narvel's seventeen-year-old son, was in the back with Shelby.

"Shelby," I said, "tell Brandon where Chockie went."

"Chockie's gone to Jesus," Shelby said.

"Well, where is Freckles?" I said.

"Freckles's gone to Jesus," Shelby said.

Knowing his answer would come from our nightly prayers, I asked, "Shelby, where does Jesus live?"

He took his blanket out of his mouth and said, "Florida?"

MY SON'S CHILDHOOD, OBVIOUSLY, WON'T HAVE ANYTHING IN COMmon with my own. People ask if I'm afraid Shelby will be spoiled, and I tell folks I know he's already spoiled, but so am I. Not many people lived the way I grew up, and not many live the way I do now. Folks know I attribute a lot of my success to the ability to work hard, which I learned as a kid from Mama and Daddy.

So it's always been very important to me that Shelby respect people who work for a living. My husband Narvel and I are very blessed with a lot of nice things and Shelby will always be required to treat these things nicely because we worked hard to get them. They weren't given to us.

Sometimes he asks Rose, my housekeeper, to play with him.

"No, Shelby, Rose can't play," I tell him, "because Rose has to work."

"Okay," Shelby says, "I help Rose work." And he does some simple job that is a big deal to him. It's cute and it's also a very effective lesson.

I've always believed that children need and want discipline. Shelby's nannies have always had my permission to discipline Shelby if they need to. I expect him to behave himself and to have good manners—and he does.

Narvel and I have made it a practice to teach Shelby to look grown-ups in the eye when he talks to them, and to call them "ma'am" and "sir." He's only four but he's definitely old enough to say "please" and "thank you." In the summer of 1993, Narvel and I took him to some carnival rides in Santa Monica, California. We let him hand his own ticket to the ride attendant while we watched from the side. He thanked the man for the ride in his little boy's voice, and I was so proud I could have cried.

Some of my friends have been very complimentary of Shelby's behavior, and I appreciate their kind words.

I play with Shelby and I try to teach him when we're together. It's quality time. But it's also important for him to play alone. And when I'm absent, I make no apologies because I don't feel any guilt. Shelby is in good hands and is totally loved at all times.

In July 1993, I went to a press conference in New York City, where the reporters began to question me about Shelby and my career. One seriously asked me which was more important to me. I said, "Shelby, of course."

Some journalists mildly applauded, as if I might have said something else. I don't understand that thinking. My personal philosophy for happiness is having my cake and getting to eat it too. I've been at that point for a few years now.

❦

I LOVE MY LIFE WITH NARVEL AND SHELBY. AND I'M BLESSED WITH really liking all the folks I get to work with.

Narvel and I had a wonderful time this past Christmas. First, we took employees of the whole Starstruck organization and their spouses to Naples, Florida, for our annual year-end retreat. We had a great time playing volleyball, golf, tennis, going deep sea fishing, shopping, and hanging out on the beach.

My bunch works very hard and they play hard too! I'm proud of every one of them.

Then Narvel, Shelby, and I took off for Aspen, Colorado,

for two weeks of rest and relaxation. We met up with our friends, Ralph and Joy Emery, and their family along with Ken and Barbara Mandrell Dudney and their kids, Matt, Jaime, and Nathan. We met at the T. Lazy Seven Restaurant, as we did last year, to eat steaks, dance, and visit. We had a great time.

Ralph and his family went home after Christmas so they weren't in Colorado to celebrate the new year with us. So Narvel and I had the Dudneys over to our house to celebrate, along with Ben and Ellen Iannuzzi, my office controller and his wife, Pam and Ken Keller, our dentist friends from Nashville, their kids Chris and Zack and their friend Pate. Rose Carter, my house-keeper from Nashville, flew in to take care of us the week after Christmas. She brought the new year in with us.

That's happiness to me—enjoying my friends and family! And personal happiness is the most important thing of all. The money, the record sales, and all the rest just make everything go a lot easier!

⚜

ANOTHER IMPORTANT SOURCE OF HAPPINESS FOR ME IS THE FACT THAT my parents have long since escaped the poverty that afflicted their lives when us kids were young. They bought a new place four years ago. There is a window in the living room that goes from the floor to the ceiling and you can see in three directions for miles. Everything visible belongs to them.

At sixty-six, my Daddy oversees a seventeen-thousand-acre cattle ranch that spreads from Chockie, Oklahoma, to the Pitts-burg County line in southeast Oklahoma where I grew up, fifty miles from the Texas border. The very first words out of his mouth when he talked to Tom Carter about his place in String-town were, "I built this ranch myself. Reba didn't buy it for me." A lot of people have insinuated that. That bruises a cowboy's ego.

Daddy calls his ranch "rough old land." But his eyes scan the earth as he speaks, and you can tell he's proud of his spread, covered with brush thickets of no use to man or beast. The cattle can't eat them and they get in the way of anybody trying to round up a herd. Vehicles can't drive through them, horses get cut on the thorns, and no chemical will kill them.

So Daddy and Pake burn the brush of their respective land in late winter when the growth is dry, brittle, and flammable. Daddy says the Forest Service takes a dim view of the practice, thinking it could make out-of-control fires that might spread to adjoining ranches.

Daddy tried to hire a man this year to burn the brush, but the fellow said he couldn't do it yet. "It's too windy, Clark."

"That wind'll die down tonight," Daddy told him without ever getting out of his truck.

"Well, what would I do if it didn't, how would I put out the fire?" the man replied.

"Pee on it!" Daddy said, and drove away.

The next morning, a few hundred acres of Daddy's land were cinders. Daddy himself burned it in the night, when the wind died down as he knew it would. He started one fire to burn into another, so that each would burn the other out. He knew exactly how to do it. Not one bush, not one blade of grass, was burned that wasn't supposed to.

But when I called Mama and Daddy this past New Year's Day, I heard that she and Daddy had had a little excitement. After she told me about Garett, my niece, getting four wisdom teeth pulled, Mama said, "The other day your Daddy had been over at Fred Smith's place trying to gather a couple of steers that had gotten out. He roped one of the steers, dangling the rope in front of him until he tangled up and fell on the ground, and then

Daddy tied him up to a tree. He left him there until he could come back with a trailer.''

When Mama heard Daddy was going back over with the trailer she said she would go with him. "Well, if you're gonna go with me, I'll take Ole Roy (a horse) and try to catch the other steer," Daddy said.

Daddy doesn't rope off a horse unless someone's with him for safety reasons. He says he might not be found for days if something happened to him.

So they took off again to Fred Smith's place and Daddy got on Ole Roy and found the other steer close to the one tied to a tree. Even cattle become buddies and stay close together. So Daddy started trailing the steer, getting him used to the horse and then took after him to rope. Just about the time he was gonna throw, the steer looked back and something told Daddy to look back too.

The pasture was on fire.

Fred Smith and his hired hands, Tom Pinner and Blue, had driven up and were talking to Mama while Daddy was "cowboy-ing." The hired hand saw Ole Roy's hooves hit a rock and the sparks catch the knee-high tickle grass on fire.

Daddy jumped off his horse, tied him to a tree, let the steer go, and took his saddle off. He got the saddle blanket and went straight to fight the fire. It took all four of the men to put it out. My daddy is sixty-six years old. That's pretty good thinking for a sixty-six-year-old cowboy.

DADDY STILL GETS UP AROUND 4 OR 5 A.M., AS HE HAS DONE ALL HIS life. In March 1993, when Tom Carter, my collaborator, went out to interview him, he told Daddy that he'd call him in the morning and make plans to meet him. Tom assumed Daddy wouldn't be up quite so early because of his age and all.

Daddy called Tom's hotel room at 7 A.M.

"I thought you was gonna see me today!" Daddy said. "Did you change your mind?"

Daddy asked him to go along while he fed the cattle. He said he'd meet him "up on the highway," and that he'd be sitting in his feed truck.

"What color is the truck?" he was asked, "so I'll know it."

"Muddy," Daddy said and hung up.

For four hours Daddy bounced Tom through the rolling and rocky underbrush that sustains virtually nothing but cattle and rattlesnakes. Daddy's 1990 truck had over sixty thousand miles on it before the odometer broke. He estimates the figure is closer to seventy thousand now. Almost all those miles were run up on his ranch when the bluestem grass turns to brown for six months every year. During this period Daddy has to feed the animals from his truck the nourishment that won't grow from the ground.

On the way, Tom asked Daddy an obvious question: how many steers did he have? Daddy said he must have about 600 head. He does, plus 2,400 more. But then the next day Daddy said, "You remember yesterday when you asked me how many steers I have?"

"Yes."

"You should never ask a cow man how many head he has. That's like asking about his sex life. It ain't nobody's business. I didn't lie to you. I just didn't tell you all the truth. I waited until I liked you to do that."

Daddy looks like the cowboy he is. He has a rugged handsomeness, his face craggy and etched with lines from outdoor work that was too hard and paid too little. He is stocky and strong, a human fire hydrant under a Stetson. He's as tough as leather, yet somehow soft as a doe. He's hardness with a heart.

I've seen him stand in a hard wind so strong I couldn't hear him yell a few feet away. But he knows how to get upwind from his herd, let the howling air carry his voice and call in hundreds of cattle with just his yelling.

"They won't come much before daylight," he says. "But that there wind ain't no problem if you know what you're doing."

And he calls, in a plaintive, lonesome yell that no man can understand, but one that sets thousands of hooves in thundering motion, even in blinding snow. Seven mornings a week, from October through mid-April, the solitary voice of Clark McEntire echoes off the Chockie Mountains.

⁂

A COUPLE YEARS BACK, MY PARENTS CELEBRATED THEIR FORTY-SECOND wedding anniversary in a way they hadn't planned. Pake, Alice, Susie, their spouses and kids, Narvel, Shelby, and I, and some friends put on a surprise party for Mama and Daddy. We decided to meet at Pete's Place in Krebs, Oklahoma, about forty-five minutes north of Stringtown.

Us kids asked some of our parents' friends, Pauline and Max Kinyon, to invite them for supper at the restaurant. Daddy said he didn't know if he could come because he had to brand cattle. So Max said he would send one of his hired hands down to help Daddy, and he did. Daddy never suspected a thing.

Instead, he walked Mama into the restaurant where a waitress told them they could use the back private room. Daddy said they wouldn't need that much space, and didn't want to go back there. But they did.

As the door opened, I could see Mama as she was partially lit by the hall light behind her.

"Well here," she said, "the lights aren't even on in here. Are you sure this is the right room?" I think she and Daddy were just about ready to leave.

Then we yelled "Surprise!"

Mama's knees buckled and she almost went to the floor and

she started crying. Daddy didn't do or say a thing. That means he was really touched by the event. Mama kept crying and hugging each of her kids and grandkids. Narvel and I gave Mama and Daddy a brand-new Chevrolet van for their forty-second anniversary present, and as of November 1993, it had logged more than 40,000 miles. It was a small payback for all the automobiles they wore out hauling us kids around.

That's one of the best things about success—sharing it and bringing happiness to those you love the most.

❧

MAYBE IT'S JUST GETTING OLDER AND SETTLED IN LIFE THAT HAS helped me recognize these things, but in some ways, I'm sure, the tragedy of March 16, 1991, has helped bring it home to me how fragile life is—and how necessary it is to concentrate on the essentials. No matter what happens to you, if you can draw strength from God and the people you love, nothing can ever defeat you.

I remember flying home alone for the first time on our new airplane in June 1991, not long after the crash, to return to Nashville after the last day of filming *The Gambler IV*. Before I got on I walked up to the plane, and I asked God to bless it.

"Now Kevin," I said to Kevin McCutcheon, my pilot, "let's agree right now in the name of Jesus that everybody who steps in this plane is protected, and that they will fly safely and swiftly." He agreed.

I stepped onto the airplane and saw that Kevin had placed little bows on top of each seat. It was like a big present! He had also reclined the seats so that I could lie down. I slept soundly and peacefully. I always feel that way when God takes over.

In early November 1992, Narvel, Sandi, and I boarded another flight to Madison, Wisconsin, where our opening act, Brooks and Dunn, was getting ready to go onstage. By then I knew the sound of my plane's landing gear returning to place after takeoff. On that night in November, I suddenly realized I wasn't hearing what I was supposed to hear.

"Something's wrong," I said to Narvel.

"Yeah," he said.

About that time Kevin looked through the curtain and motioned for Narvel to come to the cockpit. When Narvel came back, he confirmed what we'd feared. "The landing gear didn't go up," he said, "and it won't go down. It's jammed. We're going to have to fly over to the Nashville airport and make some passes to let them look at it from the ground."

We made a low sweep over the airport so the tower could see the bottom of the plane. Then Kevin's voice came over the intercom. He spoke with assurance. "The tower has confirmed that the landing gear is jammed," he said. "So we're going to fly around a while to burn off some fuel. That way, if we make an emergency landing, we won't have as much fuel on board."

We cruised for forty-five minutes. During that time, to get our minds off of what could happen, Sandi and I played cards and talked about which Mexican restaurant we'd eat at in Albuquerque, where we'd be performing that weekend.

Narvel called Madison from the cabin telephone to tell Trey Turner, our in-house promoter, to ask Brooks and Dunn to extend their set because we would be late. Then he proceeded to tell Trey the details of our emergency. Later Graeme Lagden, my tour manager, said Trey went white while he talked to Narvel.

"What's wrong?" Graeme wanted to know.

"I can't talk about it," Trey said.

But finally Trey explained to Graeme, saying that Narvel would be calling back in twenty minutes to let him know our arrival time.

So Graeme and Trey sat down by the telephone and watched it.

"I look at that now," Graeme said recently, "and I know

that Narvel very well might not have called back. You know, you hear about your heart going into your throat? I thought, 'This just can't be happening, this just can't be happening again.' "

Graeme said that when the telephone finally rang, he began to cry.

Meanwhile, Kevin was talking to the tower and working constantly with the controls. He made one more low pass in front of the inspectors and then told us the news. "They have radioed," he said, "that our landing gear is still not where it needs to be. We're going to have to make an emergency landing."

On our first approach, I saw the fire trucks on the side of the runway, waiting, just like in the movies. I hadn't been too scared until then, but then I felt my eyes fill with tears.

I honestly didn't panic, and I remember thinking, "If it's my time, it's my time."

And then we heard from Kevin again. "We are going to land on the two back wheels, slow down as much as possible, and then come down on the nose and belly of the plane," he said. "It's going to be loud. There will be metal against concrete, and we should have a few sparks."

"Just as soon as we get the plane stopped," he went on, "and I shut down the engine, the lights will go out. Then unbuckle your seat belts and come to the front."

Narvel, Sandi, and I just looked at each other.

"If he thinks I'm waiting until he shuts this engine down, and turns off the lights, he's slightly wrong," Narvel said.

The plane was probably going about 200 miles per hour when the weight of its fuselage settled onto the runway. Its scraping lasted for what seemed like an eternity, and it was deafeningly loud. The few sparks Kevin said we might see looked like Niagara Falls of fire on the news footage later.

Vice President Al Gore was scheduled to arrive at the airport minutes after our forced landing, so the place was crawling with news cameramen, who wound up filming us. The videotape made the plane look like a drag racing car with wings that were sweating fire.

The instant the plane shrieked to a halt, Narvel, Sandi, and I jumped from our seats and lined up behind Kevin, waiting for him to open the door. Once on the ground, we were surrounded by men wearing what looked like space suits and holding hoses. They sprayed the plane down with a white foam.

From the air, Kevin had ordered the preparation of another plane complete with catering. We got right on it.

People have asked me if I hesitated to board an airplane after getting off one that had emergency-landed. I didn't.

"If you have a car wreck you get right into an ambulance," I told one interviewer.

Our plane touched down in Madison and we took the limousine to the back of the concert hall, as we had done hundreds of times before. Graeme walked me to my dressing room, briefing me as he does every night we have a show.

And once we were inside the dressing room, he did something he had never done before. He hugged me.

And then I went out and I did my show.

After the concert I held my usual visit with members of my fan club. None of them knew that our lives had been in jeopardy until they went home and saw it on the news. So one fan asked me, "Why don't you sign autographs and take pictures with your fans anymore? I saw you do that with the radio and VIP folks."

I told her that autograph sessions felt so impersonal, so I decided to really get to know my fans through backstage visits instead.

"Well, I'd rather have an autograph to take home and show people," the young lady said.

That hit me wrong. I told her, "I have Patsy Cline's autograph but I'd have given it to anyone to have been able to sit this close to her and just listen to her talk."

I probably mentioned Patsy Cline to that young fan because what had happened earlier that night was more on my mind than I knew.

But then I did what I've done so many times before, and what I'll do indefinitely—I got back on my airplane. I flew home so I could fly out the next day to the next show on the way to the rest of my life.

EPILOGUE

As I finish the writing of this book, I have also just completed my one-day filming of my cameo appearance in *The Little Rascals* in Los Angeles.

At this very moment, Shelby is in Tennessee, performing in his very first school program. I missed it.

Tomorrow and the next day will be filled with shooting the video *Why Haven't I Heard from You* for the new CD, *Read My Mind*. Then it's off to Baton Rouge, Louisiana, and Pensacola, Florida, for our tour dates.

My life goes on—thank you, Lord.

If I ever write another book, I hope I have as many good memories to put in it as I have had for this one.

But I feel for the person that might suggest I do—I might try to choke a liver out of them too!

DISCOGRAPHY

REBA MCENTIRE 1978
Mercury 836 330-4

Glad I Waited Just for You
One to One
Angel in Your Arms
I Don't Want to Be a One Night Stand
I've Waited All My Life for You
I Was Glad to Give My Everything to You
Take Your Love Away
There's Nothing Like the Love Between a Woman and a Man
Why Can't He Be You
Invitation to the Blues
Right Time of the Night

OUT OF A DREAM 1979
Mercury 836 331 4

(I Still Long to Hold You) Now & Then
Daddy
Last Night, Ev'ry Night
Make Me Feel Like a Woman Wants to Feel
That Makes Two of Us
Sweet Dreams
I'm a Woman
Rain Fallin'
Runaway Heart
It's Gotta Be Love

FEEL THE FIRE 1980
SRM-1-5029

(You Lift Me) Up to Heaven
Tears on My Pillow
I Don't Think Love Ought to Be That Way
Long Distance Lover
If I Had It My Way
I Can See Forever in Your Eyes
A Poor Man's Roses (Or a Rich Man's Gold)
My Turn
Look at the One (Who's Been Lookin' at You)
Suddenly There's a Valley

HEART TO HEART 1981
Mercury MCR 4-1-6003

Indelibly Blue
Ease the Fever
There Ain't No Love
How Does It Feel to Be Free
Only You (And You Alone)

Today All Over Again
Gonna Love Ya (Till the Cows Come Home)
Who?
Small Two Bedroom Starter
Love by Love

UNLIMITED 1982
Mercury 822-882-1-M-1

I'd Say You
Everything I'll Ever Own
What Do You Know About Heartache
Out of the Blue
Over, Under and Around
I'm Not That Lonely Yet
Whoever's Watchin'
Old Man River (I've Come to Talk Again)
You're the First Time I've Thought About Leaving
Can't Even Get the Blues No More

BEHIND THE SCENE 1983
Mercury 812-781-4

Love Isn't Love ('Til You Give It Away)
Is It Really Love
Reasons
Nickel Dreams
One Good Reason
You Really Better Love Me After This
There Ain't No Future in This
Why Do We Want (What We Know We Can't Have)
Pins & Needles
I Sacrificed More Than You'll Ever Lose

JUST A LITTLE LOVE 1984
MCA 5475

Just a Little Love
Poison Sugar
I'm Gettin' Over You
Every Second Someone Breaks a Heart
Tell Me What's So Good About Goodbye
He Broke Your Memory Last Night
If Only
Congratulations
Silver Eagle
You Are Always There for Me

MY KIND OF COUNTRY 1984
MCA 5516

How Blue
That's What He Said
I Want to Hear It from You
It's Not Over (If I'm Not Over You)
Somebody Should Leave
Everything but My Heart
Don't You Believe Him
Before I Met You
He's Only Everything
You've Got Me (Right Where You Want Me)

HAVE I GOT A DEAL FOR YOU 1985
MCA 5585

I'm in Love All Over
She's Single Again
The Great Divide
Have I Got a Deal for You
Red Roses (Won't Work Now)
Only in My Mind

She's the One Loving You Now
Whose Heartache Is This Anyway
I Don't Need Nothin' You Ain't Got
Don't Forget Your Way Home

THE BEST OF REBA MCENTIRE 1985
Mercury 824-342-1-M-1

(You Lift Me) Up to Heaven
There Ain't No Future in This
I Don't Think Love Ought to Be That Way
Only You (And You Alone)
I'm Not That Lonely Yet
Can't Even Get the Blues
Today All Over Again
Why Do We Want (What We Know We Can't Have)
My Turn
You're the First Time I've Thought About Leaving

WHOEVER'S IN NEW ENGLAND* 1986
MCA 5691

Can't Stop Now
You Can Take the Wings Off Me
Whoever's in New England
I'll Believe It When I Feel It
I've Seen Better Days
Little Rock
If You Only Knew
One Thin Dime
Don't Touch Me There
To Make That Same Mistake Again

---

* Gold
† Platinum
†† Double Platinum

WHAT AM I GONNA DO ABOUT YOU* 1986
MCA 5807

Why Not Tonight
What Am I Gonna Do About You
Lookin' for a New Love Story
Take Me Back
My Mind Is on You
Let the Music Lift You Up
I Heard Her Cryin'
No Such Thing
One Promise Too Late
Till It Snows in Mexico

THE LAST ONE TO KNOW* 1987
MCA 42030

The Last One to Know
The Girl Who Has Everything
Just Across the Rio Grande
I Don't Want to Mention Any Names
What You Gonna Do About Me
I Don't Want to Be Alone
The Stairs
Love Will Find Its Way to You
I've Still Got the Love We Made
Someone Else

GREATEST HITS VOL. I† 1987
MCA 5979

Just a Little Love
He Broke Your Memory Last Night
How Blue
Somebody Should Leave
Have I Got a Deal for You

Only in My Mind
Whoever's in New England
Little Rock
What Am I Gonna Do About You
One Promise Too Late

MERRY CHRISTMAS TO YOU 1987
MCA 42031

Away in the Manger
On This Day
O Holy Night
The Christmas Guest
Silent Night
Happy Birthday, Jesus
White Christmas
I'll Be Home for Christmas
A Christmas Letter
The Christmas Song

REBA* 1988
MCA 42134

So, So, So Long
Sunday Kind of Love
New Fool at an Old Game
You're the One I Dream About
Silly Me
Respect
Do Right by Me
I Know How He Feels
Wish I Were Only Lonely
Everytime You Touch Her (Think of Me)

SWEET SIXTEEN* 1989
MCA 6294

Cathy's Clown
'Til Love Comes Again
It Always Rains on Saturday
Am I the Only One Who Cares
Somebody Up There Likes Me
You Must Really Love Me
Say the Word
Little Girl
Walk On
A New Love

LIVE† 1989
MCA 8034

So, So, So Long
One Promise Too Late
Let the Music Lift You Up
Little Rock
New Fool at an Old Game
Little Girl
Can't Stop Now
Sunday Kind of Love
I Know How He Feels
Whoever's in New England
Cathy's Clown
You Must Really Love Me
Somebody Up There Likes Me
San Antonio Rose
Mama Tried
Night Life
Jolene
Sweet Dreams
Respect

RUMOR HAS IT[††] 1990
MCA 10016

Climb That Mountain High
Rumor Has It
Waitin' for the Deal to Go Down
You Lie
Now You Tell Me
Fancy
Fallin Out of Love
This Picture
You Remember Me
That's All She Wrote

FOR MY BROKEN HEART[††] 1991
MCA 10400

For My Broken Heart
Is There Life Out There
Bobby
He's in Dallas
All Dressed Up (With Nowhere to Go)
The Night the Lights Went Out in Georgia
Buying Her Roses
The Greatest Man I Never Knew
I Wouldn't Go That Far
If I Had Only Known

IT'S YOUR CALL[††] 1992
MCA 10673

It's Your Call
Straight from You
Take It Back
Baby's Gone Blues
The Heart Won't Lie (Duet w/Vince Gill)

One Last Good Hand
He Wants to Get Married
For Herself
Will He Ever Go Away
Lighter Shade of Blue

GREATEST HITS VOL. II[††] 1993
MCA 10906

Does He Love You (Duet w/Linda Davis)
You Lie
Fancy
For My Broken Heart
Love Will Find Its Way to You
They Asked About You
Is There Life Out There
Rumor Has It
Walk On
The Greatest Man I Never Knew

READ MY MIND 1994
MCA 10994

Everything That You Want
Read My Mind
I Won't Stand in Line
I Wish That I Could Tell You
She Thinks His Name Was John
Why Haven't I Heard from You
And Still
The Heart Is a Lonely Hunter
I Wouldn't Want to Be You
Till You Love Me

AWARDS

1984	Country Music Association	Female Vocalist of the Year
1985	Country Music Association	Female Vocalist of the Year
1985	Academy of Country Music	Top Female Vocalist of the Year
1985	Music City News	Female Artist of the Year
1986	Country Music Association	Entertainer of the Year
1986	Country Music Association	Female Vocalist of the Year
1986	Academy of Country Music	Top Female Vocalist of the Year
1986	Music City News	Female Artist of the Year
1987	Grammy	Best Country Vocal Performance, Female
1987	American Music Awards	Favorite Country Female Video Artist
1987	Academy of Country Music	Top Female Vocalist
1987	Academy of Country Music	Video of the Year (Whoever's in New England)
1987	Music City News	Female Artist of the Year

1987	Music City News	Country Music Video of the Year (*Whoever's in New England*)
1987	Country Music Association	Female Vocalist of the Year
1988	American Music Awards	Favorite Female Country Vocalist
1988	Academy of Country Music	Top Female Vocalist
1988	TNN Viewers' Choice Awards	Favorite Female Vocalist
1988	Music City News	Female Artist of the Year
1989	American Music Awards	Favorite Female Country Vocalist
1989	Music City News	Female Artist of the Year
1989	TNN Viewers' Choice Awards	Favorite Female Vocalist
1990	American Music Awards	Favorite Female Country Vocalist
1991	American Music Awards	Favorite Female Country Vocalist
1991	American Music Awards	Country LP (*Reba Live*)
1991	Academy of Country Music	Top Female Vocalist
1992	American Music Awards	Favorite Female Country Vocalist
1992	People's Choice Award	Favorite Female Vocalist
1992	People's Choice Award	Favorite Female Country Vocalist
1992	Academy of Country Music	Top Female Vocalist of the Year
1992	Academy of Country Music	Video of the Year (*Is There Life Out There*)
1993	American Music Awards	Favorite Female Country Vocalist
1993	American Music Awards	Favorite Country Album
1993	People's Choice Award	Favorite Female Country Vocalist
1993	American Music Awards	Country LP (*For My Broken Heart*)

1993	TNN Viewers' Choice Awards	Favorite Female Vocalist
1994	American Music Awards	Favorite Female Country Vocalist
1994	Grammy	Best Country Vocal Collaboration ("Does He Love You"; duet with Linda Davis)
1994	People's Choice Award	Favorite Female Country Vocalist

FAN CLUB
INFORMATION

For fan club and merchandise information, send a self-addressed stamped envelope to:

Reba International Fan Club
P.O. Box 121996
Nashville, TN 37212